The
EVERYTHING
LARGE-PRINT
CROSSWORD
CHALLENGE
BOOK

Dear Reader,

Welcome! Welcome to my crossword book. Well, not my first; this is my fifth crossword book that I've written, not to mention (too late!) many other puzzles before and during those books. This goes from back to my teens when I was writing anagrams, to the late '80s when I made my first crosswords, to the '90s when I was writing palindromes as well as programming puzzle generation programs and test-solvers. Now, I'm writing a hard, large-print crossword book of original puzzles.

I try to personalize my puzzles for the intended crowd. There is no reason why puzzles can't be tailored that way. I make puzzles for teenage girls, fans of the supernatural, epicures, Bible readers, and health-conscious folks. Every place varies demographically in terms of age, interests, and taste. We are often frozen in time with what we grew up with, missing the pop culture disconnected from our generation or hobbies.

I hope you enjoy the world I've created in this book.

Douglas Fink

THE
EVERYTHING®

LARGE-PRINT
CROSSWORD
CHALLENGE
BOOK

Easy to read, tough to solve

Douglas R. Fink

Adams Media
New York   London   Toronto   Sydney   New Delhi

Dedication

This book is dedicated to my parents, for instilling in me a love of older things, be it movies, TV, stage, literature, music, lore, or legend. From silent films to ragtime, history to musical theater, Tanglewood to Broadway. Also to my in-laws, who may be responsible for me putting more big band, baseball, and jazz into this book than I originally intended. Lastly, to my wife (Susan) and kids (Hannah and Ethan) just for being there, even while I was locked away typing on the computer.

Publishing Director: Gary M. Krebs
Associate Managing Editor: Laura M. Daly
Associate Copy Chief: Brett Palana-Shanahan
Acquisitions Editor: Kate Burgo
Associate Production Editor: Casey Ebert

Director of Manufacturing: Susan Beale
Associate Director of Production:
   Michelle Roy Kelly
Cover Design: Paul Beatrice, Matt LeBlanc,
   Erick DaCosta
Design and Layout: Colleen Cunningham,
   Sorae Lee, Jennifer Oliveira

Published by Adams Media, an Imprint of Simon & Schuster, Inc.
100 Technology Center Drive
Stoughton, MA 02072
www.adamsmedia.com

ISBN 10: 1-59337-637-5
ISBN 13: 978-1-59337-637-6

Printed in the United States of America.

10 9 8 7 6 5 4

This publication is designed to provide accurate and authoritative information with regard to the subject matter covered. It is sold with the understanding that the publisher is not engaged in rendering legal, accounting, or other professional advice. If legal advice or other expert assistance is required, the services of a competent professional person should be sought.

—From a *Declaration of Principles* jointly adopted by a Committee of the American Bar Association and a Committee of Publishers and Associations

Many of the designations used by manufacturers and sellers to distinguish their product are claimed as trademarks. Where those designations appear in this book and Adams Media was aware of a trademark claim, the designations have been printed with initial capital letters.

This book is available at quantity discounts for bulk purchases.
For information, please call 1-800-289-0963.

Contents

Acknowledgments

I'd like to thank my family for putting up with me while I wrote a FIFTH BOOK. I'm gonna have to take some time off so that I can spend more time with you. I'm the one you call daddy; I think I still remember your names …

Also, I'd like to thank the staff of Adams Media, especially considering the late submission of this manuscript and the otherwise uncredited editorial work of Kathryn Powers, who finished the job started by Kate Burgo.

Introduction

We are all products of the world we're living in. Today's pop culture is tomorrow's history. Every generation has heroes and villains, inventions and fads, scandals and news.

Today, crosswords are criticized for old and obscure entries. However, crosswords should in fact be aimed at their intended audience. Older audiences should have crosswords designed with the trivia of classic *Jeopardy!* or original Trivial Pursuit, stars of yesteryear (including radio), and avoid the claptrap and hullabaloo used solely by today's kids. There should be universal appeal, without offending probable or potential readers, while drawing in the primary audience with a feeling of familiarity. Nostalgia *is* what it used to be.

How good a crossword is really depends on the clues. Are they fun? Are they fair? Are they a little unfair? Are they a little off the beaten path? Will they make you think? Do they make good use of trivia? Are they sometimes a little tricky? Will you be groaning at any puns?

Dig in and find out!

1. The Big Intro

ACROSS

1. Hotfoot it
5. Like a jigger, often
10. Cause for war
14. Towards calmness
15. Jazz nickname
16. *My Darling Clementine* role
17. What free cable did
19. Director Wertmuller
20. They had problems after 9/11
21. Cast item
23. Scalps
24. Make fragrant
25. Modus operandi
26. It's for the birds
27. Personalized hookup abbr.
30. Open, in a way
33. He founded Nemo
34. St. Anthony's cross
35. Role for Teri or Margot
36. Passes out
37. Goes for the gold
38. Emulate Xanthippe
39. Respites
40. Ponder, as evidence
41. Depressing sounds for doctors?
42. Goes no further
43. Douglas, e.g.
44. It may get developed
46. Friend of Beeblebrox
50. Free
52. Bathroom item
53. Feat for a novice pilot
54. Intel product that's under wraps?
56. "Anything You Can Do" is one
57. Oil-well capper Red __
58. Lacking zest
59. Some logic gates
60. They may go for tacos
61. Request to a teller

DOWN

1. Well-dressed de Brunhoff character
2. Colleague of Fran or Stan
3. Gazes from gigolos
4. "Is everybody happy?" guy
5. Hindsight phrase
6. Alternatives to pans
7. It's longer
8. Seashell seller
9. Those past their prime
10. Fargo lead-in
11. What Randy did at the post office?
12. Bond's first film foe
13. Shoe cover
18. City near Turin
22. Pot maker
24. Shirley Temple's assets
26. They may show approval
28. Did a number
29. Rummy
30. It's near a radius
31. Old role 30
32. Fit for swine?
33. Where tsetses are found
36. Sign of stupidity
37. Magnefique
39. CIA concern
40. Brandish
43. Coop kids
45. Historic '70s miniseries
46. Concern for FDR
47. Film maker Coen
48. Kind of wave
49. Uses a QWERTY
50. Forest Serv.'s dept.
51. Lion or tiger or bear
52. "Jabberwocky" beginning
55. Show of dedication

Addled

solution on page 300

1	2	3	4		5	6	7	8	9		10	11	12	13
14					15						16			
17			18								19			
20								21	22					
23						24								
		25			26					27	28	29		
30	31	32			33					34				
35				36					37					
38			39				40							
41			42			43								
	44	45			46				47	48	49			
50	51			52										
53			54	55										
56			57					58						
59			60				61							

ACROSS

1. Nudniks
6. Try to get an apple
9. "So long, Simone"
14. Olds model
15. Clean air org.
16. Big brass
17. Aba material
19. Rich soil
20. MIND ____
   ____ MATTER
22. Org. Bush once headed
23. Mark's replacement
24. KNEE / KOSHER
30. Gomez's cousin
31. Edible grains
32. Razz
35. Mushroom part
37. Women's group
39. Kane's last memory
40. Machines that go ping
43. Dole running mate
46. 39, to Jack Benny
47. AMONEILLION
50. Rat Pack name
51. Blanche in "The Golden Girls"

52. TOE ____
   ____ STRONG
59. Sauce served with fish
60. Repairman's words
62. Words to a hitch-hiker
63. Kodak moments
64. "Filthy" stuff
65. Borneo swinger
66. Ball-bearing item
67. 1994 movie thriller

DOWN

1. 10 preceder
2. *Rio Lobo* actor
3. It's good for the long haul
4. Large ditch
5. Role in many John Wayne films
6. Wally's little bro
7. Aunt Bee's charge
8. Stunt skater's prop
9. On the loose
10. Far Side cartoon panels, often
11. Skeptic's retort
12. Deftness
13. Country in a Beatles song title
18. Grizzled
21. Subatomic bit
24. Glancing contact, in pool
25. Anne Frank's dad
26. Pool person
27. Breakfast companion
28. Honshu port
29. Dwight's two-time opponent
33. Denmark-based toy giant

34. Bliss
36. Pear-shaped instrument
38. "Out of Time" band
41. Keeping in check
42. Half a New York prison
44. Stuck in the mud
45. "Mice" and "men"
48. Candy-bar filling
49. Abates
52. Pudding starch
53. Mezzanine, say
54. Roster, to a Brit
55. Bump on a log
56. Ten cc's, e.g.
57. Enough, often
58. Used to be
61. Got hitched

Word Wackies

solution on page 300

ACROSS

1. Water-balloon impact sound
6. Scored on a serve
10. Arrives later
14. Enjoy a joke
15. Stringy side dish
16. Humerus neighbor
17. Sanctum or circle preceeder
18. Old-time tale
19. Tab taker
20. "I barely passed," said Tom __
22. Showed up
23. Poitier role
24. Gentlemanly starters?
26. Snobs
31. War zone, for short
32. On the Azov
33. Early *Rocky Horror* cry
35. Fringe
39. Yoko's son
40. Uses scissors
42. Highway rig
43. Bovine bevies
45. Type of show
46. Nightingale's trademark
47. Have a bawl
49. Miss Yokum
51. Way to get a return
55. Detective Hutchinson of "Starsky and Hutch"
56. Its capital was Susa
57. "I got larger," said Tom __
63. Race's end
64. Mag exec Brown
65. 1903 Nobelist
66. Etc. kin
67. Mare's fare
68. Film with an egg on its poster
69. Bank
70. Artful dodge
71. Prom goers

DOWN

1. Went home, maybe
2. You can see through it
3. Breather
4. Curing chemical
5. Whup
6. Stressing
7. Adorned
8. Kind of scout
9. "A Different World" role
10. "I'm a little drunk," said Tom __
11. Comedian Sherman
12. Troll's kin
13. Overfills
21. Cockpit circles
25. Car in a Beach Boys tune
26. Leftover dish
27. Fortune-teller's phrase
28. Reverse, e.g.
29. "Taxi!" said Tom __
30. Peered secretly
34. '20s saloon
36. Jets, Mets or Nets
37. Spice Girl Bunton
38. Mature
41. Berlin's are blue
44. Mariner's "Mayday"
48. Circus
50. Winter vehicle
51. Block
52. Overjoy
53. Kind of bull
54. Dry run
58. Second word of the Golden Rule
59. Backless slipper
60. Canal opened in 1825
61. Repo req
62. Thirsts

Swifties of 10

solution on page 300

ACROSS

1. Some "To Tell the Truth" contestants
6. Coed's quarters
10. It might be grape or orange
14. Saloon sign
15. Bit of Bizet
16. Summit
17. Sleeping
18. Mrs. Sprat's dietary restriction
19. Caron film of '53
20. Pizzeria need
22. "Fernwood 2-Night" star
23. Sloppy Tracey Ullman role
24. Bush Sr, Supreme Court appointee
26. For shame!
30. Had a TV dinner, say
32. Tussle
33. Brief
37. Wing-like
38. Opera solos
39. Han's love
40. Singer who may have explicit lyrics

42. Custard desserts
43. Cut
44. Paucity
45. Single-named folk singer
48. Bull's advice
49. Single follower
50. Summertime candle
57. Plummet
58. Laugh-track sounds
59. Inbox items
60. Nash adjective
61. Lordy!
62. Clobber, old-style
63. Nursemaid
64. Walkman creator
65. Dehli wrap

DOWN

1. Fertile soil
2. Intro to Chinese?
3. Entire gamut
4. Tease
5. Talk bravely
6. Big name in Chicago politics
7. Hurler Hershiser
8. Iranian bread
9. Giant sea mammals
10. Food spoiler
11. Kind of den
12. Perry Mason's Street
13. Leaf angles
21. Informant
25. White House beagle
26. Former ruler
27. ACLU reworking?
28. Lint catcher
29. Whirling dance
30. Silly
31. One of those things
33. "Layla" singer
34. Bring up, or something to bring up
35. Isn't on the street
36. Hitch

38. Embassy staffers
41. Putrify
42. Whimsicality
44. Batman and Robin e.g.
45. Switch type
46. "V" role
47. Actress Burstyn
48. Gun control bill name
51. Emilia's husband
52. Compared to
53. Writer Lazarus
54. Sanctum
55. Lo-cal word
56. On the calm side

Scatter

solution on page 300

ACROSS

1. Tire parts
5. Not obliged
11. Many a time
14. JFK regular
15. Marine hitchhiker
16. Copacabana site
17. Tennis Open multiple winner
19. Botch things up
20. Broadway backer
21. *Bubba Ho-Tep* locale
23. Corp. dept.
26. MGM lion
27. Speculator/activist
33. At a snail's pace
37. Star Trek android
38. Green stuff
39. Lower digit
40. Berra and Bear
41. Engaged in
42. Investor's asset
44. McLaughlin's predecessor
46. Driving force
47. Disease of sheep
52. Kennedy speech writer
57. Like Gilligan
58. "So that's your game!"
59. *Roxanne* actress
62. John Lennon's middle name
63. Patronages
64. Rice of writing
65. Just kidding!
66. Up-to-date
67. Arctic barker

DOWN

1. Update an atlas
2. Massey of film
3. Shabby
4. Less up front
5. Big time?
6. They mark the spot
7. Pt. of EMS
8. Type of spy
9. The King
10. Samples
11. Cookie since 1912
12. Lawyer group
13. Ran like the dickens
18. Like some drains
22. Hex
24. O in Oahu
25. Went ape
28. Island intro
29. Gathers gradually
30. Prego rival
31. Auricular
32. It's binding
33. Cocksure
34. Easy gait
35. Golden Rule word
36. *Seinfeld* character
40. It's used in ceramics
42. Carrier pigeon's burden
43. Wall St. watchdog
45. Father goose
48. *King and I* lead and her understudy
49. Tube pasta
50. Bucky Beaver's toothpaste
51. Vivian Vance role
52. By and by
53. "Heavens to Betsy!"
54. Repeated "Take Me Out to the Ballgame" word
55. Idle actor
56. Big Board letters
60. Dykstra of baseball
61. "The buck stops here" monogram

Friends of Yoko Ono and Iggy Pop?

solution on page 300

ACROSS

1. Zeus' blood
6. "Who killed me?" film
9. He talked horse sense
13. Head shop purchase
14. Guideline
16. Role for Kenneth Branagh or Sebastian Cabot
17. Big-eyed baby
18. Get an eyeful
19. Air apparent?
20. What Simon Estes is often doing
23. Performs
24. Out for the night
25. Danson's role on "Cheers"
28. Forsakes
32. Attentive
33. Animal fat
34. Batman sound effect
35. Appear
39. Supplement, with "out"
40. Butterfly catchers
41. Craze
42. Says again
45. Usher elsewhere
46. Piles
47. Jug handles
48. One worth ignoring
54. Stylish
55. Singles
56. Relaxed
57. Ritzy
58. Homeland Security subset
59. Waste metal
60. Vino center
61. Siegfried's partner
62. Razor reviver

DOWN

1. Flapjack franchise
2. Hood
3. Hacienda hello
4. "Sure thing!"
5. Apportioned
6. Bottom-of-barrel contents
7. Kick out
8. Hawaii's 16 and England's 26
9. Put together incorrectly
10. St. Louis eleven
11. Big heads
12. Pug or boxer
15. Chem lab safety feature
21. Born, in bridal bios
22. "Growing Pains" role
25. Medieval or modern weapon
26. Came to
27. Rich fabrics
28. Em and Bee
29. Voice a view
30. Motorola rival
31. A runner may break one
33. Diner packet
36. Above
37. Green gems
38. Travel document
43. Chinese discipline
44. Lofty peak
45. Kurosawa epic
47. English Lit assignment
48. Dr. Seuss characters
49. H.S. subject
50. Tom LaGrua on *Caroline in the City*
51. Yorick's adjective
52. Exxon's ex-name
53. Answer: Abbr.
54. H&R Block employee

Something Fishy

solution on page 300

ACROSS

1. To the teeth, per-haps
6. Kid stuff
10. Warm-up
14. Miss America prop
15. Diamond protector
16. First CinemaScope film, with "The"
17. Some kind of nerve
18. Family keepsake?
19. Veiled responses?
20. Doting tsar?
22. It's dies are cast
23. Stick in the water
24. *As You Like It* hero
26. Putting all your ducks in a row
31. Blue
32. Ricky, really
33. Lois in "Lois & Clark"
35. Must, slangily
39. The facts
40. Laugher who is spotted
42. Nog time
43. Was eminent
45. Like a close encounter of the first kind
46. It's verboten
47. M&M color of yore
49. Nepali capital
51. Symbol of royalty
55. Carnival site
56. Rock that rolls
57. Messy Popsicle, perhaps?
63. A sign of things to come
64. Spork part
65. Hilarious
66. Proceed along
67. Them in *Them*!
68. Author of *The Right Stuff*
69. Slammin' Sammy
70. Ground item
71. Makes mittens

DOWN

1. Perched upon
2. Opportune
3. Akbar toon-guy Groening
4. Cleveland Indian?
5. Artificial fabric
6. Court players
7. It's raised on a farm
8. Motto
9. Simple angling needs
10. "That's Amore" singer's dresser?
11. Thinking man's sculptor?
12. WWII buy
13. Trattoria topping
21. T.V. role for Kelly Ripa
25. Jet follower
26. Tallies up
27. One of Jacob's wives
28. Syllogism words
29. Grovel big-time?
30. Like Jimmy?
34. Truly
36. Cel mate?
37. Oversee
38. Jesus with an out-stretched arm
41. Shenanigan
44. Word between two dogs
48. Ambrosia
50. High-middle hair-cut
51. Responds to excess traffic
52. Nana's brooch
53. Finger shooter's cry
54. Heavy herbivore
58. Engrossed by
59. Pressing matter
60. Film star Taylor
61. Artist's workspace
62. Tropical fruit tree

Casually

solution on page 301

ACROSS

1. "We Shall Over-come" singer
5. Malodorous
10. Letters inside a jacket
14. Farr co-star
15. *Games People Play* author
16. "Final Four" org.
17. Break under questioning
20. Long look
21. Table items
22. Future fowl
25. Fact fudger
26. Scriptural interpretation
30. Iota preceders
34. It's near Miss.
35. Heavy reading?
37. Cornstarch brand
38. Emerald City lead-in
42. Environs
43. Disorient
44. Flood control org.
45. Acceptable
48. Uses Google
50. Defeat soundly
52. End of a Burns title
53. Name giver
57. Leave out
61. Harlem Globetrotters star
64. Heating device
65. Plankton components
66. Backfire sound
67. "Candy is dandy" author
68. As a father, he knew best
69. Duel memento

DOWN

1. Big fiddle
2. Settled down
3. Best in acting
4. Capital of Croatia
5. J. Edgar Hoover's crew
6. "A mouse!!!"
7. Banyan or baobab
8. On the whole
9. Hypocrisy
10. Hammer holder
11. Examine in detail
12. Quarterback Starr
13. Some votes
18. Musically flowing
19. Asian nanny
23. Look delighted
24. Latin dance
26. Eskimo canoe
27. Olds model
28. They may be lofted in a loft
29. Droves
31. Marriage vows
32. Mescal source
33. Counter offers?
36. Teams in a game
39. Pretentious
40. Brick material
41. Core
46. Therefore
47. Model's path
49. Stars
51. *A History of Violence* actress
53. "I agree!"
54. Bristle
55. Lacking
56. Aunt Millie's rival
58. Type of Apple
59. Lady of Spain
60. RPI grad
62. Conducted
63. Kind of party

I'm Just Wild about Saffron

solution on page 301

ACROSS

1. Mundane
6. Dimwit
10. Idea iota
14. The first Mrs. Trump
15. Makes a patsy of
16. Drug-yielding plant
17. He goes "Ho Ho Ho!"
20. She requested "As Time Goes By"
21. Masters of disguise
22. Make an appeal
24. Bit of Bizet
25. Sea or moon follower
28. Fine
32. Song by Ho
38. July 4th exclamation
39. PC key
40. Davis formerly of *Trading Spaces*
41. In advance of
42. Junior's jr.
43. He goes "Hi De Ho"
46. Russian retreat
48. Triangular sign
49. Slightly
52. Warbler
54. Borge had a sound for it
58. Barbra's *A Star Is Born* costar
62. He goes "Ho Ho Ho!"
64. Not windward
65. Unctuous
66. Derisive
67. Remainder
68. Makes a doily
69. Radiant

DOWN

1. Avery Fisher's field
2. Model-train layout
3. They might be checked
4. Sad
5. West of Brooklyn
6. Peer's purview
7. Labor Dept. division
8. Stuffed deli delicacy
9. Wickerwork wood
10. Cake
11. Pollster Roper
12. Spotted one
13. Feeding time, at bootcamp
18. NBC's former owner
19. Loses it
23. Lee's man
25. Staid
26. Lashes
27. Monkeyshine
29. *Camelot* composer
30. Necklace material
31. "__ never believe me . . ."
33. "__ Lazy River"
34. Miss Streisand, singularly?
35. Pen name
36. J.F.K neighbor
37. Icky ichthyoid
43. Tart-tongued
44. Pipe cleaner?
45. Piggish behavior
47. Herbed meatloaf
50. Vernacular
51. Last name in ill-fated ships
52. Cheese by-products
53. Toon dog
54. Not shut
55. Pope John Paul II, e.g.
56. Shouts for Manolete
57. Lucy Van __
59. The third one may be dangerous
60. European intro
61. Lose sleep over
63. Govt. procurement org.

O Ho!

solution on page 301

1	2	3	4	5		6	7	8	9		10	11	12	13
14						15					16			
17				18					19					
20				■	21									
■	■	■	22	23			■	24				■	■	■
25	26	27			■					28		29	30	31
32				33	34	35	36	37		■	38			
39			■	40					■		41			
42			■	43					44	45				
46			47		■				48					
■	■	49		50	51		52	53			■	■	■	
54	55	56				57			■	58	59	60	61	
62									63					
64			■	65				■	66					
67				68					69					

ACROSS

1. Its fruit is monkey bread
7. Peppermint Patty, to Marcie
10. Lift giver
13. Earnings
14. Avails of
16. Jet follower
17. Means of NFL Chargers
18. Keeper of polydactyl cats, for short
19. Peter Pan's "__ Gotta Crow"
20. Lemmon/Matthau flick
23. '70s radical org.
26. Ally Oop's land
27. About
28. It's on many greeting cards
33. Perplexed
34. Elec. power initials
35. Pickle variety
38. Mini racer
44. *Michael Collins* actor
46. Wilderness Road blazer
47. Carson's bandleader
52. Fend off
54. Workers' gp.
55. Tango quorum
56. Legendary locale
61. Turkish title
62. It's been spotted
63. Pack animals
67. Set the pace
68. Cries of disgust
69. Climate oddity
70. Malaprop, for one
71. Start of many CA names
72. Pops, to a beatnik

DOWN

1. Hopper
2. Santa follower
3. Hept- plus one
4. 1976-80 Wimbledon champ
5. Son of Venus
6. Make inactive
7. Back
8. "Old chap" preceder
9. Defaulter's loss
10. "My word!"
11. Nevermore quother
12. Mulder or Scully
15. Item that's often tossed
21. Miss Piggy word
22. Concern of Watson & Crick
23. Rug type
24. Lattice part
25. Bema abutter
29. Pricing word
30. Babble
31. They're thrown in *Network*
32. Dave's nemesis in *2001*
36. Return address?
37. Coretta King, __ Scott
39. Sapporo sash
40. Truck weight unit
41. Part of COLA
42. From the top
43. Gambling city
45. French jets
47. Is fearful of
48. Cargo of the Edmund Fitzgerald
49. It's near Turkey
50. Conduit bend
51. Like some sushi
52. Biblical hymn
53. *Tattered Tom* author
57. It might be a big stretch
58. PTL scandal name
59. Paella pot
60. Magician's prop
64. Life or wife starter
65. Card for a magic trick?
66. Yemana's portrayer

I'd Like to Thank the Little People

solution on page 301

2. Big Deal

ACROSS

1. Homeric work
6. Plane-wreck show
10. Weight unit
14. Petrol unit
15. Road runner
16. Hold sway
17. Percussion instrument
19. Widemouthed jug
20. Is hopping mad
21. Bony
23. Collapses
26. Arthur was their king
27. Bammer
28. From this
29. "I __!" ("Search me!")
30. Play plotter
31. Brit's gun
34. Guinness suffix
35. Godot and others
38. Med. plan
39. __ ex machina
41. It gets a "b"
42. Bring out
44. Freshwater perches
46. Keenness
47. Actor Rupert
49. Splotched
50. Square dance verb
51. What to use before hiccups
52. Victor's cry
53. "We dye no honeydew," e.g.
58. Chertoff's bailiwick
59. Union contracts?
60. General Rommel
61. Big Bang precursor
62. Food fishes
63. Bottle brunettes

DOWN

1. Family
2. Golf ball position
3. Hairy cousin
4. Carson character
5. It's just a fantasy
6. Weighed down
7. It's for you and me
8. RV hookup
9. Another day to Scarlett
10. Hidden caves
11. Common sense procedure
12. Detective Pinkerton
13. What American Plan includes
18. Industrialist von Skoda
22. Potsdam pronoun
23. Yielded
24. Tickle one's fancy
25. Daring
26. Sired
28. Punch-line payoff
30. Small key
32. Billy Crystal, at times
33. Incessantly
36. Tangential
37. Started the bandwagon
40. It was Dutch Guiana, once
43. *Was a Lady*
45. Sustained
46. King of comedy
47. Instruct
48. Purchase from Pat
49. Felicity
51. Trudge
54. Hullabaloo
55. Have a debt
56. Downed space station
57. Minnesota twins

Um ...

solution on page 302

1	2	3	4	5		6	7	8	9		10	11	12	13
14						15					16			
17				18							19			
			20						21	22				
23	24	25						26						
27							28							
29					30					31		32	33	
34				35	36				37		38			
39			40		41				42	43				
		44		45				46						
47	48						49							
50						51								
52				53	54						55	56	57	
58				59				60						
61				62				63						

ACROSS

1. Item in black
6. Sennett's finest
10. Trap starter
14. Fling
15. "This won't hurt __!"
16. Wedge
17. His villains often wear gloves
18. Jermaine's brother
19. They may be inflated
20. Unrestricted funds
22. Columbo caper
23. Seaver stat
24. Peanut gallery member
26. Wonders from Whitman
31. Schlemiel
32. Columbus's home
33. Attached to
35. Elbowed
39. A place for heroes
40. Nosey Parker
42. Engrossed by
43. Surrounded by
45. Writer Lazarus
46. It's a gas
47. He played Lurch
49. Contrite
51. Songbird
55. Movie, for short
56. Dickens's Magwitch
57. Like the other long entries
63. Louise of *Gilligan's Island*
64. 'Hood
65. Bric-a-brac
66. Where a snake suggested
67. Internet gossipmonger Drudge
68. Rimes with songs
69. Need a bath
70. Option word
71. Cube's twelve

DOWN

1. Ishmael's boss
2. Auction off
3. It's a long story
4. Not one, but two
5. Studs in books
6. Hepburn, with 8 statuettes
7. *Village Voice* award
8. Epitome of black
9. Feeds a furnace
10. Reason to slow down
11. Kind of tender
12. Lost a lap
13. Tough nut
21. Shell teams
25. Mushroom part
26. Bubbly stuff
27. "Do you mind?"
28. "Bloom County" character
29. Direct
30. Jazzy dance
34. Diamond pentagon
36. Kind of jerk
37. College founded by Henry VI
38. Back off!
41. A button to push
44. Get set
48. Slander
50. Disappearing murder weapon
51. Fire fighter
52. Put up with
53. Actress Zellweger
54. Bucolic
58. Tennis do-overs
59. Regretted
60. Palisade
61. Box office formation
62. Earth's age, perhaps

It Comes Around

solution on page 302

ACROSS

1. Hard spare to make
6. Played craps
11. "Big" burger
14. Ralph Kramden's wife
15. Make __ (act)
16. Blether
17. Stable papas
18. Brit's dashboard
19. Easter lead-in
20. Young song of '72
22. Lode load
23. Ross Sea sights
24. "60 Minutes" man
26. Wasted time
30. Applies afresh
31. Involving just one operand
32. Like Sanka
35. Scuttlebutt
36. It may be slippery
37. d'Urbervilles girl
40. Projector adjustor
42. Bottleneck
43. Blob
45. Hamlet's lost love
47. Plump plus
48. British cleric
50. A high priest of Israel
51. It's a matter of degrees
57. Letter opener
58. Carpi connectors
59. Furlough
60. "Here __ again!"
61. Circumvent
62. Does some eye work
63. Downing Street number
64. Takes on cargo
65. All tuckered out

DOWN

1. Fauntleroy suit feature
2. Balletic knee bend
3. Luigi's lucre of yore
4. Champagne cooler
5. What Chuck Yeager did
6. Yellow blooms
7. Celebrity's concern
8. Keeling Islands
9. Apt anagram of vile
10. Jordan River terminus
11. Clark Kent, really
12. Renee of silents
13. Heart attack items?
21. Bullring "bravo!"
25. Em or Mame
26. MADD target
27. Bay State cape
28. Hinged appliance
29. Responds to a bell?
30. AAA map line
33. Quayle negative?
34. Cog kins
36. Have dinner
38. __ generis
39. Curative spring
41. Colleague
42. Excites
43. Easy __!
44. Compel
46. Family men
48. Ivy-covered
49. See if __!
52. Sea lettuce
53. Lover's __
54. Rose bowl?
55. Level
56. Type of stop

Metal Meddle

solution on page 302

ACROSS

1. Imp
5. "The Say Hey Kid"
9. Dined at home
14. Cryptic letter
15. "Nope!"
16. Wave over one of Columbus's ships
17. __ and the Detectives (Disney film)
18. Germ fighters
19. Black Panther name
20. "Igor lost the brain," said Tom __
23. Background computer processes
24. Lofty material?
25. Rearward
26. "That's it!"
28. Fades away
32. Household duty
35. Look into
37. Tony Orlando's tree
38. "I've got nothing to set my lectern on," said Tom __
41. Fred Astaire's daughter
42. Word replacer
43. Blackjack call
44. High plateau
46. Sega rival, for short
47. Endorsing
48. Homeric cry?
50. Galas
54. "That's a rocket thruster," said Tom __
58. Future mushroom
59. Cameo shape
60. Mother of Horus
61. Montague scion
62. Not on tape
63. Prank
64. Angles in columns
65. Flew the coop
66. Osmose

DOWN

1. Hero's need
2. Hippy dance
3. Licorice herb
4. Schussboomer's turn
5. Taboo word
6. Throat-clearers
7. Cosmonaut Gagarin
8. Thai language
9. Floundering
10. Color fabric
11. Mideast carrier
12. In a lazy way
13. Literally born
21. Show __ (appear brave)
22. Abu __
26. Pisces follower
27. Give a party
29. Door lock
30. Soother
31. Kind of terrier
32. "B.C." currency
33. Rich person
34. Wood sorrels
35. Attendant
36. Reverberant
39. Hawaiian crooner
40. Causes for shelter
45. Idolized
47. Snidely Whiplash's verb
49. Mock butters
50. Barrel strip
51. Milk pitcher?
52. Skip a sound
53. Network nabob
54. Apiece
55. Apple or pear
56. It's clubs have clubs
57. Kind of eye
58. "Sold out" letters

Swifties of 14

solution on page 302

ACROSS

1. MS. enc.
5. Panasonic rival
9. Word associated with Ayn Rand and Rand McNally
14. It's not worth much
15. Dandling site
16. Dry white quaff
17. About 17 million square miles
18. "__ be over soon"
19. Defraud
20. Place for you to duck and cover
23. Hasten
24. Uses Parseltongue
27. Kind of shot
28. Maui menu item
30. Vostok I rider
31. Rock's UB40, e.g.
34. Horn-shaped part
36. Palindromic hit by a palindromic group
37. Musical odes
40. CD collection?
41. Travels
42. Rabbit
43. Spanish girl
45. Up start?
46. Surfing spot
47. End of a Cheech title
49. *Star Trek* units
53. Sidelines seat?
56. Trim
58. Adjoin
59. Brutus' being
60. Watering holes
61. Chorus girl
62. Service
63. Nolte flick
64. *Roseanne* character
65. Cold spell

DOWN

1. Truckloads
2. Fabulous fellow?
3. Nasty
4. Showers of this and that
5. Lodged one?
6. Like some beer
7. Foster film
8. Say "Hey!"
9. Some kind of character
10. Baby's foot
11. Kitchen spinner
12. Fifth, for one
13. Hill VIP
21. Marginal worker?
22. 20th wedding anniversary gift
25. Lose ground
26. She played Loretta
28. Guided a gondola
29. Spherical bodies
31. Theorize
32. Ceramic's raw material
33. Instill
34. Troglodyte's home
35. Worrywart's woes
38. Very lean
39. They're not really red in the wild
44. Made up
46. Role for Geer or Waite
48. It's used when making beds
49. Son of Saturn and Ops
50. Acid dye
51. __ del Sol
52. Shuteye
54. False god
55. In good condition
56. *Batman* sound effect
57. Field's Oscar role

Ball Bearing

solution on page 302

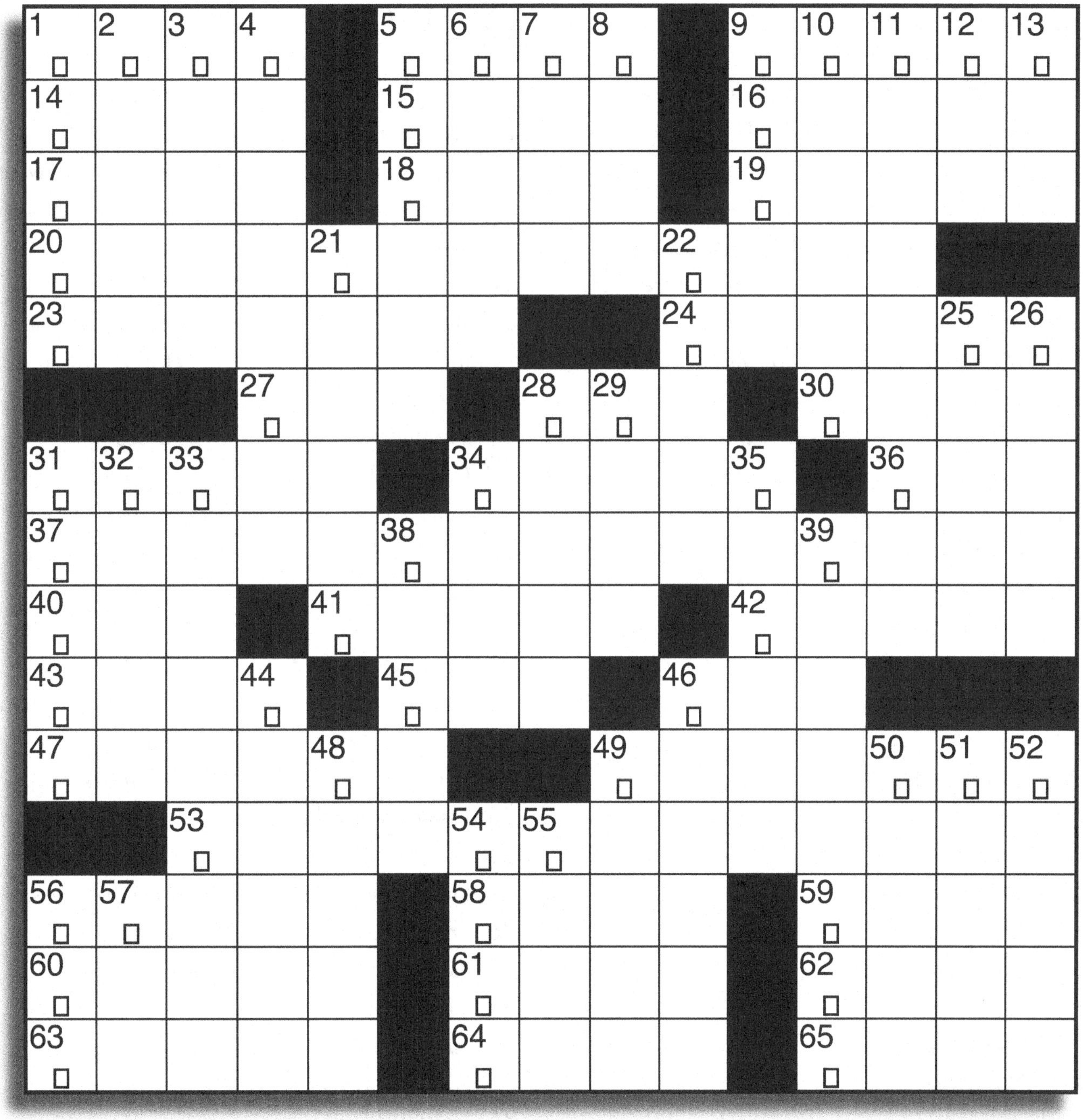

ACROSS

1. 1975-76 World Series champs
5. Evian, e.g.
8. Jetliner name, once
13. Poison plant
14. Whale herd
15. Present time
16. NAACP founder
18. Beat, in chess
19. Sky light?
20. Deface
21. La Brea goo
22. Heel-less slipper
24. MP3 site
27. It's sometimes chewed
30. Escorted group to Central High
33. Go to second proofs
34. Interrogates
35. Public procession
38. Main arteries
40. Made the perfect shot
41. Good brandy
44. Woolworth diner patrons
49. A real shocker?
50. Chess piece
51. Uppity one
53. Underdog's voice
54. Fam. member
56. Lee, to Grant
57. Ricochet
60. She refused to move
63. Weight that sounds like a fruit
64. See red?
65. They're blunt
66. Liturgies
67. It may be bitter
68. Well-rooted one

DOWN

1. Sorry
2. Blood clots
3. "Cat's in the Cradle" narrator
4. Lowlife
5. Wore
6. Taro treat
7. Junk mail
8. Expose
9. Take wing
10. Crumb lifter
11. Drink cubes
12. Cardinal
13. Done laps
17. Bondsman's client
21. Pulp fiction sleuth
23. Much Wall Street activity, these days
25. New England sch.
26. Part of NIMBY
27. Handy weapon?
28. "Puppy Love" singer
29. Kinski role
31. John Jr.'s uncle
32. DEA agents
35. Knight-to-be
36. Israeli port
37. Fisherman's tool
38. Blindness
39. Lummox
41. Murrow's network
42. Amazed exclamation
43. Took in
45. Atomic weaponry
46. Half a dozen
47. Like Mumia, at press time
48. Cheated
52. Porgy's beloved
53. "__ Together" (Beatles hit)
55. Gush forth
57. An EMT skill
58. 2001 Will Smith biopic
59. Tire mark
60. "Dizzy" singer
61. Personal
62. Dian Fossey subject

solution on page 302

ACROSS

1. Unsuitable
6. Vamp's relative
11. What an RN provides
14. Ventriloquist Wences
15. Letter standout
16. Galley item
17. Jot down
19. School starter
20. Rodin art
21. In disagreement
23. Colorful Apple
24. Rotten
25. Seven-time AL batting king
29. Fiscal concern
30. "To a ... " work
31. Acting baseball commissioner Bud
33. Awaken
36. Florida locale, for short
38. Wooded valleys
40. Ernie's Nairobi group
41. Not on all fours
43. Campaign tactic
45. Moving-day rental
46. Fly, for one
48. Opposites
50. Puget Sound city
53. Occasional runner
54. Voracious fish
55. Went berserk
59. Edible tuber
60. Break down
62. Not dis
63. Toughen
64. Admit knowing
65. Prior to
66. Foxe portrayer on *Remington Steele*
67. Ain't right

DOWN

1. Beliefs, slangily
2. Bar request
3. Vegas headliner
4. Kind of license or justice
5. Shocks
6. Kind of triangle
7. Dolphin hazard
8. Crush underfoot
9. Raised Cain
10. Krupke, e.g.
11. Upside-down
12. "Whip-snapper" of films
13. *Rocky* fighter
18. Approached
22. Clunky shoe
25. Cassock
26. Incense emanation
27. Slow down
28. Colonel Deering
32. "The Heat is On" singer
34. "Owa tagu —"
35. Earth's age, perhaps
37. Integra maker
39. Zen goal
42. Followed popcorn predictions
44. Reason for retribution in *The Mirror Crack'd*
47. Colorless gas
49. Less remote
50. Verse form
51. British cleric
52. Ryan's daughter
56. Cole Porter title character
57. 007's alma mater
58. Ballplayer Bucky
61. All alternative

Going Down

solution on page 303

ACROSS

1. Highly religious Jew
6. "Now I get it!"
9. Polyphonic
14. Banana plant
15. WKRP newsman
16. Pacific Rim bay
17. They have ties
19. Take five
20. Sterile
21. Part of ACLU
23. Shrill scream
24. Dreamed up
28. Brit's potato chip
30. Silver __ (cloud seed)
31. Verbal abuse
34. Bee bunch
36. Genesis creator
37. Informant
38. *The Phantom Menace* kid, ace short
39. Jam ingredient?
40. Escape clauses
42. Technical details
44. Ghostly variant
45. It might force you home
47. Spock's forte
49. Spanish ranch
51. It's major or minor in tarot
55. "Adieu!"
56. Drugged
57. Smallest amounts
60. *Ally McBeal* singer
62. Meander
63. Laid up
64. Be of use
65. Cupolas
66. She played Miss Van Owen
67. True partner

DOWN

1. Laugh-track snippets
2. Disconcert
3. Cavalry blade
4. Prop for Yukon Cornelius
5. Freshwater fish
6. Obi-Wan portrayer
7. Female pronoun
8. Indian tea center
9. Precede
10. Cyber-names
11. Liquid meas.
12. Police blotter abbr.
13. Not taut
18. West African garments
22. Hurt severely
24. Girl's place
25. Bridget, to Jane
26. Mystery writer's award
27. Hon
29. Barter
31. Foam
32. Mary's "Oh, Rob!" role
33. Room at the top
35. Jambalaya base
41. Saliva
42. Shipped out
43. Hasty and careless
44. Houdini, notably
46. Auto deals
48. Least wet
50. TV producer Susskind
52. Early game console
53. Chutzpah
54. Threw in
56. Merely
57. Bankroll
58. Hosp. plan
59. Co. called "Big Blue"
61. "Bravo!"

Gotta Dash!

solution on page 303

ACROSS

1. Herb used with cucumber
5. Recovery room
11. Lay down the lawn
14. Sills solo
15. Bam man
16. Like some humor
17. Unarmed woman?
19. It might be crushed
20. Emcee's open
21. Sot's tot
22. Marilyn's *Some Like It Hot* role
24. Talcum powder helps do it
26. Wodan, to a Viking
28. Spirit
34. Wipeout
38. "Children should __ ..."
39. Sole feature
40. Auric measure
42. Words after "sit" or "step"
43. A sea-going one can only be found at the Galapagos
45. Mini MP3 player
47. Alias for espionage
49. Meadow mothers
50. Know-how
55. Simple rings
58. Kind of cat
61. Convoy chaser
62. R and R stop
63. Mauritius, once
66. Hopkins' title
67. Moneymaker
68. Dundee native
69. Edible root
70. Penance unit
71. Ben's boy

DOWN

1. Actor Duchovny
2. Dunne of *Cimarron*
3. Fluffs
4. 1944 Gene Tierney film
5. Foot that leads
6. Peck film, with "The"
7. 18-wheeler
8. Camera support
9. Gland lacked by anhingas
10. Like the "p" in "pop"
11. Big gulp
12. Richard Harris movie of 1977
13. Beautician, at times
18. First name in skating
23. Concord
25. One in a pier group
27. They have red letters
29. Fin. fund
30. Like a King novel
31. __ cava
32. Hold in
33. "Within" word form
34. Large pipe
35. Golden Fleece ship
36. Dregs of humanity
37. Like tree-lined walks
41. Credit card letters
44. More full of gossip
46. Protest
48. Flashlight carriers
51. Discomfit
52. Popeil's agcy.
53. Cantina order
54. Undoes a dele
55. Kind of signal
56. Gobi's locale
57. George Wendt role
59. Irish author O'Brien
60. Milord
64. Thai language
65. Use a wok

Deployment

solution on page 303

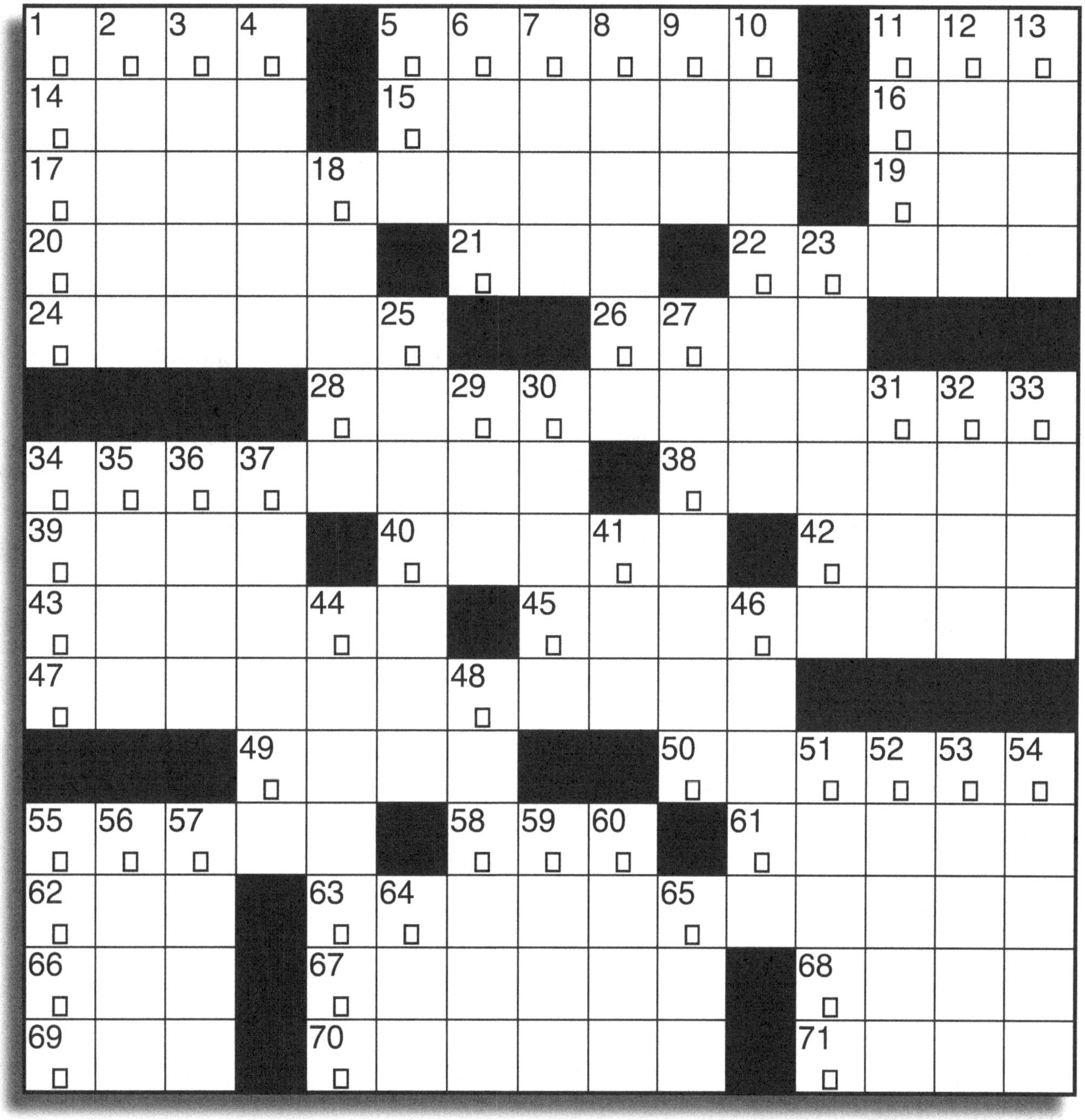

3. Big Quotations

ACROSS

1. Johnnie Cochran's org.
4. Be plentiful
10. Mock fanfare
14. Chat-room chuckle
15. Limit
16. Aladdin, for one
17. It might keep a watch
18. Part 1 of quote
20. Chisholm Trail terminus
22. A la Oscar Madison
23. Like a wolf
24. Ignore a physician's oath
25. Org. Bush once headed
26. Ottoman empire?
30. Actor Young of *Mr. Ed*
31. Jack or jenny
32. Noted DC office
33. High point
34. Part 2 of quote
37. Lint trap?
40. Start of a Hitchcock title
41. Blaxploitation star Grier
44. Sammy Davis Jr.'s *Yes __*
45. Part 3 of quote
48. Militarize
49. Fat one's nickname
50. Hardy heroine
51. Well-behaved one
53. It might be muted
56. End of quote
58. Black bird
59. Level in Liverpool
60. They're history
61. Churchill's "so few"
62. Tropical fruit tree
63. Field
64. Bridge guru Culbertson

DOWN

1. Darla adorer
2. Tots' scrapes
3. Ones like Silas in *The DaVinci Code*
4. Top
5. __ there, done that!
6. My treat
7. Martha Raye's gp.
8. Everyday
9. They blow hair
10. Former news org.
11. A, for example
12. Showy flowers
13. In cold storage, perhaps
19. Belief
21. Rent out
24. Religious time
27. Dirty
28. New Deal org.
29. Galley blade
30. Finesse
33. H.S. math class
34. Hideout
35. Sesame seed
36. Prince of Broadway
37. It might be a barrel of fun
38. Wirewalker, e.g.
39. Git!
41. Ready
42. Powder room?
43. Perplex
45. Brave's home
46. Turbine
47. $$ dispenser
49. Festival time
52. Lodge fees
53. Khon Kaen native
54. Run the realm
55. Powers' crash site: abbr.
57. "Babylon 5" channel

Wilde Quote

solution on page 304

1	2	3		4	5	6	7	8	9		10	11	12	13
14				15							16			
17				18					19					
20			21					22						
23							24				25			
26			27	28	29					30				
31				32					33					
		34					35	36						
37	38	39				40					41	42	43	
44					45	46				47				
48				49						50				
51			52					53	54	55				
56						57					58			
59					60						61			
62					63						64			

ACROSS

1. Wood sorrel
4. Loses traction
9. Like #1 pencils
13. Castle collider
14. Sleeper, perhaps
15. Annoying one
16. Choice word
17. Less normal
18. "SpongeBob" Baldwin
19. Part 1 of 4
22. October birth- stones
23. Impose, as a tax
24. Get the fat out
26. Bout
30. Part 2 of 4
35. English 101 assignment
38. Omega rival
39. Legume container
40. Part 3 of 4
45. Grassy plain
46. Moves like a crab
50. Thick soups
55. Barely legible
56. Part 4 of 4
59. Same old same old
60. Excessive fondness
61. Even as we speak
62. Homeless tot
63. Clara Bow, with "The"
64. Farm femme
65. Rustic hotels
66. Unified
67. Trip cause

DOWN

1. Demosthenes, e.g.
2. Soiree snack
3. Author of *The Joy Luck Club*
4. Merganser's kin
5. Where Inchon is
6. They may climb the walls
7. Loses, perhaps
8. Launch a tennis ball
9. Less dense
10. Olive products
11. Cut and run
12. R.N.'s skill
14. Name in math
20. *The Four Seasons* star
21. "In __" (basically)
25. Bus-sitter Parks
27. It may be blown
28. Chuang Tzu prin- ciple
29. Anomalistic
31. Homer's neighbor
32. "Amscray!"
33. Ring dec.
34. Ponderosa name
35. He gives a hoot
36. "Runaway" singer Shannon
37. Defeated 1982 Amendment
41. Swallows up
42. Kind of grapes
43. French engineer
44. Netherlands cheese
47. Model train name
48. Bequeaths
49. Tipsy
51. Floppy disks, e.g.
52. Dora's traveling companion
53. Expenses
54. Blemish
56. Chinese money
57. *Chocolat* actress
58. Brutish sort
59. Crime that makes MADD mad

Billboards

solution on page 304

ACROSS

1. Disobey
5. Blofeld had 'em
10. Clan history
14. Gin fruit
15. Citadel student
16. Pod of sorts
17. Milano moola, once
18. Bout site
19. Red sauce brand
20. First half ...
23. Test drive
25. Post-op stop
26. Describable
27. Dog-eat-dog
30. Polo Grounds hero
31. Former Davis Cup captain
32. Mindful
34. Marks a ballot
37. Oddity about this quote
41. Covert org.
42. "Who's there?" response
43. "White Flag" performer
44. Offensive holiday?
45. Airport employee
48. Dodgeball pro
52. Grp. into genealogy
53. Java server
54. ... second half of quote
57. Party pooper
58. Yogi was behind it
59. Not one __
62. Chemical compound
63. French beans
64. Chew steadily
65. Nerve network
66. Gets sight of, biblically
67. Classroom call

DOWN

1. Personal connection
2. Clinton or Bush at one time
3. Early spring bloom
4. "She Loves You" word
5. Scanty
6. Benders
7. Arabian seaport
8. Richards of tennis
9. American Crossword Tournament site
10. Cow catcher
11. Reach rival
12. Bright Orion star
13. Give the slip
21. Feel yucky
22. In pursuit of
23. Many an inhabitant of the island of Sodor
24. Oxidizes
28. Cock and bull
29. Dog-paddles
33. Stories
34. Classic sci-fi radio show
35. Place to get down from
36. Contempt
38. Michelangelo's only signed sculpture
39. Goes for
40. "__ to Joy"
44. Three-bag hit
46. Least rampant
47. Age of note
48. European viper
49. Nemo's creator
50. Crime fighter Ness
51. Appomattox man
55. Hoopster Archibald
56. Euphoric state
60. Old salt
61. Overwhelm

Chanukah Greetings

solution on page 304

ACROSS

1. It's in the background
6. Colorful expressions
11. Jam ingredient
14. Quickly
15. With less color
16. Lisa, on *Green Acres*
17. Part 1 of quote
20. Put down
21. Twiggy places
22. Psyche's love
26. Part 2 of quote
29. *Apocalypse Now* incendiary
31. Doce meses
32. "Chances __"
33. Pipe cleaner
34. Roulette bet
36. Part 3 of quote
42. Trikester of *Laugh-In*
43. March along
45. Jackie's O
48. State VIP
49. The Donald's daughter
50. Part 4 of quote
54. Mallrat, most likely
55. Zee, to Zeno
56. Not fooled by
58. Part 5 of quote
65. Costar of Betty and Rue
66. "No man is an island" writer
67. Restricted
68. RR stop
69. Antennaed slowpoke
70. Critic with a thumb

DOWN

1. Director Peckinpah
2. IRS expert
3. Made tracks
4. Sleet-covered
5. Ground grain
6. Place in Eliza Doolittle's exercise
7. Role for Billy Dee
8. TV cat-hater
9. Largest US union
10. Yukky Yankee
11. Lear jet rival
12. Incarnation
13. Go to the mat, slangily
18. Yes or no follower
19. Loop for Lilo?
22. "Tell me more!"
23. K follower
24. Colorful fish
25. Punjab princess
27. Pay hike
28. Cross letters
30. Actor of many faces
34. It might be raw
35. Supper scrap
37. Siegfried's org.
38. VH-1 rival
39. Fall preceder
40. Unattached
41. It locks an ox
44. Slide the camera
45. Nuclear weapons
46. Get together again
47. Chest filler
48. Sentries
49. :, sometimes
51. In history
52. Anwar's successor
53. Chip maker
57. Move like the Blob
59. Thither
60. Actress Claire
61. Old salt
62. Three Dog Night hit
63. Finish'd
64. Rachel Carson subject

1	2	3	4	5		6	7	8	9	10		11	12	13
14						15						16		
17				18						19				
				20					21					
22	23	24	25		26			27	28					
29				30				31				32		
33						34	35							
	36				37					38	39	40	41	
					42				43					44
45	46	47		48				49						
50			51				52	53			54			
55							56		57					
58					59	60					61	62	63	64
65				66					67					
68				69					70					

ACROSS

1. Malaprop, for one
4. Range backbones
11. Drift off
14. Signal
15. Skelton feature
16. GI mail drop
17. Part 1 of quotation
19. Exemplar of easiness
20. Flower holder
21. Feelings, nothing more than feelings
23. Easy to manage
25. She "outed" on TV
26. Sights at Oxford
29. Letter to Santa, maybe
32. "Yessir," e.g.
33. Concerned with
34. Part 2 of quotation
40. Lively dance
41. So-called
42. Disclosed
46. Words from the town crier
47. Pong creator
48. Furry growth
49. Certainty
53. One year in four
55. Anti-ICBM plan
56. Last part of quotation
60. "Fever" singer
61. Hitting precisely
62. In times past
63. Kind of curve
64. Lacking courage
65. Dissenting vote

DOWN

1. It merged into WorldCom
2. This can be monotonous
3. Earthquake activity, collectively
4. Blind trio
5. Early man
6. Fifth of a series
7. Exclusive
8. The same as before
9. Generic dog's name
10. Legislature's place
11. Place known for gelato
12. Thinks out loud
13. Refrains
18. You might get this after mono
22. Green around the gills
23. Bolshevik target
24. Choir recess
27. Boarding an Acela
28. Carnegie's industry
29. Handle with skill
30. Follower of Models or Murder
31. Bacterial genus, briefly
35. Comb user
36. Able fellow
37. Old-world
38. Pastoral poem
39. Like some stockings
42. Try to get a pin
43. Piano pieces
44. Keeps changing
45. ". . . __ he drove out of sight . . ."
50. Biblical patsy
51. Dither
52. Trade for cash
53. Light focuser
54. Bits of work
57. Do battle
58. Turkish title
59. Dale's hubby

1	2	3		4	5	6	7	8	9	10		11	12	13
14				15								16		
17			18									19		
		20					21			22				
23	24								25					
26				27	28		29	30	31					
32						33								
34					35				36	37	38	39
			40				41					
42	43	44	45				46					
47								48				
49				50	51	52		53	54			
55				56			57				58	59
60				61						62		
63				64						65		

4. Big Films

ACROSS

1. Promenade
5. China setting
9. Sacred song
14. Pilothouse position
15. Calf meat
16. Roomy dress cut
17. Commuter's hope
18. Ship to Colchis
19. Burn a bit
20. Swanson movie of 1950
23. "The Scourge of God"
24. Live and breathe
25. Alcoholic dessert
29. Adjective for McCullers's cafe
32. Poodle-adorned item of the '50s
35. Auction actions
36. "I Remember It Well" musical
37. Musical film of 1950
40. Sticky stuff
41. Epitome of thinness
42. Something to dress to
43. Admit, with "up"
44. Parts of some hats
46. Reagan program, briefly
47. Chinese fruit
51. Lunar-aimed film of 1950
57. Impromptu quip
58. Window part
59. Seals, as a deal
60. On the whole
61. Bargain type
62. Traditional stuff
63. Pricy fur
64. Calls at poker
65. In the cellar

DOWN

1. A son of Ishmael
2. Attu native
3. Was biased toward
4. Proceeds full force
5. Bodily manifestation
6. Sarajevo citizen
7. Othello's deceiver
8. Last name in baseball
9. Lesotho's capital
10. Red-topped film role for Shelley Duvall
11. Ike's ex
12. Tech sch. grad
13. Prepared to drive
21. Blue bloods
22. Dogie snarer
26. Phrase with bend or lend
27. Main theme
28. Pastoral poem
29. Convey via Ameslan
30. Fluish feeling
31. Cacophonies
32. Edible starch
33. Have no doubts
34. Not excluded
36. Flour factory
38. Kernel
39. Detach
44. Good to eat
45. Wahine welcomes
46. Moonshine machine
48. Brownish color
49. Weed whackers
50. Hawaii in a state map, often
51. Emcee's post
52. Writer Buchanan
53. Thick cut
54. Indiana Jones perils
55. The stuff of legend
56. Crystal-gazer's words

'50s Films

solution on page 305

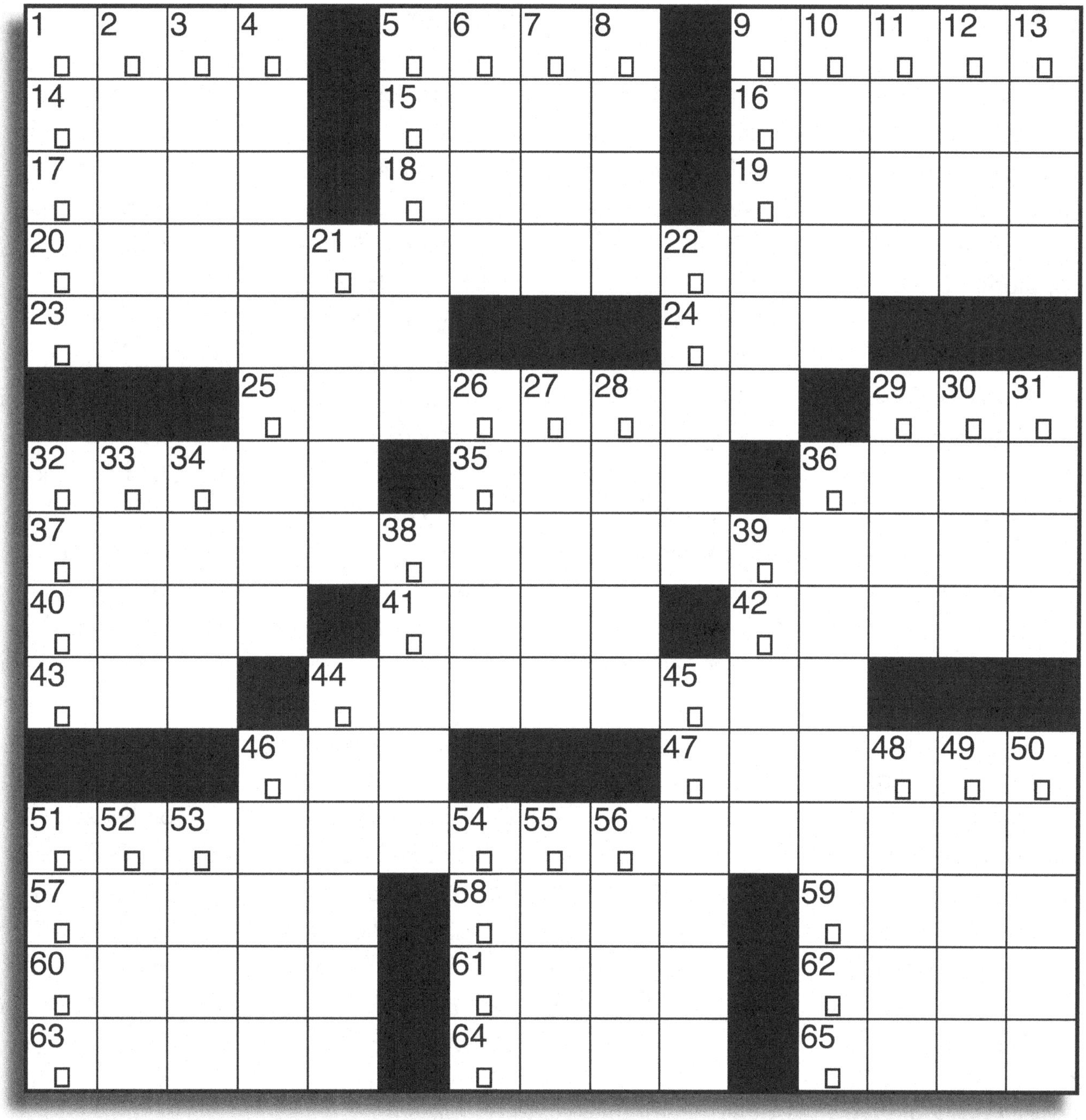

ACROSS

1. It may be a cross but not a down
6. Good grade
10. Bring down the house?
14. Storied other reindeer
15. Welk lead-in
16. Heavy haulers
17. Notorious name of '51
20. Holder in the hacienda
21. Words of inclusive discovery
22. Passion
23. Cafeteria carrier
25. Big-chinned host
27. Expensive eggs
30. Easing
34. Theater of old
35. Met score
36. Former orbiter
37. Cartoon begun in '51
41. "I'm Alive" gp.
42. Slightly
43. Unknown aircraft
44. Kennedy or Clinton
47. They weep
48. In vogue
49. T follower
50. Word with pen or Penn
53. Circle of light
55. Folk singer Jenkins
59. '51 vehicle for Katherine and Bogie
62. Monopoly piece
63. Rural hotels
64. Icy water transport
65. Obscure character
66. Type of arch
67. Expo '70 site

DOWN

1. Austin Powers power
2. It's after Av
3. Seasoning sometimes with Havarti
4. Icarus' attempt
5. A hundred bani
6. Type of line
7. Swag
8. Still pure
9. Diocese
10. Sir Walter Scott novel
11. Let go
12. Gene's *Producers* co-star
13. Many an RPI grad
18. Burn somewhat
19. Darling dog
24. The Buddha's mother was one
26. *Easy Street* actor
27. Like medical files
28. Maid in *Die Fledermaus*
29. Malevolence
30. Enlightened Buddhist
31. Word with mirror or spitting
32. Not so nasty
33. Lady Jane and Zane
35. Jigsaw puzzle work
38. Lahore wrap
39. Like obsidian
40. Pesky insects
45. They're usually in the 80's
46. Child or Puck
47. Grebe's cousin
49. World-weary
50. Use a spoon
51. Traffic word
52. Forever and a day
54. Undesirable spots
56. She looked like she had Danishes on her ears
57. Valerie Plame's career ender
58. "Puppy Love" singer
60. Copacabana site
61. Status follower

solution on page 305

ACROSS

1. Treats for Archie and Jughead
6. Beloved, to the Bard
10. It might be hanging
14. Consumed
15. Escorts
17. Beckett play of 1952
19. Cereal box abbr.
20. Docile
21. *Airplane!* heroine
22. Petal oil
23. Urban blight
24. Masked mammal
27. "Angela's Ashes" sequel
28. Blessing preceder, often
29. Sudden flight
30. __ Raton
34. Title role in Ralph Ellison book of 1952
38. Stitched
39. Call it quits
40. Skewed
41. "Crossfire" network
42. Loom device
44. Ridiculous
48. Robin Hoods' Nottingham
49. Plains home
50. Coffee shop
51. Old Pan Am rival
54. His "Old Man ..." came out in 1952
57. China type
58. *Cider House Rules* star
59. Aromatic herb
60. Dumbstruck
61. Flanges

DOWN

1. Bryn __
2. Somewhat
3. Solo's love
4. "Pshaw!"
5. Barroom target in Westerns
6. Gofer
7. Deduce
8. WWII arena
9. The radius goes about halfway across it
10. Southern Slav
11. Was talented
12. Past
13. Forestall
16. Wrinkly fruits
18. Former Haig command
22. Flip __
24. Charlie Brown's "Darn!"
25. Crick
26. Enjoy taffy
27. Randy's ice partner
29. It was dropped in the 1960s
30. *Baby Jane* portrayer
31. Pass over
32. Telemarket
33. Put into a pot
35. Feud
36. Rest stop
37. Dustin's *Marathon Man* co-star
41. Salad green
42. Disgraced
43. LP player
44. Enjoyed home cooking
45. Quotable catcher
46. Handmeister Wences
47. Put another way
48. Landscape
51. Slender shoot
52. Dwindle
53. Thumbs-ups
55. Greeting, in oaters
56. Ramble

New in '52

solution on page 305

ACROSS

1. Duel tools
6. PETA kin
11. Elbow poke
14. Stuffed deli delicacy
15. Like Samson, once
16. Kid of Jazz
17. Watson & Crick discovery
19. It's picked by the picky
20. Like batteries sometimes
21. Harangue
23. Matters of will
24. Reverent
25. First word in a Robert M. Pirsig title
26. Willed items
29. Arts schools, of a sort
32. I Love You, for one
33. Fooled ya!
34. Part of two Seuss titles
35. Cockney coppers
36. Lush valley
37. Coat for cooking
38. Run-down
39. Bathroom bars
40. Fall movies, often
42. Brit's belly
43. Lingerie purchases
44. Tips badly
48. Part of R.U.R.
50. Part of a clergy hierarchy
51. Workers' fed.
52. Arthur Miller classic
54. Jaws sighting
55. True-blue
56. Range ridge
57. High part of a weir
58. They have ears and wide mouths
59. Less normal

DOWN

1. Smarmy neighbor of the Beav
2. Drudges
3. Burp
4. Decorate brilliantly
5. Greets, in a way
6. Hibachi heap
7. Take off
8. Baby kisser
9. Commentary
10. On edge
11. Polio conqueror
12. Like Mars
13. Computer character?
18. Jeannie portrayer
22. *Less Than Perfect* lead
24. He's green on the island of Sodor
26. Tight spots
27. You, a long time ago
28. Without
29. Short swims
30. Kind of surgery
31. He prefers shaken to stirred
32. Zigs or zags
35. It might be XXX
36. Quail or grouse
38. Saliva
39. Willemstad is its capital
41. "Do Ya" gp.
42. Off-limits
44. Permanent result?
45. Receded
46. *48 HRS* star
47. Pilot
48. Abundant
49. *thirtysomething* star
50. Harry Potter had one
53. Cyclops standout

The Year: 1953

solution on page 305

ACROSS

1. *The Power of Now* author
6. Like Jumpin' Jack Flash
10. Recuperate
14. Sorbonne send-off
15. Muted trumpet sound
16. Part of M*A*S*H
17. Item first sold in 1954
20. Men of many words
21. Boater's behind
22. Private address?
23. Apollo 11's LEM
25. With Murrow, hunter hunter
30. Vamp Bara
32. Immature salamanders
33. Tofu source
34. In what manner?
35. Postal creed word
37. Ball caller, for short
39. Half a chocolate candy?
40. Baby blues
42. Fawn or stag
44. "Happy Birthday" medium
46. She married DiMaggio in 1954
49. Howlers
50. Bit of granola
51. Assignments
54. Flag stuff
58. White House hostess
61. Bator lead-in
62. Knight time
63. Jung's inner self
64. Clique
65. Barbershop sound
66. Church council

DOWN

1. Sonoran snack
2. Bloodhound's enticer
3. Quartermaine role from *General Hospital*
4. Acrobat's attire
5. Spaniard or Swede
6. Flabbergasts
7. Sal of song
8. Blow away, so to speak
9. Ferocity
10. Makes a beeline
11. 15 miles of song
12. Don Juan's emotion
13. Actress Whitfield
18. Crushed underfoot
19. Man, e.g.
23. Gee's preceder
24. Maestro Toscanini
25. Lesser amount
26. Never existed
27. Maynard's pal
28. *Lolita* actress
29. Chinese masculine force
30. Big ant film
31. Georgetown athlete
36. Extended journeys
38. Vicious fishes
41. Common activity when you close
43. These types are rather wide
45. Not just soft
47. Minstrel's item
48. It may be proper
51. Cocksure
52. Western Samoa money
53. Model from Somalia
54. Roadrunner's cry
55. Victor's cry
56. James Mason sci-fi role of 1954
57. June celebrant
59. Bit of positivity
60. Hindu title

ACROSS

1. Type of treatment or thing needing treatment
5. More than a mere success
10. Type of chicken
14. Canal opened in 1825
15. Centric starter
16. Malaria symptom
17. CA tourist attraction opened in '55
19. *Marty* director
20. Hankers
21. Must
23. Bob of Bob and Ray
25. Start of a Spike Lee film title
26. Heavy metal
28. Trite
32. Like some funds
37. Go!
38. One of the Waughs
39. Edible bulbs
41. Falstaff quaffs
42. They have shoulders, but no arms
44. Dastard's forte
46. They're often recalled
48. Have the look
49. It gets hammered
51. Like a Muppet chef
56. A Monroe hubby
60. Jambalaya kin
61. Like Moriarty
62. *Winds of War* author
64. Crowsnest cry
65. Promo gimmick
66. Actress Heche
67. Signs
68. Muggle haters
69. Joplin tunes

DOWN

1. Tint anew
2. A Disney princess or Israeli leader
3. Rug fiber
4. Painter Toulouse-Lautrec
5. Snake oil salesmen
6. Dick Van Dyke Show scapegoat
7. NPR book reviewer Cheuse
8. Trig ratios
9. Cab call
10. Epitome of rebellion, from '55
11. Holy mackerel!
12. Speck of the litter
13. Vegas game
18. Tibbets' mom
22. Farmer's place
24. HBO UFO miniseries
27. *The Ballet Class* painter
29. Martyr of 1776
30. Former ova
31. Kinski title role
32. Jurist Warren
33. Popular number
34. Twenty quires
35. Ray Kroc's company
36. Prescribed amounts
40. Kitchen vessels
43. Hitch
45. "In other words ..."
47. Tourist highlights
50. __ wait
52. John, or one of his sons, namesake of a scotch whiskey company
53. Massey of the screen
54. Hurled
55. Codlike fishes
56. Chopped liver purveyor
57. *Stop! Or My Mom Will Shoot* director Reitman
58. End of a Marilyn Monroe film title
59. Modern ice cream flavor
63. Smith and Jones flick, briefly

New in '55

solution on page 305

ACROSS

1. Feel pain
5. A dollar in Kuwait
10. Prized items
14. Nursery purchase
15. Eleve's place
16. Month after Av
17. Village, of yore
18. Gene Vincent hit of 1956
20. Dated
22. Unflappably
23. In a tizzy
25. Notions
26. Doris Day song of 1956
32. Egg-shaped
33. Ties one's shoe
34. Ovine utterance
37. Nibbed tools
38. Star of *Capricorn One* and *M*A*S*H*
39. *Jungle Boy* star of '56
40. Holds
41. Col. Tibbets' mom
42. Expressed wonder
43. Little Richard rework of 1956
45. Type of fund
49. Bronx cheer
50. Amigo
54. Tenderfoot
58. Loesser song of 1956
60. Places for posies
61. Orchid-expert detective, to friends
62. Give a wide berth
63. Gene Simmons' group
64. Kremlin dynast
65. Hounds' sounds
66. Syllogism words

DOWN

1. Raspy Ray
2. Like Fonzie
3. Like this book
4. Stress
5. Shark's victim, at times
6. Luger's surface
7. Cribbage jack
8. Not just a little
9. __ *Man* (Estevez film)
10. Frozen
11. Artfully dodge
12. Ancient jester __ Nasrudin
13. Defeats a dragon
19. Aka
21. Like fine wine
24. Funny fellow
26. Hebrew letter, not a cold symptom
27. Eye layer
28. Ages upon ages
29. __ Sainte Marie
30. Filled pastry
31. Like Rudolph's nose
34. Siamese coin
35. Act as accomplice
36. German carmaker
38. Serengeti stampeder
39. Type of long-necked lute
41. Phillips of "Benson"
42. Ricelike pasta
44. Capacitance measurements
45. In short supply
46. Hoop sites
47. Eclipse shadow
48. Hunter's guide
51. 6/6/44
52. All-night party
53. Hydroxyl compound
55. *Miracle on 34th Street* role
56. *Meet Me __ Louis*
57. Gas brand outside the U.S.
59. Kind of code

Say What Songs of '56

solution on page 306

ACROSS

1. Loses strength
5. Commits a deadly sin
10. Caesar or Cleopatra
14. Use a hammock
15. *Paper Moon* star
16. Jon Arbuckle's dog
17. Ice chunk
18. The "U" of UHF
19. Narthex neighbor
20. 1957 jury drama
23. Some passes
24. Gives the boot to
25. Less wild
27. Mxyzptlk, for one
28. Sewing-machine man
29. Shell lining
32. Beer outlet
35. Hemingway adaptation of '57
39. Gunpowder Plot's Fawkes
40. Armbones
41. Wine hub
42. In behalf of
43. Snob of a sort
46. Valuable strings
49. Watched
51. Ingmar Bergman classic of '57
54. Defeat soundly
55. Late bloomer?
56. Type of lift
58. Caesar's being
59. It's over the fence
60. Cosmetic additive
61. Sod spoiler
62. President before Polk
63. Plateau

DOWN

1. Keebler worker
2. Cloth roll
3. Slays, Dirty Harry-style
4. More apt to nod off
5. It's blown up in *The Great Race*
6. Ignorant
7. Of bristles
8. Mountain lakes
9. Foundry refuse
10. Settle the score
11. "Dilbert" cartoonist
12. Rosie's concern
13. Mall rats
21. Box top
22. Friend of Mercutio
25. Austin Powers verb
26. Vegan staple
27. N.Y.C. subway
30. 2001 Will Smith biopic
31. People who patronize
32. Fit for future service
33. Roadie's haul
34. HS exam
36. Lose ground?
37. Kids' card game
38. McClellan victory site
42. Ate nothing
44. "Element Song" singer
45. Wallet papers
46. Disperse
47. Yonder items
48. Don't waste
49. Peevish
50. "__ Tomorrow Comes" (Sammy Kaye hit)
52. Far-reaching
53. Indochina country
57. *Crying Game* star

Films of '57

solution on page 306

1	2	3	4		5	6	7	8	9		10	11	12	13
14					15						16			
17					18						19			
	20			21					22					
		23							24					
25	26							27						
28						29	30	31				32	33	34
35			36	37						38				
39				40						41				
			42					43	44	45				
46	47	48				49	50							
51					52							53		
54					55						56			57
58					59						60			
61					62						63			

ACROSS

1. He resigned on 10/10/73
6. Pinnacle
11. Quick to learn
14. Pasta sauce
15. Small primate
16. Type of date
17. Spicy seasoning
19. Prankish pipsqueak
20. Vaulted recess
21. Plimpton book
22. Big Bopper hit
27. Mel of football
29. Western capital
30. Chuck Berry song
34. Laertes, to Polonius
35. Yiddish yikes
36. Dorothy on *The Golden Girls*
39. High-pitched song
45. Proboscis
47. Pinball start
48. Presley hit of '58 in Britain (and '57 in the U.S.)
52. Couturiere Schiaparelli
53. ESPN subj.
54. Joan Cusack, to John
55. Derby pro
62. Map altering org.
63. Quitter's comment
64. *The Necklace* had it
65. Spanish or Japanese honorific
66. Aussie city
67. *Hans Brinker* author

DOWN

1. Dragnet letters
2. Mousse cousin
3. Spy org.
4. Inclusive abbr.
5. Taipan pan
6. Caught some Z's
7. "Uh-Huh Girl" co.
8. Spur
9. French street
10. Bungle
11. Reebok rival
12. Bubbly rock
13. Little house on the prairie?
18. Word with hose
21. Nobelist Wiesel
22. Mindy of *The Facts of Life*
23. 4th c. nomad
24. Dancer Miller
25. Corp. takeover
26. Yeshiva head
27. East Coast membership buyer's club
28. John, to Ringo
31. Gillespie's genre
32. Sock hop site, maybe
33. Buckeyes' sch.
36. Verb for Danno
37. Roxy Music co-founder
38. Stretched-out *Star Wars* word
39. Pop
40. "Whazzat?"
41. He played Quincy's aide
42. *WarGames* org.
43. Stark of England
44. Part of ASPCA
45. Aid to digestion
46. New name of Datsun
48. Pulls one's leg
49. Free
50. Obsession, e.g.
51. Gort almost destroyed it
55. In fashion
56. "Wings" nickname
57. EMS aim
58. Hit trio
59. Scuttle
60. H.S. course
61. It might be seeded

Songs of '58

solution on page 306

ACROSS

1. Union defier
5. Composer Bartok
9. Nestling pigeon
14. Aaron's acting daughter
15. Etc. kin
16. New currency of 2002
17. Go up against
18. Tackle box item
19. "Behold!"
20. Youngest U.S. chess champ (January of '58)
23. Knights, at times
24. Seals up, in a way
28. Cooking leaf
29. Share of profits
31. Type of onion
32. Run a meeting
35. Red dye
37. Kind of wind or will
38. Seuss title of '58
41. *Miss Saigon* setting, briefly
42. Eastwood's "Rawhide" role
43. Deadener for youth?

44. Part of Ripley's title
46. Large cask
47. "Nova" network
48. Metallic auto trim
50. Bead art
54. Surrounder discovered in '58
57. Dyeing method
60. Ump's call
61. Whoopsy!
62. Like Tom Hanks, with "Wilson"
63. First fratricide
64. Early 007 foe
65. Trudges
66. Sub chaser
67. Takes before Wapner

DOWN

1. Shots in the dark
2. Early computer language
3. Oranjestad's island
4. Gradually
5. Batty place?
6. Vanity cases
7. Director Von Trier
8. Pianist Templeton
9. Vegas natural
10. Least needed
11. Providence sch.
12. Time Warner name dropper
13. "Be Prepared" org.
21. Annually
22. Jazzman's "Go!"
25. Grammy-winner Bonnie
26. Euchre variant
27. Proctor-__ (appliance brand)
29. Humorist Myron
30. A Swiss Army knife has many
32. Skeptic
33. Uncultivated land
34. Mail room item?
35. Famous last words

36. Pencil stub
39. Like Baby Bears porridge
40. Bush offerings
45. Like some reporters
47. Spanish dish
49. Toyota and Ford
50. Ways up and out
51. Gandhi's dad
52. Dolly for one
53. More mores
55. Not even close
56. Gray wolf
57. It's a relief
58. Given amount
59. Excessive

The Year: 1958

solution on page 306

ACROSS

1. Detail, for short
5. Penne or fusilli
10. Mayor's bailiwick
14. Legal lead-in
15. Just over a quart
16. First $100,000/ year netman
17. "How sweet __!"
18. Word with false or fire
19. Discovery of 1898
20. Gleason's vehicle
23. Gave rise to
24. Wall St. intro
25. "... nattering __ of negativism"
28. Wine-and-soda drink
33. Hodgepodge
34. Journalist Goodman
35. Beehive State brave
36. Annette, Cubby et al., with "The"
40. Grandpa Simpson
41. What botox does
42. European carmaker
43. Graduates' certificates
45. Skilled
47. It may be slippery
48. *La Boheme* updated
49. Long-running kid's show
57. "Here comes trouble!"
58. Refrain after animal sounds
59. Road shoulder
60. Cleopatra portrayer in '17
61. Huskies' burdens
62. Frilly trim
63. *J'Accuse* director Gance
64. Present, for example
65. Joie de vivre

DOWN

1. Patio turner
2. Maze choice
3. Albany's canal
4. Accountant's need
5. They smooth things out
6. Felt below par
7. Gallows reprieve
8. Kind of insurance
9. Wardrobes
10. Is unable to
11. Fortuneteller's start
12. *Adventures in Babysitting* deity
13. Wistful thinking
21. Spinner in space
22. Add one's two cents
25. Wanderer
26. Why not
27. Arm muscle
28. Oscar Madison and others
29. As well
30. Bantu people
31. Paganini offering
32. Bridge move
34. Madame Bovary
37. First name among bombers
38. Most tasty
39. Like desserts at some restaurants
44. Deadly
45. Veinlike
46. Part of ESL
48. Speakeasy stings
49. "Show me the money!" shouter
50. Pequod captain
51. Hole in your head
52. Cleo's barge carrier
53. Alert
54. True-to-life
55. Shamu or Willy
56. Writing on the wall

1	2	3	4		5	6	7	8	9		10	11	12	13
14					15						16			
17					18						19			
20				21					22					
			23					24						
25	26	27				28	29				30	31	32	
33					34						35			
36			37	38					39					
40				41					42					
43			44					45	46					
			47				48							
49	50	51			52	53					54	55	56	
57					58						59			
60					61						62			
63					64						65			

5. Time Machine: The '50s

ACROSS

1. Beautify, in a way
5. Room design
10. Airline with very good security
14. About a third of Earth's land mass
15. Baked brick
16. Vineyard valley
17. Abused
19. Banjo part
20. *High Society* song
22. Bonnet dweller
23. Comprehension
24. Stray securer
28. Ledger entry
30. Like Humpty Dumpty
31. Rough up
32. Ernie's TV partner
36. Severe lunch date excuse song
39. *Easy Street* actor
40. Bounce off the walls
41. Brings up
42. Assortment
44. Father figure, to a hipster?
45. One with pressing concerns?
48. Bk. after Exodus
49. "Can-Can" hit song
55. Mirror shape at times
56. *I Remember Mama* actress
58. Use the microwave
59. Rarely-mentioned James Bond portrayer
60. Medical suffix
61. Legendary septet
62. McCarthy's trunkmate
63. Snowpeas, essentially

DOWN

1. Slangy leg
2. "__ Mommy Kissing Santa Claus"
3. Checkout headache
4. Wonka's writer
5. Ire
6. Axel, in *Beverly Hills Cop*
7. Duck or turkey preceder
8. Debated wedding-vow word
9. Do again
10. Chained up
11. Early animal form
12. Anchor position
13. Machine tool
18. Astronomer's light ratio
21. Reuters rival
24. Where the heart is
25. Force in King novels
26. Bus rider Parks
27. Takes apart
28. Elegantly showy
29. Dollar starter
31. Flaky mineral
33. Kind of reckoning
34. Exerter's words
35. U.S. gas brand renamed after a Standard Oil suit
37. Contour map features
38. With children
43. "Shiny Happy People" group
44. Protect
45. Computer pix
46. Musical show
47. 1970 World's Fair site
48. Eye makeup
50. Cheshire Cat feature
51. Glacier coating
52. Witticism
53. Golden Rule word
54. It's an OK place
57. Every ship has one

You're the Tops

solution on page 307

1	2	3	4		5	6	7	8	9		10	11	12	13
14					15						16			
17			18								19			
	20									21				
				22					23					
24	25	26	27				28	29						
30					31					32	33	34	35
36				37				38					
39				40				41					
		42	43					44					
45	46	47					48						
49					50	51				52	53	54	
55				56									57
58				59					60				
61				62					63				

ACROSS

1. Postal creed obstacle
6. Cartoon Chihuahua
9. It lacks backing
14. Gandhi, for one
15. Org. symbolized by a caduceus
16. Manga movie style
17. True up
18. One on top
20. READY
22. Stretched *Star Wars* word
23. WWII journalist
24. High muck-a-muck
28. Gambit
29. Eagles' org.
32. Century plants
33. Ye preceder
34. Gumshoe, at times
35. AIM
38. Burden
39. Formerly
40. Feudal lord
41. Posthumous duettist of 1991
42. Calf-mate
43. Like Dutch shoes
44. TV threesome
45. Mother, in the Ozarks
46. FIRE
54. Gallant
55. Home movie
56. A chicken in __ pot
57. Little green men
58. Fencing items
59. Work stations
60. TVA spin-off
61. Scolds, with "out"

DOWN

1. Iranian ruler, once
2. Actress Taylor of *Mystic Pizza*
3. Sir Geraint's love
4. Leading follower
5. Charlie, for one
6. Leave time
7. Grounded birds
8. ID plate
9. In a sinister way
10. Full of wonder
11. Role for Marlon
12. Love, in Lorca
13. Square
19. Pooh pal
21. Pick pick pick
24. Twirler's tool
25. Massey of film
26. Date
27. Volstead's opponents
28. *Goodfellas* actor
29. Spoke sheepishly?
30. Burn a bit
31. Colonist asked to speak for himself
33. Less ugly
34. Tony Orlando and Dawn, e.g.
36. They might be scored
37. Pass
42. Saunters
43. Prankster
44. Conceited smile
45. They might play bingo with no markers
46. Ran in the wash
47. All-night party
48. Tax Day, for one
49. Cager Thurmond
50. Dry dishes
51. Figment
52. Swarm
53. Dan Blocker role

Ready, Aim, Fire!

solution on page 307

solution on page 307

ACROSS

1. Saudi garment
4. Prepare for painting
9. Louisiana native
14. Quagmire
15. Type of candle
16. Staring intently
17. Frat whose members are barely passing
19. Type of contract
20. Tops
21. Twosome
23. Changes location, perhaps
25. Lets off the hook
30. Platters
32. Infamous cow owner
33. Demolished in Devon
36. Amerind tribe
38. King leader
39. Downspout feeders
40. It issues fed. docs.
41. Household canary, e.g.
44. Attract a trooper perhaps
46. Fraidy cat
47. More up-to-date
49. Belongs
51. Effulgent
55. Europe's tallest active volcano
57. One or two
58. Prefix equivalent to -ish
62. Opera star singing to the troops?
64. Made an "oopsie"
65. Observe Yom Kippur
66. Letters on McGwire's cap
67. Coins for cheap novels
68. Small anchor
69. Immigrant's subj.

DOWN

1. Despise
2. Memorable trailblazer
3. Malarial fevers
4. Not COD
5. Perches
6. World currency org.
7. Anti-DWI activists
8. Follow
9. Luminosity unit
10. Give it __
11. Boxer's blow
12. Magazine holder?
13. Hammett detective Beaumont
18. Napped leather
22. Nerve-cell conduits
24. Junkyard fodder
26. Rusty Staub, once
27. Pitcher Satchel
28. Figure of speech
29. Where fathers may gather
31. Vegas natural
33. Kid's song performer
34. First *Tonight Show* host
35. Dentist's request
37. Discourage
39. Plumed wader
42. Great fury
43. Sea nymphs of myth
44. One taken
45. *Big Night* role
48. Diminishing
50. Kind of attack
52. Treat badly
53. Places for a diet of worms
54. Bridge resident
56. Buy a hand
58. Math proof abbr.
59. Mentalist Geller
60. Chair part
61. Check out
63. Dowsing tool

Cargo

solution on page 307

ACROSS

1. Hindu noblewomen
6. Exchanged for Powers in 1962
10. Swarm
14. Retro poster genre
15. Diana's supplanter, on *The Avengers*
16. Word in two Bond titles
17. Site of many mysterious disappearances
20. Salad green
21. Burr or Hamilton, once
22. Toothpaste option
23. Lazy ones
24. Entertains
28. Bottled spirit
30. Con game
31. Trapper's trophy
32. God of destruction
36. Critter in a faked picture
39. Chemical suffix
40. Judo class protectors
41. Borden spokescow
42. Spews
44. Kansas City nine
45. Colorful lizards
48. It's not free of charge
49. South Americans
50. Stone engraving
55. Obsession for Fox Mulder
57. Gangster's gal
58. Sunbather's or fisherman's catch
59. Place on a list
60. Withdraws, with "out"
61. Skull & Bones school
62. Refuse

DOWN

1. Bench outfit
2. *Greystoke* extras
3. *French Connection* cop
4. Cookbook author Rombauer
5. Maker of roe
6. In any way
7. Diminish
8. Bobble the ball
9. Verbally assaulted
10. With a robotic voice
11. *A Wrinkle in Time* author L'__
12. *Oklahoma!* aunt
13. Press secretary Dee Dee
18. They might go for a few bucks
19. Autobahn auto
24. Up to snuff
25. Particle of cosmic radiation
26. Extraordinary: Scots
27. Unlucky ones
28. Hero's exploits
29. Street liners
31. Coll. entrance exam
33. "__ raid!"
34. Thin disguise?
35. Mythical hawk
37. Delegate
38. Newborns
43. Jazz flutist Herbie
44. Campus recruiting grp.
45. An affair to remember?
46. Lively dance
47. Like Pisa's tower
48. Occupied
50. Pastoral poem
51. Hit for Mathis and Bolton
52. Colorful parrot
53. A party to
54. 1993 peace negotiations site
56. Cote call

Mysteries

solution on page 307

ACROSS

1. Persuade
5. Kid's place?
10. Wonka writer
14. Wander
15. It has many layers
16. Drive the getaway car
17. Eugene Maleska staple
20. *West Side Story* song
21. Singer Seeger
22. Role in *The Right Stuff*
24. Fez frill
28. Type of opportunity
31. Boot out
33. "Bird" word form
34. Mary Kay rival
35. Powdered drink since '59
37. Poet Nash
39. Protein at a blood drive?
42. Norse goddess
43. Rick's old flame
44. Start of N.C.'s motto
45. Hope provider
46. Like the King in *The King and I*
48. Allure
50. Renter
52. Ancient Greek city-state
54. Nutmeg coat
56. Profit
60. Ack-ack generator?
64. Dunderheads
65. Post of properness
66. Longest armbone
67. Stand up to
68. Flaxlike fiber
69. Legendary loch

DOWN

1. Nocturnal bear
2. Kind of service
3. It blows
4. Dire time
5. Orchestral piece
6. Quechuan
7. Connery title
8. Group shop
9. Beginnings
10. Vice President or gymnast
11. Red crescent system
12. One of L.B.J.'s beagles
13. Soho co.
18. Miss equivalent?
19. Rotor housing
23. Like some surfaces
25. Brutality
26. All the same
27. Tarry
28. Pool limit
29. Unwilling
30. Buster's venues
32. Blechs
36. Flu source?
38. Lube job tool
40. MPAA, and others
41. Good looker
47. It's home on the range
49. Dancer Bambi __ (*Your Show of Shows*)
51. Full of spunk
53. Printing daggers
55. City in Peru or Ohio
57. Do office work or nails
58. Wayside havens
59. High times
60. One way to send a pkg.
61. Cheech's pal's daughter
62. Spoiled
63. Hoop part

Crosses to Bear

solution on page 307

ACROSS

1. Hemsley series
5. Bingo kin
10. Delta House, e.g.
14. "__ Hey Hey Kiss Him Goodbye"
15. Lowermost deck
16. Gofer, perhaps
17. Pacino film of '75
20. "Well, __ be!"
21. Broadcast
22. Aspiring actress
26. Middle Eastern treat
30. Minx
31. Stable food
33. Thunderstruck
34. Coast Guard off.
35. Bud Abbott's bud
36. Transitions
37. Peter Sellers comic caper
41. Housewife's sack
43. Quarrel
44. Hole goal
47. Advantage
48. Assent asea
49. US border state
51. Cesta sport
53. Venture a guess
55. Prickly shrub
57. Kyoto honorific
58. Chuck Norris, in '83
65. By-and-by
66. "Ditto!"
67. *High Noon* climax
68. Cheeky
69. Black-ink item
70. "Ods bodkins!"

DOWN

1. In addition
2. Big Red?
3. A Siamese twin
4. Bottom lines?
5. *Young Frankenstein* star
6. Clemens stat
7. Italian sports car, briefly
8. Inform
9. Beethoven wrote just one
10. Spanish dance
11. 1947 Hope-Crosby destination
12. Hullabaloo
13. Countdown beginning
18. McBeal on TV
19. "We Are the World" goal
22. Girl's pronoun
23. Wine cask
24. Zulu spear
25. Hammer wielder
27. Mistake
28. Herd heroine
29. "This is where WALLS will be" guy
32. Singing cowboy of films
35. Shank
36. Baste
38. G-man
39. Candle ingredient
40. Broke up soil
41. Indian chief
42. *Evening Shade* role
45. Cry of triumph
46. Actor Scheider
48. Supermarket lanes
49. OPEC member
50. Strip
52. Java quality
54. Race site since 1711
56. Small lizards
58. Indy measure
59. Almost none
60. Hide-hair link
61. Mop-topped Stooge
62. Only mo. without a U.S. holiday
63. ATF's cousin
64. Antiquity

Canines

solution on page 307

ACROSS

1. Jane Austen novel
5. Snippet
10. Raincoat, in London
13. Perjurer
14. Lauer's cohost
16. B'way Burrows
17. Alien damage
19. Cast off
20. Concerning
21. Oceanfront
23. Super's needs
27. Made amends
28. Playing marbles
29. S. California city
31. Took a stab at
32. Donald's nephew
33. Econ. news no.
36. Chick watchers
37. Reveals
38. Halt, horse!
39. Coterie
40. Costs, with "to"
41. Word with eye or pie
42. Spheres
44. Gives a leg up
45. Values
47. Secretive
49. Permits
51. Facilitate
52. Campfire fallout
53. Like a physician's oath
58. *Citizen X* actor
59. Remorse
60. Skip
61. It needs a PIN
62. Ends one's case
63. Smitten

DOWN

1. Peyton Place's main street
2. Mamma's follower
3. Scratch up
4. Virtuosos
5. Petrifies
6. Mead need
7. Bad toupee
8. Eventful times
9. They're what ails you
10. Why Cheech might screech
11. Put up with
12. Handed over
15. Talkative
18. Signed a contract
22. Earth's star
23. Trajectories
24. See eye to eye
25. Revered Galloping Gourmet?
26. Cassandra, for one
30. Dumbfounds
32. Edna of TV
34. Fawn Hall's boss
35. Winner of "The Lottery," in essence
37. "Feel Like a Number" singer
38. Without reservation
40. Nab
41. Sometimes it's clear
43. Family dog, for short
44. Creatures
45. Ben's mom
46. Kickoff
48. Credo
50. Chef's herb
54. Collection agcy.
55. Doc bloc
56. Oil derrick
57. Kingston Trio hit

Anagram This!

solution on page 308

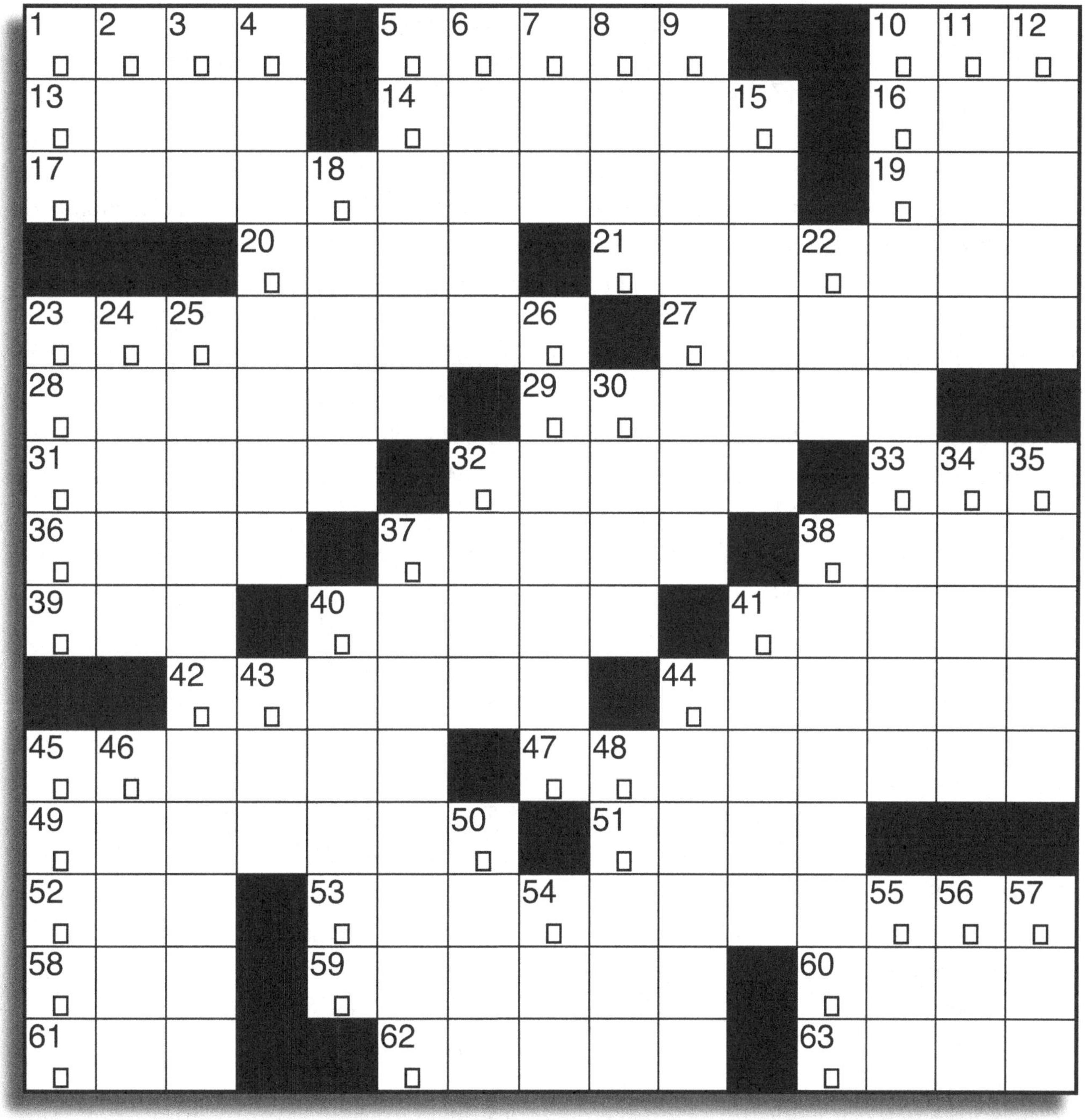

ACROSS

1. Miss who regrets
5. Refrain words
10. Bit of bickering
14. Airplane stunt
15. Cavities
16. Fairy tale heavy
17. Letting 'em have it
20. Jungle crusher
21. Desmond played by Swanson
22. "I lack iniquity" speaker
23. Clown of old TV
25. Penance prayer unit
28. Tied tresses
32. "__ never fly!"
33. Ancient Roman marketplace
34. Capacity-crowd letters
35. Exclamation in a baby's game
39. Pre-, wordwise
40. Shoppers' meccas
41. Flat fee
42. Drifters' needs
44. Pole vault items
46. Aphrodite's squeeze
47. Like Hamelin's piper
48. Tell-all title starter
51. Brings charges
55. It contains many single numbers
58. Hydroxyl compound
59. Deal with
60. Auctioneer's first offering
61. Bulky book
62. Dutch master Jan
63. *I Dream of Jeannie* star

DOWN

1. Paella pot
2. Betty Boop, e.g.
3. Part of the Corn Belt
4. Total rival
5. Widget
6. Sonata section
7. Pond tidbit
8. Tennis do-over
9. Bat wood
10. As well
11. *M*A*S*H* cook
12. E-mail heading
13. Brownie was its boss
18. Crowd sound
19. Digestive aid
23. "Monster Mash" sender
24. Heavy load
25. Less green
26. *SNL* comedienne
27. Sack out
28. Forms a common fund
29. Heretofore
30. It's twisted
31. Oafs
33. Pleats
36. Lacking ethics
37. Buck-naked
38. Subject to wear and tear
43. Chess maneuver
44. Fake diamond's source
45. CIA concern
47. Chatter idly
48. "__ a Song Go ..."
49. Skid row bum
50. Film director Egoyan
51. Not aweather
52. Adjective for "no news"
53. Do or sol
54. Potato part
56. Initial for Superman
57. Reno risk

Boo!

solution on page 308

ACROSS

1. Mocks
6. Women's gp.
9. Bridge call
14. Plump plus
15. Prior to
16. Host Edwards of *This Is Your Life*
17. Ogden Nash specialty
18. Hump day
20. North Pole helper
21. Hindu sage
22. Where the buck stops
23. Corroded
26. Slow haulers
28. Rankled relative
31. Held court
32. One up to no good
33. Bottom line
35. No-go call
36. __ City (video game)
38. Bulgarian capital
42. Bad start?
44. Like a non-believer
46. Entertainment unit units
49. Role for Astin or Julia
51. Forcible ejection
53. Tools for duels
54. Role for Shirley in '63
55. Anoint, old-style
57. Bank aud.
60. High-pitched hairdo
62. Ring-toss item
64. Bumped impolitely
65. WWII theater
66. Like man, in a way
67. Hot sauce
68. Hybrid vehicle?
69. Records

DOWN

1. Roman god to a poet
2. First victim
3. Just right, slangily
4. Draft letter
5. Diocese
6. Presence of morning droplets
7. Land measures
8. Cinnamon candy
9. Incense
10. Titled Turk
11. Wetland trees
12. Athens' rival
13. Most bashful
19. Vetoes
21. Mtg. sub
24. Claxon
25. Camp accommodations
27. Holy war
28. Dos Passos work
29. Collar
30. R.E.M. vocalist
34. Cousteau's world
37. Congrats!
39. Abject failures
40. Tenet
41. Relief sounds
43. *Mean Girls* star
45. Hang open
46. Some shakes
47. *Romeo and Juliet* setting
48. Playwright Beckett
50. They might be escrowed
52. Ming things
56. Brute preceder
58. Select
59. ABA people
61. Actress Lupino
62. Proof letters
63. New England sch.

Chas Did 'Em

solution on page 308

ACROSS

1. Hood's blade
5. It's turned when it's driven
10. Daddy-o
14. One with a hood and a muffler
15. Saw things
16. Noodle creation
17. ATONE
20. Marsh plant
21. Animator Bluth
22. Game rooms
25. Strict person
29. Nikita's successor
30. It goes right to the heart
31. Like ballet movements
32. Convex moldings
33. Vitality
34. NOTABLE
38. Deep black
39. Bitter herbs
40. Racer Andretti
42. Surpasses
45. Fencing moves
46. Make desolate
47. Raises in value
48. Mr. Ziegfeld
49. White flag's message
50. GOAT
57. Smart guy?
58. Notoriety
59. Classic Belafonte refrain
60. Prom night woe
61. Get togged up
62. Litigates

DOWN

1. Musical item
2. Puzzled remark
3. Midori of skating
4. Like igneous rock
5. Did a do
6. Gets plastered, perhaps
7. Sofer of *General Hospital*
8. Mail Boxes __
9. Movie genre
10. Eat out
11. Keats opus
12. Speed word
13. H.S. exam
18. Hoity-toity
19. Myrna's role
22. TV ET
23. Soothe
24. Barroom slider
25. Actress Gilpin et al.
26. Greek cafe
27. Eagerness
28. Site of '60s service
30. Italian talk
32. Neutral shade
35. Incited
36. Punish by fine
37. Posteriors
38. Book after Esther
41. WWII agency
43. Update the siding
44. Soft stone
45. Tennis flubs
47. Malayan outriggers
49. Roof piece
50. Tiny battery
51. RN's forte
52. Bowling frames in a game
53. It might be a Beta unit
54. Greek cross
55. Pipe cleaner
56. Nick's *Family Ties* hellos

Space Invaders

solution on page 308

ACROSS

1. Zoroastrian scripture
7. Chevy Chase bit
15. Terminal
16. Alters an itinerary
17. Some cephalopods
18. Like the Fugitive's prey
19. It may be financial
20. Redress
21. "Minnie the Moocher" singer
24. MPG rater
27. 100%
28. Yule drink
29. Rocky Lane spoke for him
30. Luau loop
31. Kind of hopper
33. Fetters
35. One of Charlie's Angels
38. All the little people
40. Sewer line
41. Taper off
44. It may be Dutch
45. Not sqr.
46. For example
47. Paw part
48. __ runway (prepare for takeoff)
53. They might have mints on their pillows
54. It fits a thole
55. Elbows on the table?
58. Emulate 5 o'clock Charlie
61. It's self-serving
62. He lays his cards on the table
63. Prosper
64. Meshuga

DOWN

1. Tumult
2. "__ and Sade" (radio show)
3. Cornerstone word
4. Stiff-upper-lip type
5. Carson, after a joke that bombed
6. Bard of boxing
7. TV teaser
8. Avoid a Time lapse
9. Coliseum
10. Wormwood, to Voldemort
11. Some coats
12. S&L device
13. Auto racer Petty
14. It was dropped in the '60s
20. Star of computer languages
21. James Dean role
22. Collier's cooler
23. Loiters
24. CHiPS star
25. Type of name
26. Junk mail
29. Raser's raincoat
32. "__ Bones"
33. Pants cloth
34. Knitted
36. Baby sitter?
37. Cloth measures
38. Man from Moo
39. America's largest power co.
42. Cry to Cratchit
43. Toodle-oo!
48. It's read on Saturdays
49. Observe Yom Kippur
50. City near Dayton
51. Troy story
52. Secretaries may file these
53. Planet of the Apes doll word
55. Little Women sister
56. Aquarius, e.g.
57. Bivouac bed
58. Bon __
59. Downing Street number
60. Aforetime

This Car

solution on page 308

ACROSS

1. Masticate
5. It's behind the altar
9. Curly-tailed pooch
14. Use a strop
15. Pot contents
16. Housed in a hotel
17. Little bit
18. Bart's brother
19. Has to have
20. VW slogan
23. Ingested
24. That __ say . . .
25. Enlarge the staff
28. Not outgoing
29. He's taxed in April
31. Dresser
33. Dirk Diggler effort
35. Wail
36. Wendy's slogan
39. Electron tubes
40. Poi roots
41. Seeps
43. Lit one
44. Go a-courtin'?
47. Overrun
48. Young girl
50. Maladroit
52. U.S. Army slogan
55. Expertise
57. Flight paths
58. Big bucks, perhaps
59. Support, in a way
60. Storied place for a finger
61. Little Engine's thought
62. Shell type
63. Flip talk
64. Fixed fee

DOWN

1. Reproves
2. Sideline shout
3. Being
4. Contrive
5. Lt. or gov.
6. Some cats
7. Turns anger inward
8. Heirs split it
9. "__ She Sweet?"
10. Golddiggers get them
11. Unfit to eat
12. *Airplane!* character Striker
13. They surround the news hole
21. Repeat performances
22. Monk, in most fight scenes
26. Shipwreck site
27. Be wrong
30. Market before building
32. Like Shields and Yarnell movements
33. Walker's device
34. Polo Grounds hero
36. Lays rival
37. Domestic beer?
38. Puffy footstools
39. E, in Morse code
42. Diet dishes
44. Iroquoian people
45. Positive
46. Always, in verse
49. Half the UAR, once
51. Low point
53. Eagle's nest
54. Avails of
55. Stern watchdog
56. Knowing cry

Ads of 13

solution on page 308

6. Big Entertainment

ACROSS

1. Bonfire remnant
4. Boys in the 'hood
8. Diamond shape
13. Time co-founder
14. Coin on the Spanish Main
15. Tidal bore
16. Leaning ltr.
17. Not fooled by
18. Bob Mackie creation
19. Part 1 of quote
21. Eyeglasses
22. Weds
23. "Forbes" profilee
24. *Airplane!* character Striker
25. Jesus' tongue
29. Pasted
33. *Xanadu* band
34. Mrs. Colin Powell
35. Part 2 of quote
39. Supernatural force
40. "All the Things You __"
41. High muck-a-mucks
42. Clinton cabinet member
44. D-Day craft
46. Sternward
47. Ocean's shoreline
52. *Golden Girls'* town
55. Sayers of the quote
56. Billy Crystal, at times
57. Cherub with a bow
58. __ 51
59. Sri Lankan native
60. Grown-up filly
61. Alligator __
62. Blue-pencil
63. Passed easily
64. Exasperate

DOWN

1. Detroit output
2. Sell hot tickets
3. How do
4. Window-shop
5. Like many tuxedos
6. Solemn vows
7. Fizz flavor
8. Bible miracle scene
9. Comedian of few words
10. Arch type
11. Richie's mom, to Fonzie
12. She preceded Mamie
13. Flora and fauna
20. Best
23. Gator kin
25. Actress MacGraw
26. African lily
27. Apple variety
28. Dastards
29. Places for reps
30. Rachel's sister
31. Radius partner
32. Battleground of 1942
33. Palindromic preposition
36. Cartoonist Kelly
37. Burned item in the '60s
38. Yawl cousin
43. Away from home
44. "The Raven" name
45. Kind of cow
47. Poison ivy is one
48. Giraffe kin
49. Broadcaster
50. Furtive one
51. Kremlin dynast
52. Dole (out)
53. Caliph
54. Zenith
55. One of the Three Bears

Oz

solution on page 309

	1	2	3		4	5	6	7		8	9	10	11	12
13					14					15				
16					17					18				
19				20						21				
22									23					
				24				25				26	27	28
29	30	31	32				33				34			
35					36	37				38				
39					40					41				
42				43				44	45					
			46				47				48	49	50	51
52	53	54				55								
56					57					58				
59					60					61				
62					63					64				

ACROSS

1. Cracker brand
5. Oar holder
10. *Goodbye, Columbus* author
14. Amu Darya's outflow
15. Has rank
16. Norma solo
17. He was born Bernard Schwartz
19. Burst
20. Last on the list
21. Uses an acetylene torch
22. Poe woe
23. Render unreadable
26. Baby
29. He got his start in the circus
33. Molten rocks
34. Rivers in England and France
35. Eastern belief
36. Dentist's request
37. Having lots of lots
38. Flying start?
39. Antepenultimate word of the Declaration of Independence
40. George of *Star Trek*
41. Rock singer
42. *Boys Town* actor
44. Finicky one
45. Superhero accessories
46. Make a memo of
47. Light source
50. Snow removers?
54. You might make it a double
55. Star of *Missing*
58. Eh
59. PC letters
60. Jacob tricked him
61. Scout creation
62. Yellow-brown
63. Bargain price?

DOWN

1. Can't stand
2. Monopoly piece
3. Hired help
4. Gold seeker
5. Depend
6. "B.C." cartoonist
7. "Master Melvin"
8. "Fantasy Island" accessory
9. Bush has one
10. Like most modern horror films
11. Former hurler Hershiser
12. Neck and neck
13. Upstagers
18. Prepares to strike
21. Attic sight
23. Galas
24. Legalese term
25. Buy by Benny
26. One-master
27. __ New Guinea
28. In-your-face
29. O preceder
30. *SNL* star
31. Merchandise
32. High times
37. "Modern Maturity" org.
38. TV listings
40. It might give you a lift
41. Morel start
43. Andean feline
46. Toast topper
47. Job to do
48. It works on impulse
49. Baja buck
50. Matching
51. Kid's retort
52. Concern for George Bailey
53. Comfy
55. Deep black
56. Its sym. is the caduceus
57. Crow's cry

ACROSS

1. Boob tubes
4. Mexican liquor
10. Hippo's wear in *Fantasia*
14. Wet behind the ears
15. Get a lungful
16. Osiris' sis
17. Flamenco cry
18. Ultimate rider
20. Exhaust too much
22. NPR or PBS
23. The President, and two other roles, too
26. Utters loudly
27. Afflicted
28. Mole
31. Pauline had them
33. Trivia buff's forte
35. Falstaff quaffs
36. Side for Larson
37. *Mod Squad* role
38. Paper with colored graphs
41. Beach Boy helper
43. Played the first card
44. Dastard
45. Doozy
46. Fighter in the war room
50. Stiller's spouse
53. Wang or Versace
54. Title role
57. Tome starter
58. Riches alternative
59. Football squad
60. Recipe amt.
61. Alka-Seltzer-in-water sound
62. They have run-on sentences
63. Comment before "I told you so"

DOWN

1. Girl Scout group
2. Trombone slide
3. Gland meat
4. Cold north wind
5. Signs up
6. Devon and Dorset
7. Joe of cigarette ads
8. Matterhorn, e.g.
9. *Fantasy Island* item of greeting
10. Hawaiian lights
11. "Surfer," so to speak
12. Antler prong
13. '84 Olymmpics no-show
19. *The Very Hungry Caterpiller* author
21. Go back to ERA, say
24. False witness
25. It's pretty shady
28. Some Japanese people
29. Scummy place?
30. Community ctr.
31. Kevin Arnold's buddy Pfeiffer
32. If not
33. Like old Paree
34. Lazy person
36. Dress-wearing actor
39. Vegas thief of filmdom
40. It takes two
41. Get better
42. Hurries
45. Verb for a dear one
46. Hold tight
47. Staff leader
48. Pouf the coif
49. Figure of speech
50. Car letters
51. "And others," briefly
52. Golden Fleece ship
55. Thicken
56. Ivy Leaguer

Mushrooms in the End

solution on page 309

1	2	3		4	5	6	7	8	9		10	11	12	13
14				15							16			
17				18					19				
20			21							22				
23							24	25					
	26						27			28	29	30
31	32					33			34			
35					36				37			
38			39	40			41	42				
43			44			45					48	49
	46				47						
50	51	52				53				
54				55	56				57		
58				59				60		
61				62				63		

ACROSS

1. Bungle
5. Italian treats
9. Tear
14. One of the Simp-sons
15. Shortened legal plea
16. Saints and Devils
17. Type of car
18. Peas, to a prank-ster
19. Believe without question
20. Capra villain
23. Gold-watch recipi-ent
24. Highlanders
28. Bargain price?
29. Haberdashery items
31. Aforetime
32. Some pasta
34. Words of optimism
37. Villainous Lemmon role, with theme music
40. Tandy's hubby
41. Join
42. Flapper's haircut
43. Metal-stamping tools
45. Places to get in hot water?
48. Sugarcoat
51. Dollar store pur-chase
54. Asylum villain
56. Time off
59. Champagne cooler
60. Elvis's title
61. Not of this world
62. Take off
63. Best of the movies
64. Coats with gold
65. Cereal-pitching tiger
66. Bygone ruler

DOWN

1. Element #9, in com-binations
2. Fine knits
3. Familiar with
4. Court game
5. Fatuous
6. Strives
7. Sailor's saint
8. Apply balm to
9. Blue hue
10. Hester Prynne's daughter
11. Bean spiller
12. Green-egg layer
13. It's not an easy read
21. Dispute
22. When Yom Kippur and Rosh Hasha-nah are
25. Competition
26. Angus' tongue
27. Innovator's prefix
30. Put forth
33. Pub crawler's spree
35. Counterbalance
36. Friday handout
37. Wave cutter
38. Judicial cover?
39. Like some celebri-ties
40. Murrow's network
44. Give no ground
46. Insects hated by fruit farmers
47. "Burnt" crayon color
49. Over and done with
50. Chances to play
52. Start of a Kram-den laugh
53. Candice's dad
55. Off-the-wall reply?
56. Scott Joplin tune
57. "Thrilla in Manila" victor
58. It's nothing at all

Film Villains

solution on page 309

ACROSS

1. Soho stroller
5. Lock up
10. It's a long story
14. She gets what she wants
15. Establish communication with
16. Tough-guy actor Ray
17. Dion and the Belmonts hit
19. Slide follower?
20. Look up to
21. Relinquished
23. Motive
25. Gentlemen of Portugal
26. Sugar alcohol
31. Nipper's co.
32. Pre-supposed
34. Adams, of the Sierra Club
38. Reverse, on a PC
39. Paul's pal
41. It's quite a fete
42. Reserves
44. Sayonaras
46. Plate decision
48. Inner ear items
49. Like some grape leaves
53. Kingston Trio hit
54. They might be revealing
56. Noted rug weavers
61. Pastiche
62. Gene Chandler hit
64. Norwegian saint
65. Role for Sinatra or Clooney
66. Round, twistable snack
67. Little feller
68. Cauldron additives?
69. Its bell rings at 4 P.M.

DOWN

1. Ballet bend
2. Donnybrooks
3. More than a little
4. Lion or horse feature
5. Religious recluses
6. It's bleu on maps
7. Floozy
8. Overdoes the exercise
9. Mother Goose or Eminem
10. Hit for The Penguins
11. Last in a famous nonet
12. Lotus-eater
13. Some Yalies
18. Make a flat?
22. Pachacuti was one
24. Recurring theme
26. Word with pencil or ticket
27. Mr. Bill's cry
28. *Trading Spaces* verb
29. Hit by the Monotones
30. New Hampshire's state flower
33. How to break (from behind)
35. It may follow the pitch
36. Folk singer Jenkins
37. Miss
40. Loges, say
43. Like many a whirling dervish
45. One place for angling
47. It's close to the bone
49. Bamboo unit
50. English channel viewer
51. Kayak's kin
52. It may be wild
55. Throw out of kilter
57. Many millennia
58. A soul leader
59. Ruffles one's feathers
60. Sour fruit
63. Spilled tea?

Doo-wop Hits

solution on page 309

ACROSS

1. Phooey!
4. Kind of tea
10. Bond studied here
14. Draft pick
15. Contaminated
16. Assess
17. She played Ernestine
19. Cry of woe
20. Exclusive
21. *Tale of Two Cities* site
23. One more
25. Young in the cinema
26. Made back
28. Increase
32. Hitching post
36. LSD nabbers
38. Regale
39. Bank claim
40. "Rope-a-dope" boxer
41. Tynan portrayer
42. Contingency strategy
44. Hudson contemporary
45. Balloon material
46. *Silkwood* star
48. Educator Young
50. Store
52. Car mogul
57. Ticket riskers
61. Can man
62. Hot rock
63. *Baby Snooks* star
65. "Ain't She Sweet?" writer
66. Fan
67. Chooser's word
68. N.M. sight
69. Warning word
70. Held court

DOWN

1. Glider wood
2. Ripley foe
3. Parrot's word
4. One with a thumb
5. Was a ham
6. LP speed
7. Light component
8. Puccini pieces
9. You can see right through them
10. She came back to acting for *Small Time Crooks*
11. Fill in
12. Date's shape
13. Its main building is at 18 Broad Street
18. At any rate
22. "See ya!"
24. It has blips
27. Brouhaha
29. Yank
30. Steak letters
31. Juicy fruit
32. Yodeling locale
33. Happy tune
34. Kind of gas
35. Jerry Stiller's partner
37. Spicy sauce
43. Form droplets
45. Gruesome
47. Like some houses
49. Bar man
51. It may be fair or free
53. Hockey idol
54. Works out with a bar
55. Winter warmer
56. Klaxon cause
57. Type of dancing
58. Call at a hotel
59. Arden and Plumb
60. Bank deposit?
64. FDR agency

Funny Gals

solution on page 309

ACROSS

1. Get a whiff of
6. Former NSA and CIA head
11. Bo Derek's number
14. Courtyards
15. *Irma la __*
16. Workers' fed.
17. Game show where yes/no questions are asked
19. He broke Lou's record
20. Did kid's art
21. Father's Day gift
22. Millinery adjuncts
26. Has a preference
28. Couples cruise destination
29. They may be deafening
32. Internet destinations
33. Loud insect
34. Toppers
35. 1973 Rolling Stones hit
36. Enter
39. Flat fillers
41. Make laugh
42. Big stinks
44. Likenesses
45. Actress Lenya
46. Tennis overhands
47. Don Larsen stat
48. Of a taster's pride
52. Finless fish
53. '70s version of *Amateur Hour*
58. Eminent leader?
59. Accumulated, as a tab
60. End of a Garbo line
61. Message in a bottle?
62. Endless finish
63. Beat, in chess

DOWN

1. It has teeth and can sing
2. Highest degree
3. George's #1 lyricist
4. Fill the bill
5. Connective tissues
6. Pastoral poems
7. Agnew's plea, for short
8. Mrs. of TV and film
9. Noriega's affliction
10. Ribbed
11. Game show where you get X's and O's
12. *Seinfeld* gal
13. To boot
18. Butte's st.
22. Breakfast fare
23. *Turandot* tune
24. "How'd your mate answer this?" game show
25. Here!
27. Mysteries
29. Wise guys
30. Sufferer's suffix
31. Strong soap
33. Baby bouncer
35. Grate stuff
37. Psychiatrist's reply
38. 1987 Costner role
40. Ruler's rod: var.
41. Alloy
42. Catches some Zs
43. Manolo Ortega, e.g.
44. Old cowhand's intro
46. Orders to a broker
49. Surprise cries
50. See-through item
51. Malarial symptom
54. '70s radical grp.
55. How some like it
56. A quarter of four
57. Take the plunge

Game Shows of 11

solution on page 310

Big Entertainment **109**

ACROSS

1. Make unproductive
5. Polonius's hiding place
10. Doc Bricker of *The Love Boat*
14. Something to hum
15. Cur's curb
16. Carrot on a stick
17. Coloratura piece
18. High-IQ group
19. Nimble-fingered
20. Game show where you might get a zonk
23. Star of *Sherlock Jr.* and *The General*
24. Jannings of *The Blue Angel*
25. "A drop of golden sun"
27. Pass by
32. Show hosted by Hugh Downs
36. Abdul Aziz ibn __
38. *The __ of Pooh*
39. Makes a choice
40. Game show with 1 (or 3) bachelorettes
45. Timmy's dog
46. Tell-all bk.: Brit.
47. Defeat decisively
50. City of Florida and Italy
55. Game show with whammies
58. Carla on *Cheers*
60. Produces interest
61. Not a pretty fruit
62. Big name in cereal or etiquette
63. Subsequently
64. Eagles or Falcons
65. Apportion
66. Orchard, essentially
67. Remains after dinner

DOWN

1. Track prey
2. Turn to liquid
3. Clarence's accuser
4. It also rises
5. Book of handy facts
6. Need a bath
7. Rajah's wife
8. Indian silk center
9. More nefarious
10. Burghoff's TV co-star
11. Spielberg's first full feature
12. Sandy's bark
13. Strawberry, once
21. Bard's sunup
22. Actress Joyce of *Roc*
26. Hairy Himalayan
28. It was smashed in the 40's
29. King Cole's request
30. Tippler
31. Annie's pair
32. Snooker items
33. Likelihood
34. Bread that might accompany biryani
35. Deli option
36. MO metro area
37. "Take on Me" group
41. General's gofer
42. Superlatively short
43. Biological groupings
44. Purim's month
48. Name on jetliners, once
49. "Kookie" actor
51. Mickey Mouse's dog
52. Olympic racer of a sort
53. Renown
54. Thumbs through
55. Irksome one
56. Emulate Ebert
57. Enough's companion
58. Record number?
59. Tiller's tool

Game Shows of 13

solution on page 310

ACROSS

1. __ snuff
5. 1-59337-120-9, e.g.
9. Dogie catcher
14. Like Felix Unger
15. It's full of baloney
16. 39th Veep
17. Hussy
18. Andean tubers
19. Labor leader's cry
20. Game show with fakers
23. *SNL* comedienne
24. Begets
25. White edible root
28. Ingratiate
32. Cryptic mystery
35. Language of the Gaels
36. TV game show for over 30 years
41. Frosty covering
42. Mr. Roarke's sidekick
43. Some cephalopods
45. Memory traces
50. Identify a caller
53. Jazz pianist Blake
54. Game show where vowels will cost you
58. Hosiery color
59. In Timbuktu, perhaps
60. Osiris's sister
61. Barkin in *Switch*
62. Developer's interest
63. Carnival's end
64. Lip application
65. Dick Tracy's love
66. Proof word

DOWN

1. Turn off the pause control
2. Jai alai ball
3. Less slack
4. Frolicsome aquatic mammals
5. "White Wedding" singer
6. Like-minded group
7. Depressed state
8. Some first-generation Americans
9. Actress Tewes of *The Love Boat*
10. Literally, lamb of God
11. Fit of anger
12. Clockmaker Thomas
13. Carry a mortgage
21. Shea shot
22. Arnold's crime
26. Acknowledge, in a way
27. Elite alternative
29. Joule's kin
30. Tree, or burnt wood remnant
31. Emeritus, for short
33. Procure
34. Plant pest
36. Even if, for short
37. Ad follower
38. Absorb, as a loss
39. Ones under mentors
40. Understood over radio
44. Dresses carefully
46. TiO_2
47. Privilege loser, often
48. Going for the gold?
49. Takes care of
51. It might be clear
52. Bergen dummy Klinker
54. Jack Benny catchword
55. City near Mauna Kea
56. Jazzman Waller
57. Bauxite and cinnabar
58. Seek alms

solution on page 310

ACROSS

1. Decorative knotting
8. Speed trap operator, at times
15. Important gland
16. Kind of dye
17. The Clown Prince of Basketball
19. Musical Chipmunk
20. Recoils, with "away"
21. She gets what's coming
22. It's in the bag
24. Snap companion
27. Bad to the bone
29. Acquire
32. Horizontal coordinate
36. Copy, briefly
37. N.B.A. scoring leader: 1960-66
40. Sneak __
41. Unlike Mr. T's fool
42. Rusty
45. Cornerstone word
46. Bridge builder's letters
47. Brainy bunch
49. Do KP work
53. Sleep soundly?
55. Lamb Chop's voice
56. The first Clown Prince of Basketball
61. Wanted by the police, maybe
62. Venezuelan river
63. Anybody's and Jo March
64. Moms and dads

DOWN

1. Half of a '60s rock foursome
2. Fred's dancing sister
3. Hanker for
4. Sent through multiple URL's
5. Author unknown, for short
6. Hillbilly matron
7. Annex of a sort
8. Skating server
9. Blacker
10. Scrabble piece
11. London libations
12. Afflicted Cratchit
13. "Sail __ Ship of State"
14. Toon dog who sounds like Peter Lorre
18. Present a poser
22. "Don't be absurd!"
23. Film actress Lanchester
24. Chrysalises
25. Gold braid
26. Peasant laborers
28. Tiny Tim's wife
30. Senator Hatch
31. *Chicago* Mister
32. Cy Young, e.g.
33. Man or bird
34. Iditarod vehicles
35. Mosh pit items
38. Leaning
39. Frequent erupter
43. Like East St. Louis
44. Long lunches?
48. Classic start
50. Iacocca's Chrysler successor
51. Burp
52. Oscar night lineup
53. Picket-line crosser
54. Agrippina's tyrant son
55. Kind of crazy
56. Hamelin pest
57. Ike's command, for short
58. Freddy's street
59. The usual routine: Abbr.
60. Fab competitor

Harlem G.

solution on page 310

1	2	3	4	5	6	7		8	9	10	11	12	13	14
15								16						
17							18							
19							20							
21					22	23					24	25	26	
		27	28				29		30	31				
32	33	34			35			36						
37							38	39						
40						41								
42				43	44		45							
46				47	48				49	50	51	52		
		53	54					55						
56	57	58				59	60							
61						62								
63						64								

7. Time Machine

ACROSS

1. Flame followers
6. Git!
10. Place for change
14. Tale of Troy
15. Gentle stroke
16. Furnace fuel
17. Freed-Brown song of '29
20. Kink
21. H.S. course
22. Slips away from
23. Like some threats
25. Type of sheet or item with sheets
26. Entertains
29. Is past
30. B as in Barak
34. Posed
35. Sudoku solving skill
37. The press, e.g.
38. Berlin classic of '29
41. He threw to Chance
42. Fernando's farewell
43. Tea, in Tours
44. Fiddler or pianist
45. FedEx rival
46. Middle managers?
48. One-dimensional item
50. Baby birth intro words
51. Put on the back burner
54. "__ you sure?"
55. Sourpuss
59. Fats Waller song of '29
62. Mayberry sheriff
63. Prop for Chaplin
64. Go by bike
65. M*A*S*H meal
66. Was in hock
67. Crackerjack

DOWN

1. Young lady
2. Big name in chemicals
3. Yothers of *Family Ties*
4. Scottish dish
5. Anti-ICBM plan
6. Coward's lack
7. High-selling *American Idol* dud
8. Polo Grounds hero
9. The rest
10. Steel wool user
11. Semi's haul
12. Dust Bowl denizen
13. Hamiltons
18. Trafalgar victor
19. Crimson rival
24. Some are kosher
25. Sonora sights
26. Quaking tree
27. Purple hue
28. Absolute
29. Zephyrs
31. Meathead's mom-in-law
32. Church's 10%
33. Dusty mists
36. Run amok
37. Tablelands
39. Clangers
40. Inn's kin
45. Org. that promotes World Press Freedom Day
47. Like some cows
49. Trellis traipser
50. Grated on
51. Impostor
52. Make more acute
53. A weir's are raised
54. Problem for Noriega
56. Used cars?
57. P.D.Q.
58. Smack
60. Flint org.
61. Reg. agency

Songs of '29

solution on page 311

ACROSS

1. He bore a heavy load
6. MS-DOS popularizer
9. Valerie Harper role
14. Philly sub
15. PBS supporter
16. He finished with 755
17. Tried
19. What tug-of-war ropes lack
20. Andrew Sisters hit on '39
22. Jima's intro
23. Sure, Cap'n!
24. Snowman's go-with, in a film title
28. Reserved
30. It might form tears
34. Go with the flow
35. Used flexible straws?
37. A queen can make you this
38. Frankie Carle's theme
41. Baby's need, briefly
42. Rock at the Oscars
43. The in things
44. One-pot dish
46. It's a matter of pride
47. Ones with sizzle
48. Brown brew
50. Self-proclaimed greatest
51. Johnny Mercer song from one year before '39
60. Iowa religious sect
61. Got happy
62. Skinflint
63. Slim battery type
64. Els of the links
65. *Miss America* author
66. McCourt memoir
67. REM song

DOWN

1. Pequod pusher
2. Popular PBS gift
3. Past due
4. Stress, for one
5. Mutually beneficial
6. Opening bars
7. It has a head and hops
8. Whipped up
9. Gravelly
10. Circled with light
11. Kind of tradition
12. It's slip is often showing
13. Singer of "Diana"
18. "Mongo only __ in game of life"
21. Hen, at times
24. Forfeits food
25. Type of education or bookstrore
26. First name in bicycling
27. EMT skill
28. Timex rival
29. Torero ta-da's
31. Water bill word
32. You get pomace when you make it
33. Head lock?
35. Titanic problem
36. Ends
39. Almost straight up
40. Thumbs down
45. Time, to Rain Man
47. Amscray
49. Find out
50. Territories
51. Tight spots
52. Reverse time
53. Wiz verb
54. Torme forte
55. Trendy tea
56. Quite fresh
57. Dame who is a drag
58. Undoing
59. Went like mad

Songs of '39

solution on page 311

ACROSS

1. Ottoman VIPs
5. Improvise
10. Has to
14. Lipinski leap
15. "V" villain
16. Chip in
17. Bridges of Hollywood
18. Peter Falk played this actor's henchman
20. Chitchat
22. Even though
23. Hosp. scanner that might be open
24. Open
25. She's usually with Lucy
30. Disney princess or Israeli leader
31. 43,560 square feet
32. Q-Tip, generically
36. Clothing store section
37. Scornful smirk
38. Home for some crocodiles
39. "Hey, you!"
40. Mah-jongg piece
41. *Ulee's Gold* actor
42. *Gypsy* movie star
44. Brief rundown
48. Like sushi
49. All __!
50. Lily Tomlin persona
55. Bernard Schwartz, today
57. I like what __
58. Greasy spoon sign
59. Humdrum
60. The item here
61. "Leave it be"
62. Blows the whistle on
63. Sargasso Sea swimmers

DOWN

1. Batgirl Gordon
2. CEO or CFO
3. "She Loves You" word
4. Worst of places to live
5. Be next to
6. *Shrek* actress
7. Lingerie trim
8. Squid's squirt
9. Long pole on the tightrope, say
10. African snake
11. Like some expectations
12. Disciple of Zeno
13. Agent's cut
19. *Legally Blonde* lead role
21. Grueling exam
24. Let out line
25. Jazz accompaniment
26. Ticks off
27. French wines
28. Table type
29. Amtrak's bullet train
32. Fairy-tale heroine
33. Bowery character
34. Ray of film
35. Abacus unit
37. Hoagy Carmichael song
41. Adroit exploit
42. Popeye Doyle was one
43. Showy blooms
44. Gratifies to the max
45. WWII sub
46. Three-card con
47. Thou __ rise
50. Catchall phrase
51. Havarti spice
52. 1975 Wimbledon champ
53. Sea of Tranquility explorer
54. Eerie loch
56. 66, e.g.: abbr.

The Great Race

solution on page 311

ACROSS

1. "Tommyrot!"
5. Igneous rock
11. Kingdom come preceder
14. Sills' solo
15. Risk parties
16. Make a bed
17. Trust
18. They often have rides
20. Toys to be tossed
22. Pouty look
23. Fiddle with a flute
24. Looks
25. __ Bay (Khan's craft)
28. River of no return
30. Speedily
31. One with a handshake
33. Dedicated lines?
36. Sticky toy that's thrown
39. USPS limbo
40. Beer named for a First Brother
41. Fraction of a rupee
42. Charlie, for one
43. They're not originally from around here
44. Church lady's nemesis
47. It might test your metal
50. Windows alternative
51. Twister's challenge
55. Tiny
57. Michael Jackson's early do
58. Nice friend
59. Lawn tool
60. Something borrowed
61. Nancy Drew's beau
62. Evaluate
63. D-Day landers

DOWN

1. Tree skin
2. Lunch box snack
3. Minuteman's home
4. Needler's place?
5. Diamond worker
6. Enlightened Buddhist
7. Whiff
8. Without purpose
9. Cask dregs
10. ⅙ fl. oz.
11. Pang
12. Malarkey
13. Nods of the head
19. "Little" board
21. Sweetheart
24. Flow of ideas
25. Floozy
26. Glassy silica
27. Snack in a shell
29. Type of ski lift
31. Alaskan sled pullers
32. Bar none
33. Tom Joad, e.g.
34. "Babaloo" singer
35. Epochs
37. Take the cake
38. Barkeep's yell
42. Prepare to fly
43. Slangy signers
44. Home of the Nubian Desert
45. *Princess Mononoke,* for one
46. Retiring
48. Stand for
49. Feeds the pot
51. Laments
52. Crop circle makers?
53. Whippersnapper
54. Many eras
56. Fleming Hamill's gp.

Fad Toys

solution on page 311

1	2	3	4	■	5	6	7	8	9	10	■	11	12	13
14				■	15						■	16		
17				■	18						19			
20				21						■	22			
■	■	■	23					■	24					
25	26	27			■	■	28	29			■	■	■
30				■	31	32				■	33	34	35
36				37					38				
39			■	40				■	41				
■	■	42				■	43						
44	45	46		■	47	48	49				■	■	■
50				■	51						52	53	54
55			56					■	57				
58			■	59					■	60			
61			■	62					■	63			

ACROSS

1. Let in
6. Join firmly
10. Dagon, e.g.
14. It doesn't hold water
15. Borodin's Prince
16. "Well done!"
17. Bike part
18. Fashion fad meant for dancers
20. New family
22. Bamboo eaters
23. Humorist Burrows
25. Menu phrase
26. Set a price
27. Eden exile
28. Glowing visual fad
31. Pa Clampett portrayer
33. Lags behind
34. *Pal Joey* writer
36. 1952 Olympics site
37. One of the Carpenters
39. Forefather
43. Absorb in class
45. Podia
47. Part of Iberia
50. Dangling fashion fad
52. "Dig in!"
53. The way, in China
55. Dumbo wing
56. Heckle
57. Troop groups
59. Elaborate
61. Color-changing fashion fad
63. Headlights?
66. Moreover
67. 1996 runner-up
68. Shi'ite's deity
69. Wallendas lack
70. Meadow mowers
71. Substantive

DOWN

1. Cleo's undoing
2. Do alternative
3. Middle Age
4. Nobelist Pavlov
5. Like some bios
6. Home on the range
7. They may be swollen
8. Yule item
9. Plummets
10. Not excluded
11. Vacuum tubes
12. Do to do
13. Taper off
19. Doughboy?
21. *Northern Exposure* locale
23. Benny Carter's sax
24. Captain's insignia
26. *Off the Court* author
29. Sauce for fish
30. Film for Dirk Diggler
32. Musical Count
35. Incan, e.g.
38. He sang about Officer Obie
40. Rossellini of *Big Night*
41. Fix up
42. Exxon's ex-name
44. Door sign
46. Father of Isaac
47. Able fellow
48. Conditional release
49. Not more than
51. They often have feet
54. In reserve
58. Unity bonds?
59. Lewd look
60. Folk item
62. "Move it!"
64. Mare's morsel
65. Lacking

Fads

solution on page 311

ACROSS

1. Become corrupt
6. Backside
10. Glinka's *A Life for the __*
14. Olds model
15. Out fishing, perhaps
16. Kid's retort
17. Castle dwellers who are really brine shrimp
19. Pocket item?
20. Dame, slangily
21. Labored
23. He'll humiliate you
26. Foilers
27. Willow-borne harbingers of spring
28. Like some blankets
29. Part of one of Columbus' ship names
30. Pens or lighters
31. Worshiper's place?
34. Center of valor?
35. Avow
38. Great Emancipator's nickname

39. Cause for Chapter 11
41. Nice jug
42. Praline nut
44. A truckload
46. Most cunning
47. Attempted yet again
49. Part of some party platters
50. Aim
51. They might be proper
52. Heath for Heathcliff
53. Mimi's desktop fad
58. "Blondie" tyke
59. Disney opener
60. March 17 marchers
61. Act the wisenheimer
62. Start of a Hitchcock title
63. Role for Cooper or Sandler

DOWN

1. Get-go?
2. Zorro cheer
3. Clown leader
4. Crossing guard's ID
5. Threshold
6. Senegal capital
7. __ *People*
8. *SNL* head writer who gave birth
9. Rapidity
10. Food on the first *Survivor*
11. Fad emblems
12. September bloom
13. Map lines
18. They might be heard a thousand times
22. Dedicated lines?
23. Old hat
24. Rousseau hero
25. Clothing fad
26. Worrier's complaint
28. They go with drums
30. Did obeisance
32. Mock
33. Lets out
36. Fix calligraphy

37. Excellent
40. Ring bearers?
43. Blight
45. Hullabaloo
46. Synagogue
47. "How Do I Live" singer
48. First name among bombers
49. Pigment
51. Director Ephron
54. Deplore
55. Commit perjury
56. Dropped item
57. Library censures

More Fads

solution on page 311

ACROSS

1. It's like green fur
5. Bench parts
10. Boxers do it
14. Coyote's favorite company
15. Ulysses S. Grant's real first name
16. *Jaws* boat
17. Agitate
18. Peanut gallery task?
20. Terse talker born 7/4
22. Whopper topper
23. Dickens lass
24. End of a ring count
25. Gen. material
28. Humble home
33. 7/4 birth who gave his regards to Broadway
37. "White Wedding" singer
40. Greek weeper
41. Holds up
42. Contraption cartoonist born 7/4
45. "Farewell, Francois!"
46. Enjoy Okemo
47. Ottoman ruler
50. Blue river
54. Dog tag datum
56. Deep-voiced crooner born 7/4
61. Transformer site
62. Bohemian
63. Sailing direction
64. Ghana's capital
65. Dark cloud
66. They go with dolls
67. 1989 French Open winner
68. Scottish isle

DOWN

1. Animal icon
2. Pump factor
3. When you do this, so does the world, in a song
4. Tom __ (MST3K role)
5. Eschew
6. *Mod Squad* role
7. Heated offense?
8. Chevy SUV
9. Whiff
10. Auction cry
11. Prude
12. Mars and craters
13. Jazz piece
19. Purple shade
21. Dictator's phrase
26. Command to Nanette
27. Testa kin
29. Foes in cubes
30. Taunter's cry
31. Pomade dollop
32. No one has two
33. Mirth
34. Deity
35. Peters out
36. Mousy
37. Creation of Sen. Roth
38. Fizzler
39. Geisha's sash
43. "Hit the engine!"
44. Cut-up
47. Arctic parka
48. With T.L.C.
49. Diamond motif
51. Designer Mizrahi
52. Fastener
53. Emmy role for Susan
55. Shawls
56. Oner
57. Abide by
58. Dupes
59. Bard's sunup
60. Fly in the ointment
61. Droop

Born on the 4th of July

solution on page 312

ACROSS

1. Borg units
5. Water holder
10. Respecting
14. Bickering
15. Diminish
16. Mrs. DeVito
17. Columbus tricked them in 1504 with a known lunar eclipse
20. Sally Struthers role
21. Neuron gap
22. Ike's adjutant
25. Support for a plea
26. Former *Face the Nation* host
30. Toss out
33. Emanate
34. Molokai dance
35. Apr. workhorse
38. Apr. 15 busybody
42. Gp. in *The Crying Game*
43. Acreage
44. Jazzman Blake
45. They make cubes in the kitchen
47. Mining cars
48. He explored with Clark
51. Keister
53. Lasagna herb
56. Cap
61. On 2/29/1940, the film with the first African-American Oscar win
64. Bookies' concerns
65. Small role
66. Never again
67. Cozy place
68. Cap-and-gown bandleader
69. Pastrami preference

DOWN

1. Blabbed
2. List ender
3. Yugoslav leader
4. Mix it up
5. Glitter
6. Prairie
7. PIN place
8. Petitions
9. Peppy
10. Esoteric
11. Mold
12. Rigid
13. Refuges
18. "Peanuts" girl
19. Pen refills
23. Hold fast
24. UPI rival
26. Spanish ayes
27. Movie bigwig
28. Far East
29. Barbarian
31. Tickle pink
32. Propel a shell
35. West Indies island
36. Very proper
37. Lifetimes
39. Lobbying org.
40. Seat for two
41. Prickle
45. Swallow
46. "Vidi," literally
48. Start work on the PC
49. Lose ground?
50. Moves forward
52. Loathe
54. Small cut
55. Our Gang affirmative
57. GI no-show
58. Mudville count
59. Pizarro foe
60. Bliss
62. __ *Pinafore*
63. Football holder

On February 29th

solution on page 312

ACROSS

1. Ladder rung
5. African iris, for short
9. Radio character with a crowded closet
14. Munchausen, e.g.
15. Agitate
16. 1999 World Series champs
17. Chancellor Bismarck
18. Devilkins
19. Mold overflows
20. "Chantilly Lace" singer
23. Egrets' kin live there
24. Not permitted
28. Star Wars, to RWR
29. "Like that would happen!"
30. Fire proof?
31. Predecessors to slide rules
34. Derek, of Derek and the Dominos
35. Guitar's kin
36. "... his widowed bride"
39. *Lucky Jim* author
40. Glassy sound
41. Harnessed
42. *Sopranos* airer
43. On-line banter
44. Sega rival, for short
45. Chinese fruits
47. Boon
51. *La Bamba* guy
53. Lug
56. Bourbon Street veggie
57. Cinders of comics
58. 1492 discovery
59. It might by given or kept
60. Apple spray, once
61. Actress Burstyn
62. New Age singer
63. Actresses Wray and Bainter

DOWN

1. A deadly sin
2. Church gift
3. Nosher
4. Nose
5. Amulet
6. All arms and legs
7. Chow chow
8. Hating
9. Me
10. Bay of Naples isle
11. Oxlike critter
12. Squeeze (out)
13. It makes a cat scat
21. Part of IPA
22. Fold of skin
25. Fill a crack
26. Cordage fiber
27. "__ never believe me . . ."
29. "You __ serious?"
31. Gian Carlo's kid
32. 1942 Disney classic
33. Hilarious
34. He has many people in stitches
35. Like some notebook
37. Moral code
38. "Laughing" animal
43. Ante
44. The Silver State
46. El Greco's birthplace
47. Jam fruit
48. *The Most Happy __*
49. Dental filling
50. Kaiser cousins
52. Admired one: var.
53. Any ship
54. *2001* computer
55. Diamond gal

American Pie

solution on page 312

8. Big Time

ACROSS

1. Autobahn auto
5. Apple's place?
10. Mrs. Peel's follower
14. It's a crock
15. Some nobles
16. Son of Venus
17. LOCK
20. Catches Carson, back when
21. Rare-book binding
22. Brazen
24. This may be striking
25. Squushed
28. Tea Party inciter
31. One who's "agin" it
32. Galley goofs
34. Velcro's inspiration
37. STOCK
40. Part of BYOB
41. Denver and Houston
42. "Three Sisters" sister
43. Wheels with room
44. Chaplin munchies
45. Crimean casa
48. Hite height?
51. Makes mad
54. Hebrew school
58. BARREL
60. Cosmetic ingredient
61. Miss Kitty city
62. Reduce a sentence
63. Tear to bits
64. Range roamer
65. Zhivago, for Sharif

DOWN

1. Sounds of awe
2. Sometimes it thickens
3. Regretful miss of song
4. Way to address a peeress
5. They might drop down
6. Squawks
7. Show humanity
8. It was the first stuff
9. Little Oil Drop was its mascot
10. Raptors have them
11. Friends, in Firenze
12. Big name in TV infomercials
13. Vacuum-tube gas
18. "By Jove!"
19. Lionel's basis in *Murder by Death*
23. Telling tales
25. Shark variety
26. From scratch
27. Brit's gun
29. Grandchild in "When I'm Sixty-four"
30. Eliza's dislikes
32. Oklahoma city
33. Hollywood's Hayworth
34. Bit of cotton
35. Root on
36. Showy rugs
38. The big chill
39. More appetizing
43. Under the elms
44. McGwire's homer rival
45. __ flask (inspiration for the Thermos)
46. Arboreal lizard
47. Sing like Bing
49. *The Tinker's Wedding* playwright
50. Title role for Sandy
52. Heels
53. Kilt wearer
55. Chinese leader?
56. Thin disguise?
57. Prado display
59. It requires dedication

Lock, Stock, and Barrel

solution on page 312

1	2	3	4		5	6	7	8	9		10	11	12	13
14					15						16			
17				18					19					
20							21							
			22			23		24						
25	26	27				28	29	30						
31				32	33						34	35	36	
37			38						39					
40				41					42					
		43					44							
45	46	47				48	49	50						
51				52	53		54				55	56	57	
58						59								
60				61					62					
63				64					65					

ACROSS

1. What Misery does in *Misery*
5. "We try harder" company
9. Ghana's capital
14. Role for Shirley or Marie
15. Cardinal's quarters
16. Atoll material
17. Trace
19. Pioneer's path
20. "Let the prisoner come down," said Tom __
22. Scorer on a serve
23. Noah's scout
24. Averse
27. Valhalla VIP
29. Boulle film extras
33. Give the OK
35. Snake eyes
37. The O in AWOL
38. "Hence, it's carbonated," said Tom __
41. "Get my drift?"
42. Fed lines to
43. Wooden coin not to take
44. Grub
46. Eye ailment
48. Colecovision rival
49. Lock name
51. Little Red Hen retort
53. "It's darn busy away from the tables," said Tom __
60. *Dick Van Dyke Show* plea
61. Big bucks at the dentist
62. She played Alice on TV
63. Concerning, in legalese
64. Healthy muscle condition
65. Unlike a rolling stone
66. Juror, in theory
67. *Support Your Local Sheriff!* actor

DOWN

1. File sect.
2. Chevron rival
3. Anteing words
4. Court orders
5. Cordial flavor
6. Bur-based material
7. Cartographer's speck
8. Olympic concern
9. When Ophelia goes bonkers
10. Pupil's protector
11. Tor
12. Travel mode
13. Treaty associate
18. Study of a process
21. Bumped off
24. Insurance interruption
25. *Barbarella* actor
26. Heretofore
28. Third word in response to the time
30. Weird Al revue music
31. Swiss mathematician
32. Art pens
34. Muss up
36. Of the hip
39. "Proceed!"
40. Turn on
45. Church councils
47. Theater cry
50. In check
52. *Animal House* brother
53. Meaney of two Star Trek's
54. Drew Carey's state
55. Grounds keepers
56. Start of Welk's introduction
57. Chemical compound
58. Natalie Wood's sister
59. Stuff before the Big Bang

Swifties of 15

solution on page 312

ACROSS

1. Utah Beach craft
5. TRW's concern
9. "As if __!"
14. Lhasa __ (terrier type)
15. Trickle
16. Stockholm prize
17. Anything goes
20. Trying to get again
21. Goof up
22. Long fish
23. Part of the U.K.
24. Amateur's opposite
27. Daisy-like flower
29. Hostility
31. Like most colleges
32. Omega rival
34. Used a certain pigment
36. Wagner's indentured agent show
39. Reproductive cell
40. From Cuzco
41. Ice cream thickener
42. *One Day at a Time* mom
43. Struggles for air
47. Title role for Demond Wilson
48. Sardine container
50. Gas-station freebie
52. Big foot?
53. Servility
56. Slots
59. Composer called "Papa"
60. Broadway King
61. __ -yourself
62. Double curves
63. Inoculants
64. New Yorker cartoonist

DOWN

1. Doomed dinosaur spot
2. Big Brother
3. Casual cover-up
4. Pronto
5. Journalist Roberts
6. Tethering underground
7. Pound of poetry
8. Creditor
9. Disguised, briefly
10. Kind of meal
11. Blood-type group
12. '20s car
13. Deer's kin
18. Pig out
19. Chinese cosmic principle
24. Ruminate
25. Atoll feature
26. Puzzling
28. Banana oil, e.g.
30. Violinist's need
31. 20th wedding anniversary gift
33. Likeable president
34. Like NASDAQ trades
35. Embarrassment
36. Classic villain
37. Capone catcher
38. Michigan city
39. Driving force
42. Photog Adams and others
44. Alumnus-to-be
45. Jelly ingredient
46. Takes care of
48. Rotates
49. MS-DOS popularizer
51. An ex-Trump
53. Radio's *Vic and* __
54. Singer Brickell
55. Snorri story
56. "So that's it!"
57. Kvetch
58. Cyclone center

Yeggs Over Easy

solution on page 313

ACROSS

1. Central part
6. Kind of shirt
10. Musical featuring "Memory"
14. Potato type
15. Calla lily family
16. To some degree
17. 180 degrees of arc
19. "Don't look at me!"
20. Pool jumper's cry
21. Gulf in 1991 news
22. *Nixon in China* character
23. Colorful flower found in rocky terrain
25. Dove
30. Subsequently
31. Mater preceder
32. He directed Marlon in '54
34. Harry Potter sneerer
37. It's under the dedication here
38. Pulls apart
40. Yank's place
41. Pens an ode about
43. Group with flower pot hats
44. Pull apart
45. Vega's constellation
47. Niches
49. Place for a bag
52. Bravo preceder
53. Mrs. Tom Hanks
54. Certain melon
60. Ages and ages: var.
61. Stases
62. Soggy soil
63. *Sister Act* roles
64. Ceramic pieces
65. Sushi sauce sources
66. Food stabber
67. *Steppenwolf* author

DOWN

1. This and that: abbr.
2. Comic-strip light bulb
3. Butler's last word
4. Kicker's target
5. On its way
6. Scalded
7. Bo Derek's debut film
8. Calm periods
9. Diner order
10. Kitchen gadgets
11. Loathes
12. Atlas was one
13. Great fuss
18. More absurd
24. Drinker's sounds
25. Beach toy
26. *Born Free* lioness
27. Up and about
28. Striped confections
29. '50s home-run king
33. Make spots
35. Corn concoction
36. Drops the curtain on
39. Kind of climber
42. "No seats today"
46. Rise
48. Glacially worn flint, not a Piltdown tool
49. Mining cars
50. "Farm" follower
51. Arizona Amerind
55. Former Georgia senator
56. Tony's little brother
57. Web sites components
58. Many props in *The Great Race*
59. Good life

Can Can

solution on page 313

ACROSS

1. Strumpet
5. Mercedes rival
8. Soft throw
14. Healing plant
15. She played Caroline on TV
16. Toboggan
17. Feed the cable through
19. Guard
20. Wilder play
21. Cauterize
22. Place to wear lingerie
24. Fjord city
27. D-Day town
30. Kettle metal
32. Out of sight
33. F __
35. *Chico and the Man* actress
36. East of Ill.
37. Desi role
38. Make bisque
40. Reg. agency
41. Performs a Lutz
46. Bids one club
47. Everything
48. Clown Kelly
50. Verbal jab in the ribs
51. Cheesy sandwich
53. Pacify
55. Haven
57. Ladies and gentlemen
61. Church supper
63. Henhouse collective
64. Florida fruit
65. Barbarian
66. Golden Rule word
67. Punched
68. Como's "__ Impossible"
69. Dry run

DOWN

1. Fiesta fare
2. Jesus in the outfield
3. Holler
4. School reading matter
5. Enlarge, as a photo
6. Wander
7. Car-wash option
8. Reaches for
9. Custard treat
10. Onset
11. Staff needed for *Tron*
12. Long chaser
13. Orr's org.
18. Cote quote
21. Habitat
23. Run a tab
25. Bedding
26. Least typical
27. Rivulet
28. Sec leader
29. Anesthetic without glucose
31. Bank take-back
34. Famous WWII correspondent
39. Type of jab
42. Forwarded, perhaps
43. Band aids
44. Spunk
45. Take a breather from
49. Condor claws
52. Besmirch
54. Dine
56. Mint plant
58. The best
59. A jillion
60. Catch sight of
61. Kind of sister
62. You can dig it
63. Frat X

Double Trouble

solution on page 313

1	2	3	4		5	6	7		8	9	10	11	12	13
14					15				16					
17				18					19					
20							21							
			22			23				24			25	26
27	28	29			30				31		32			
33				34		35					36			
37									38	39				
40				41	42	43	44	45		46				
47				48				49		50				
51			52		53				54					
		55		56				57				58	59	60
61	62					63								
64						65				66				
67						68				69				

ACROSS

1. Book jacket info
4. More tender
10. Pro adherent?
14. Alley closing
15. Draw idly
16. Mingo portrayer
17. NYC transit org.
18. Eel host?
20. Arab land
22. Providence sch.
23. He played an uncle in *Mary Poppins*
24. Sent out a certain wagon
29. Peter Gunn's girl
31. Snarls
33. Caron-Ferrer film
34. Super Bowl QB Dawson
35. Dictator's phrase
36. Stopovers
37. Honalee dweller
39. Santa's reindeer, e.g.
40. Crop
41. Heartland unit
42. Horseradish dye
43. "__ of these days, Alice ..."
44. Takes in
45. Thong
47. Private escape
48. Treks
50. WWW address starter
52. Part of EEC
53. Esiason and others
56. Fishy player?
61. Puffin's kin
62. Francesco Rinaldi rival
63. A Dionne quint
64. Cereal box abbr.
65. Hotcakes acronym
66. Red-berried shrubs
67. Minor miscue for Martina

DOWN

1. Fall flat
2. Scintilla
3. Colorful hostess?
4. Jingle writer
5. Dovelike
6. Cornucopia
7. Gem State, for short
8. TV Tarzan
9. Grossed out
10. They're stuffed at restaurants
11. Jack Horner's last words
12. Shamus
13. Fire proof?
19. Tolkien beast
21. Highball ingredient
24. They're filled with desire
25. Proofreader's targets
26. Little comedienne?
27. Weatherman's scapegoat
28. Drive off
29. 1959 Marty Robbins hit
30. Confounded
32. Delicate point
38. Ate crow, in a way
39. Witnesses
46. Light-based
47. PIN requester
49. Mystery writer Grafton
51. Carryalls
53. Martin's role in *Ed Wood*
54. Worthy of a slap
55. Card game for three
56. Madras mister
57. Inga Swenson's cry
58. Long trailer
59. Green-egg layer
60. Flange

Fishy Fish of 11

solution on page 313

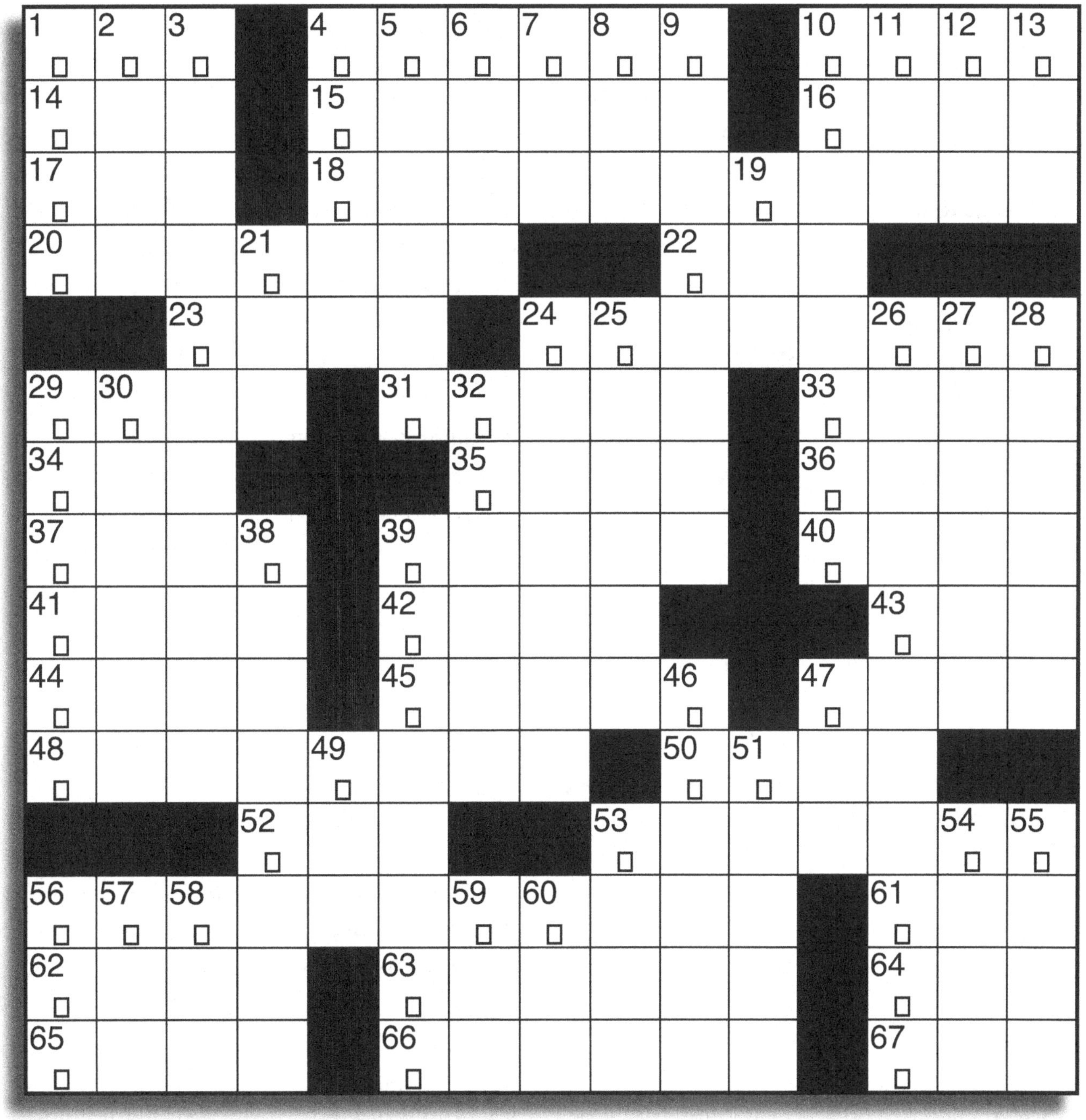

ACROSS

1. *Norma*, e.g.
6. AM word
10. Problems
14. *Wings* role
15. Cineplex wheel
16. Bicycle part
17. Sickening spread?
20. All-male
21. Fictional governess
22. Zenith's opposite
23. Dunderhead
25. Fix, as a clock
27. Bachelor's last words
28. Coloring competition?
34. P.D. alert
35. "Heat of the Moment" group
36. Decide
37. Chinese food request
39. Telecom that merged
41. It has depth
45. Actress Wallace of *E.T.*
47. Fridge trip, often
49. Cain raiser
50. Bio title for Rev. John Mason Neale?
55. Homer's dad
56. Long chaser
57. Deadly biter
58. Gentiles
60. Moonfish
63. Eastern bishop or Swedish quartet
67. Attach a heroine?
70. Eye colorer
71. 2000 title role for Julia
72. Eldritch
73. Purviance of silents
74. Egg carton letters
75. Ethyl acetate, e.g.

DOWN

1. They offer resistance
2. Bog fuel
3. Actress Joyce of *Roc*
4. Dukakis defeater
5. Clause connector
6. Kind of brat
7. A stone's throw away
8. James Bond's wife
9. Freddie's street
10. Mallorca, for one
11. Intro
12. Too-too
13. Solid alcohol
18. Go-aheads
19. Opposites, globally
24. A burlesque girl may have one
26. Ike's area
28. Flay, review-wise
29. G.I. address
30. MS-DOS popularizer
31. Canyon edge
32. Shell lining
33. AMEX rival
38. Shield, to RWR
40. Jethro Tull's Anderson
42. That's a moray
43. *Evening Shade* wife
44. Sega rival, for short
46. Head start?
48. TWA mogul
50. Chatterbox
51. Word in Amtrak's slogan
52. Enters, as data
53. Pitchers, of a sort
54. Trump, at times
59. TV's __ *Living*
61. Invoice stamp
62. Patty Duke's first name
64. S.F. train system
65. Camembert kin
66. Perfect-grade recipient
68. __ de mots (puns)
69. Shaq's shoe width

The Parent Trap

solution on page 313

1	2	3	4	5		6	7	8	9		10	11	12	13
14						15					16			
17					18					19				
20					21					22				
			23	24				25	26			27		
28	29	30				31	32				33			
34				35					36					
37			38			39		40		41		42	43	44
			45		46		47		48			49		
50	51	52				53					54			
55				56					57					
58			59			60	61	62			63	64	65	66
67					68					69				
70					71					72				
73					74					75				

ACROSS

1. Cook's herb
6. "Too bad!"
10. They follow some music notes
14. Must, slangily
15. Dusky white
16. Nope
17. Poet's almost
18. Pass over
19. Old gray matter?
20. Roadster feature
22. Soft cheese
23. Not dis
24. Putty, e.g.
26. The whole enchilada
31. Dusk
32. Drill type
34. Embrace
38. It's wrapped in red
39. Vocalist
41. He's at Bee's knees
42. "She Blinded Me With Science" singer
44. Order takers
46. Relay opener
48. Gives way
49. Suffering memory loss
53. Tarnish
54. Puss' plaint
55. Buzzers
61. Canal of song
62. Tiny case
63. Buoy up
64. Wall St. biggie
65. Ms. Coolidge
66. Twangy
67. Coaster
68. Spotted
69. Ledge

DOWN

1. Seaweed
2. Not ritzy
3. Commodity
4. Knife thrust
5. Noble's territory
6. Renegades
7. Unconvincing
8. Fugitive's moniker
9. Chair for two
10. Potter's mentor
11. Mitchell surname
12. Host of the 2006 Winter Olympics
13. Toga party attire
21. Nettle
25. Gardner of *Mogambo*
26. Sprinted
27. Detach
28. Type of ticket
29. Wind-driven plant
30. Particle speeder-upper
33. John Leguizamo, in part
35. Angled page?
36. Item for Frosty
37. Guarded movie character
40. Of the kidneys
43. But of course!
45. Filters
47. Hecklers
49. Solemn assents
50. Sophie's portrayer
51. Racket
52. Charmer
56. TV-remote button
57. Sans pizzazz
58. Let up on
59. List curtailer
60. Kind of portrait

Be It Ever So 'Umble

solution on page 313

ACROSS

1. It's unfathomable
6. PETA cousin
11. Gremlin
14. Date
15. Farm blocks
16. Easter lead-in
17. Arrow holder on a $1 bill
18. Last words
19. Edmond O'Brien film
20. Sergeant's oxymoron
22. *Newhart* setting
23. "Vogue" rival
24. Expose
26. Beacon
29. All for naught
31. "Double Fantasy" singer
32. Wankel engine part
34. Less calm
37. Jejune
39. *Frisco Kid* traveling prop
41. Like an owl
42. Keep Time
44. Boris Badenov's boss
46. Davenport visit?
47. Lustrous
49. Flap
51. Menu noun
53. Run, as a noun or verb
54. My and thy
55. Angsts?
61. Unfilled, on a TV sched.
62. Intent look
63. Title TV role for Dwayne
64. In the know
65. Frenzy
66. Get away
67. Consult with
68. Compel
69. Hamper

DOWN

1. Made mellow
2. Thai meat option
3. Boo Boo's buddy
4. Blue
5. Dramatic
6. Fall off
7. Common bar order, with "the"
8. Marry me, e.g.
9. It involves lots of questions
10. Agrees
11. Chai?
12. Has a loose end
13. Short-sheeting, e.g.
21. Carve up
25. Cat call
26. Get high
27. About
28. Curtains for a curtain?
29. Alfred E.'s verb
30. Damascene
33. Felix and Garfield
35. Birthright seller
36. Agents
38. Gateway rival
40. Took on
43. Alas!
45. Like some looks
48. Way with words?
50. Crawfish cooking style
51. Flame followers
52. Jazz pianist Blake
53. Doggie reward
56. Grandma, sometimes
57. "The Red"
58. Bump up against
59. Carnie's milieu
60. He gets what's coming

Who Makes House Calls

solution on page 314

ACROSS

1. Gung-ho
5. On and off items
10. Juxtapose
14. River in Russia
15. Worth a ten
16. Mitsubishi rival
17. Hand line study
20. Becomes extroverted
21. Greeting for Dolly
22. Like the White Rabbit
24. Drop off
25. Place for vows
29. Boat people
31. "M" star
32. Bruce of N.F.L. fame
33. Accord
37. Usable by anyone
40. First Lady after Eleanor
41. "How clumsy of me!"
42. At the right moment
43. Rumple
44. Some chocolates
45. Pantry
49. Grand includer
51. ESL class conundrum
52. Emphatic words
57. Improperly formed
61. Look furtively
62. Timer button
63. Play a child's game
64. Tries for a tan
65. On top of it
66. Earlier

DOWN

1. Designer Gucci
2. Senate stalemate ender
3. Legalese phrase
4. $5000 movie word
5. Ceremony
6. Take on
7. She played Sister Agnes
8. Crony
9. Shrewd
10. Fire proof?
11. Prepares eggs
12. Quitter's word
13. He caught Holyfield's ear
18. In the arms of Morpheus
19. "That was close!"
23. Overshadow
24. She plays Doug's TV wife
25. Golf item or golf site
26. Strop
27. Three-point lines, e.g.
28. They get paid
30. Prearranges illegally
32. A friend of Antony
33. Gives no stars
34. "Sesame Street" lesson
35. This, for one
36. Holders
38. "__ Cheatin' Heart"
39. It's heard in *All in the Family*
43. Kind of pad
44. Form of self-defense
45. Goes like Tiny Tim
46. Au revoir
47. No longer abed
48. Wharves
50. Part of a Lemmon title
53. Cuban cash
54. Bliss
55. Smart guy?
56. Youngster
58. Gp. that's fond of firing
59. One of the tribe, colloquially
60. John Dos Passos trilogy

No Repeats

solution on page 314

1	2	3	4		5	6	7	8	9		10	11	12	13
14					15						16			
17				18						19				
20										21				
				22			23		24					
25	26	27	28				29	30						
31					32					33	34	35	36
37				38					39					
40					41				42					
			43				44							
45	46	47	48			49	50							
51						52		53	54	55	56
57				58	59	60								
61				62					63					
64				65					66					

ACROSS

1. Brylcreem unit?
4. Garden shelters
10. The way you walk
14. Choler
15. Precisely correct
16. "My Way" song-writer
17. Hearst-napping org.
18. Stu Erwin's wife
20. Catch fire
22. VW predecessors
23. Deplete
25. Cleans, as a deck
30. Brief bursts
33. Car trip break spot
36. Some bridge players
37. "Whip It" group
38. In order to avoid
39. Kind of cut
40. Becomes an also-ran
41. Auctioneer's first offering
42. Egg carton letters
43. Hurling stats
44. One with a bounc-ing eye

45. Attempting again
47. Colorful parrots
48. Diminish over time
49. Poet's muse
51. Ditty
54. Not precise
58. Go-getter
63. Travel with a trailer
64. Aussie hello
65. Involve
66. Clay today
67. Reason for a PG-13 rating, per-haps
68. Work device
69. *Roseanne* or *Night Court* role

DOWN

1. Type of jockey or brakes
2. Alice's chronicler
3. Exude joy
4. Fixes
5. Applies afresh
6. Swahili or Zulu
7. Canticle
8. Fabulous birds
9. It's right under your nose
10. Guy's date
11. Whichever
12. Likable guy?
13. La Brea goo
19. Intense longing
21. Robin portrayer
24. Foreboding
26. TV's Underdog
27. Ring around a pupil
28. Present, as a gift
29. Glossy fabrics
30. Bolt down
31. Grammarian at times
32. Familiar with
34. Holiday nights

35. Palindromic hit by a palindromic group
37. Worf portrayer
40. Circle of life
44. Blondie, for one
46. Date part
47. Horsemanship
50. Antagonist
52. "Yeah, right!"
53. Divorce center
55. Slightly
56. Burger and fries go-with
57. Bed size
58. Horton hatched one
59. Brouhaha
60. Long fish
61. Gaze upon
62. Long chaser

All in the Family

solution on page 314

ACROSS

1. Grant's landmark
5. Smackers
10. Eddie Munster's pet
14. Bean sprout?
15. Antiseptic acid
16. Bay of Fundy feature
17. They come around in time of need
20. Some quidditch players
21. Orient
22. Leveled in London
24. Artist Chagall
25. Is wearing
28. Cold-day feature
30. Hot under the collar
33. Melodic passage
35. Chelsea neighbor
38. Dogpatch nickname
39. Tycoon known for his appetite
42. Doctrine
43. Taboo thing
44. Transparencies
45. Abound
47. Give a hand to
49. Concerned words
50. Maple fluids
53. Paddock sound
55. "A Horse With No Name" band
58. Actor Fraser
62. Make a fresh start
64. Highland hillside
65. Ridicule
66. Moral wrongs
67. *Hud* director
68. Bicycle wheel part
69. Leave in

DOWN

1. Muscle spasms
2. "Garfield" pooch
3. French mother
4. Deal spot
5. Most truckers
6. Give some slack
7. Kennel sound
8. Perturb
9. Vamoose!
10. Takes the tiller
11. Rum drink
12. High roller's concern
13. Pop quiz
18. Pressures, in a way
19. *Deathtrap* writer Levin
23. Quit a group
25. Reached one's limits
26. Face the day
27. Pet with blue eyes
29. Luau staple
31. Entertainment with Knight or Easy
32. *Family Ties* mom
34. Lennon's missus
36. Brit. seagoing letters
37. Accommodating one
40. Gene ID
41. Opulence
46. Advertise
48. Prove fake
51. Kind of boss
52. Nae sayers?
54. Burned up
55. MS or SASE
56. Le Havre hubby
57. "Pronto!"
59. Just conclusion?
60. Green Gables Girls
61. Aerie home
63. Status follower

Keeping in Shape

solution on page 314

9. So Big

ACROSS

1. It might get filtered
6. Campbell of country
10. Metal shapers
14. Hide-and-seek game cry
15. Home for Yeats
16. Bit of land
17. Veggie (TV) fare?
20. Shed item
21. Prefer charges
22. "But of course!"
23. Distributors
25. Explosively, in music
29. Site of the *Potemkin* mutiny
30. Expunges
31. Turndowns
32. Later!
34. Engaged in
35. Veggie topper?
38. Rum-soaked cake
41. She's riveting
42. Hartford hrs.
45. Keep up
48. Svengali's forte
50. Pretender
51. Narnia hybrid
52. Taxing letters
53. Actress MacGraw
54. Huff and puff
55. Veggie plea to baby?
60. Jai-alai cheers
61. Apple tenders?
62. Worrier's risk, so they say
63. ABBA fan, perhaps
64. Polanski film
65. Grace word

DOWN

1. Feeling
2. Gets by
3. Places for Polonius
4. He got too much sun
5. Pasture sound
6. Family subdivision
7. Magazine or cereal
8. Botch up
9. Must
10. Serves
11. Kay Kyser's Kabibble
12. '70s rock gp.
13. Give a darn
18. UN member since 1949
19. Ski tent
24. Ovid's "to be"
25. Overwhelms with yuks
26. Leading
27. Carter discovery
28. Judge with many sandtimers
30. Supreme Court Justice White
33. Uncanny
35. Most prudent
36. Ade acid
37. Penthouse, another way
38. Mercedes rival
39. They're tied to towers
40. Crib
42. Intensify
43. Light holders
44. Bivouac buddies
46. Field cover
47. Missing
49. Shock
51. Showy flowers, briefly
53. Indy hates them
55. Elephant's org.
56. U.N. labor arm
57. Winning sign
58. Pro vote
59. Chicago, for some

Just Vegging

solution on page 315

1	2	3	4	5		6	7	8	9		10	11	12	13
14						15					16			
17					18					19				
20					21				22					
23			24				25				26	27	28
29						30							
31				32		33				34			
			35					36	37				
38	39	40				41					42	43	44
45			46	47				48		49			
50							51						
			52			53				54			
55	56	57				58			59				
60				61					62				
63				64					65				

ACROSS

1. Nimble
5. Made a lap
8. Food of many shapes
13. Border lake
14. Pugilistic org.
15. Doughnut, slangily
16. Dribble glass?
18. It may be pending
19. "Honest" prez
20. Feed-bag morsel
21. Penalized
22. Corporate coach
24. Went around
27. Motown mistake
28. Up start?
29. "300" spoiler
30. Fugitive
33. Morrow of *Quiz Show*
34. Nukes
37. Oak-to-be
38. Comfy spot
39. Fed. watchdog
40. Layered entree
42. Romeo and Juliet
45. "Runaway" singer Shannon
46. Hirshhorn Museum offerings
50. Ran
52. Kid comeback
53. Scheherazade's offerings
54. *Mystery!* channel
55. Dubya, as a collegian
56. Funds
58. "WAH! I dropped my ice cream!"
60. Tack on
61. It needs refinement
62. "Um-hmm"
63. "Touched by an Angel" star
64. Speed word
65. Mary Poppins chimney sweep

DOWN

1. Bagel seed
2. Explored
3. Matures
4. "Positively!"
5. Talk a blue streak?
6. In __ (soon)
7. Abolished M&M color
8. Props in *The 5,000 Fingers of Dr. T*
9. Pay before a deal
10. Hard-to-find RR posting
11. Boxing count
12. Finesse
15. Barbecue rod
17. Hammer and sickle
21. Part of FDIC
23. Driving needs
24. Toppled from the throne
25. Desirous deity
26. Red-ink total
28. Building fronts
31. Iron man Ripken
32. A Siamese twin
34. Round number?
35. Per
36. Stuff that's hard to read
38. Scruff
41. Like Thor
43. Gets the lead out
44. Containing NaCl
47. "Ten-hut!" canceler
48. It'll curl your hair
49. It'll make you flush
51. Cultivate
52. General Double-day
54. Hit the books
56. An eagle is two under this
57. Koko, for one
58. Friday, for one
59. Tiny tale

Paging Reverend Spooner

solution on page 315

ACROSS

1. Bogart role
9. More than enough
14. Footwear fasteners
15. "Mack the Knife" singer
16. Loud alerts
17. Companion of Artemis
18. Unbroken
19. Sirens
21. Ms. Salonga of *Miss Saigon*
22. Annapolis grad.
24. Like Ellington's doll
25. Went stealthily
27. Sound flyer?
30. Place at an auction
34. Fill with glee
35. *thirtysomething* star
36. Fizzy drinks
38. Chills and fever
39. They're often out on a limb
41. Well-rounded dessert
43. Few and far between
45. Arrogant gait
46. Lineage
48. Dog days mo.
49. Good name for a cook?
52. Deceitful
55. Sitting Bull defeated him
57. Take the blame
58. Taking in
60. Drawn-out fight
61. Social newcomer
62. Internet destinations
63. Winter wear

DOWN

1. Piano prodigy film
2. It comes from the heart
3. Butte's kin
4. Deli machines
5. Law-firm bigwigs
6. 1 or 11, in blackjack
7. Make a bad impression?
8. They make a bloom blossom
9. One taken in
10. Fighting discipline
11. Engine verb
12. Fact fudger
13. Loaf parts
14. Flying jib, e.g.
20. Indy 500 month
23. Dish's beloved, in rhyme
25. Separatist?
26. Hubbubs
28. Small holder
29. Projection room item
30. Business partners, perhaps
31. He played Obi-Wan
32. *A Different World* actress
33. Skate's kin
37. Make smart
40. Predicaments
42. Bates College is near it
44. And so forth, briefly
47. Coin toss option
49. Bit of work
50. Collapsible shelters
51. Impulse
52. Deposit in the "circular file"
53. "The Big One"
54. It's yucky
56. Laurel of *Babes in Toyland*
59. A solo HR earns one

My Fill

solution on page 315

ACROSS

1. Drink or computer language
5. Rachins and Bates
10. Minotaur's milieau
14. Sale caveat
15. Junkyard dog command
16. Like much of Saudi Arabia
17. Jefferson's home
19. Tear
20. Make cryptic
21. End-all product
23. Filtering through
25. Big Band, for one
26. Obloquy
29. Get used to it
33. UK isle
37. *Monster-in-Law* star
38. Ask
39. To do with
40. He hit 511 home runs
41. Popular Surgeon General
42. Quivers's boss
44. Prior to
45. Feel in one's bones
46. Creator of Mush-mouth
47. Mollifier
49. Poem pt.
51. Googlers
56. Be lost?
61. He's mortgaged
62. Player at "The Big O"
63. Mozart opera, with "The"
65. Honest-to-goodness
66. Local life
67. Garnish
68. Twice tetra-
69. *Full House* twin
70. Takes in

DOWN

1. Miss Moneypenny addressee
2. Unified
3. Wrestler McMahon
4. Put __ to (halt)
5. Emulate Hillary
6. Cock-and-bull story
7. Rights grp.
8. Little Dickens girl
9. What David did to Goliath
10. Big dog, smaller than Clifford
11. Carpet concern
12. Voltaic cell element
13. Turning point?
18. Ding-dong
22. Mesopotamia now
24. Dolls for boys
27. Far-out
28. Stopover spots
30. Too long a time
31. Tourney vets
32. Cast leader
33. Mich. neighbor
34. Fond of
35. Tests for Sr.'s
36. *Moonlighting* role
43. Refusenik's refusal
45. It's a fine line
48. Pon four sufferer
50. Sly role
52. Hat fabrics
53. Adapt, in a way
54. Link again
55. Is apparent
56. Long lunch?
57. CEO or COO
58. Hit the cuspidor
59. Whodunit shadower
60. Some are easily bruised
64. Four-time Japanese P.M.

Strings Attached

solution on page 315

ACROSS

1. A tieback ties it back
6. Burns flick of 1977
11. Wee whopper
14. *Roseanne* role, eventually
15. Fogg's creator
16. Gaslight time
17. "Exit stage left" toon
19. Sonnyboy
20. Sanctum
21. Snooze alarm activity
23. Any of several *Grey's Anatomy* leads
26. Mrs. Norton of *The Honeymooners*
27. Applaud
28. They might be goo-goo
32. Asian fete
33. PIN acceptor
34. Broadcaster
36. Starbucks offering
39. Social events
41. One who might get rubbed out
42. Grown-up grigs
43. Purviance of silents
44. *My Fair Lady* lady
45. Terse President
46. Feature-filled film format
48. Over one's head
49. Bor-r-r-r-ring
50. Captains' seniors
53. Snapshots
55. Engorged oneself
57. Phony coin
58. Cosmonaut's home
59. His theme? "Here I come to save the day!"
64. Scuff
65. Pond growth
66. School kid
67. Random selection
68. Percussive dance show
69. Great fuss

DOWN

1. He gives oral exams: abbr.
2. Did a 10K
3. One of Mickey's wives
4. Pooh pal
5. Mortimer's voicer
6. Egg order
7. Like some cats
8. Vittles
9. Beginning
10. Sandy expanse
11. Lindbergh's mascot
12. Persian today
13. ID for Friday
18. Totem pole's story
22. Pie part
23. Hopping mad
24. Distinguished
25. Early Hanna-Barbera duo
29. Triangular sign
30. Newsman Pyle
31. Take forcibly
35. Submit another resume
37. Crockett's Waterloo
38. Guam and Bali
40. Relish
47. Ibsen works
49. End your computer session
50. Train throwee of film
51. Like dinosaurs, we now suspect
52. Clown prop
54. Camels have 'em
56. Waffle brand
57. Dance move
60. Green eggs go-with
61. Reuters rival
62. Moral lapse
63. Member at lodge?

Cats and Mice

solution on page 315

ACROSS

1. Main theme
6. British interviewer
11. Coterie
14. Midway alternative
15. *My Fair Lady* composer
16. Money maker
17. One from Maine?
19. Wabash st.
20. Feral pig
21. Bedelia of kid's lit
23. Saunters
27. *Cocoon* star
28. Exhausted
29. Sticky note
30. Divine archer
31. Triumphant cry
33. Fictional Frome
36. Trumpeter Adderley
37. Poem parts
39. Hebrew judge
40. It's a steal
42. Mutual bonds?
43. Pain may yield it
44. Resting places
46. Suggestive state
48. Newborns
50. Ladieswear
51. "My Time Is Your Time" singer
52. Stereo knob
53. Personal story
54. Swear by your hatchetman?
60. One of Mickey's wives
61. One might be rubbed out
62. Poppycock
63. Jewish grant of divorce
64. Return
65. Type of power

DOWN

1. She goes with apple pie
2. Taunting cry
3. *The __ of Pooh*
4. It has many forms
5. Lame
6. Tiny circus performers
7. Crowd sound
8. Lge. ref. source
9. Takes or minces an oath
10. Home wreckers
11. Look in the back of this book
12. Bilko nickname
13. "Who's on First?" catcher
18. Cautionary phrase
22. Put out
23. Depleted
24. It lacks vowels
25. Parade item for the fans?
26. Rhea, to the Romans
27. Reagan coworker
29. Walden et al.
32. Bides one's time
34. Looking-glass girl
35. Something to dress to
37. Prehistoric time
38. Heavenly
41. Stable newborn
43. Great time
45. *Family Ties* dad
47. Bowling-alley buttons
48. Hospital hanger
49. Gullible
50. Ham or onion prep tool
52. Soft cheese
55. Tolkien or AMA character
56. "But is it __?"
57. Go head-to-head
58. MPG modifier
59. Deep sleep letters

Begone!

solution on page 315

ACROSS

1. Yodeler's perch
4. Gambler's quest
10. Order
14. Polar explorer
15. Hawaiian lama
16. Roughly
17. 1951 Bob Hope film
20. Robin portrayer in '38
21. Folk dances
22. Disconsolate
23. Sign away
25. Former Red Cross head
27. They might have rings
31. Respectable
35. In times past
36. Passes by
38. Too
39. Certain Latin lands
43. Ningpo nanny
44. He bee
45. "Calvin and Hobbes" bully
46. Zesty dips
49. Hides from prying spies
51. Job-safety org.
53. Head for
54. Empty talk
57. Kind of test
59. Deceptions
63. 1966 Beatles song
66. Mimic a mantis
67. Isolate
68. TiVo, for one
69. Vague amount
70. Stand-up comic or mythical sailor
71. CBS symbol

DOWN

1. Jocular Johnson
2. Cowardly Lion actor
3. Social equal
4. Halloween hanger
5. Popeye verb
6. Tern or ern
7. You might carry one
8. Put a halt to
9. Matthew's *Freshman* costar
10. Popinjay
11. Pesters
12. Most people live there
13. Bridges on TV
18. Lomond, for one
19. Home of the Kon-Tiki Museum
24. Old Russian diet
26. Roster wrapup
27. Rum cakes
28. Old World lizard
29. Having a key
30. Metric unit
32. Super Bowl sight
33. Site of Eliza's first public outing
34. Portions
37. He lives in a pineapple under the sea
40. Facetious "I see"
41. Weird, for a Scot
42. Philosopher Russell
47. Now about . . .
48. Oboes of yore
50. Part of BYOB
52. Very, in music
54. Swindles
55. Dynamic leader?
56. Poetry event
58. U, for one
60. Fries or slaw
61. That green feeling
62. Desiccated
64. It's good for seals
65. It'll never fly

I'm Still Just Wild About Saffron

solution on page 316

ACROSS

1. Too
7. Just eh
11. U.N. Day month
14. You might get it after mono
15. It might give you a lift
16. Sauce for the wok
17. Emmett Kelly's character
19. Item in a lock
20. Travel guide listings
21. One way to cook a steak
22. Opera villainess, often
23. Potential perch
24. "Evil Women" gp.
25. Gomer's cousin
27. Trip cause
28. Invisible Jet flyer
31. Not so many
32. Susan Lucci's Emmy role
33. It's spent in Iran
36. Stuntman Robinson
38. Casino tip
39. Choice words
41. Repasts
44. Hard-to-find striped-shirt guy series
47. Columnist Smith
50. Pick-me-up
51. Single's so long
52. Fenced gems
53. Pal of Kukla and Ollie
54. Violet shade
56. Geraldine portrayer
57. Circle of life
58. Victim of bringing down the house
60. Coda
61. Peter's *A Shot in the Dark* costar
62. Eager for company
63. Downed dinner
64. Costner role
65. Over thar

DOWN

1. Eddying
2. Pool people
3. Detached
4. Messes up
5. Rocketman Willy
6. Cad's move
7. WWII site
8. Be accommodating
9. Swabby
10. You can dig it!
11. Caruso rendition
12. Holder of sorts
13. Rookie
18. Decreased
22. Scrubs
24. Girl on a ranch
26. Have markers
29. Moliere's forte
30. Dumfries denial
31. European coin
33. Wet behind the ears
34. Unlearned
35. *Guys and Dolls* gal
37. Do deja vu
40. Sophocles title word
42. What's more
43. John of London
45. Good as gold, e.g.
46. Distresses severely
47. Harmonized
48. Cold stick
49. Gentle breeze
53. Pet peeve?
55. Tiny Tim's tiny items
56. It might be slipped
58. Cyst type
59. Pitched item

1	2	3	4	5	6		7	8	9	10		11	12	13
14							15					16		
17					18							19		
20					21						22			
23				24			25		26					
27				28		29								30
			31							32				
33	34	35				36		37			38			
39				40			41		42	43				
44					45	46						47	48	49
	50						51					52		
53					54		55				56			
57				58						59				
60				61				62						
63				64				65						

ACROSS

1. Opening night dos
6. *What's My Line?* panelist
10. They can be essential
14. Admiral Byrd book
15. Sub in a tub
16. CD player problem
17. Cop show catchphrase
19. Miss's equivalent
20. It seats 100
21. Systematic
23. Not him!
25. Fretful
26. Superficial
31. Kind of pool
34. Worms or sponges, say
35. Biblical verb
37. Milk, in a way
38. Jiffs
39. Wine can dissolve it
40. Indian name meaning "ruler"
41. Deluge refuge
42. Rush to sell, on Wall Street
43. Comprehensive
44. Urging of Longfellow or Joaquin Miller
46. Gift list
48. Jose Carreras, for one
50. "Savvy?"
51. Naked
54. Say it again
59. Like Franklin's Richard
60. Phrase from Lorelei Lee
62. Tab-taker's phrase
63. Grand Canyon sight
64. They moved in a Bowl
65. Nostradamus, e.g.
66. Like certain trays
67. Proceeds on one's way

DOWN

1. Is a yenta
2. Lily plant
3. *On Golden Pond* bird
4. Vegas headliner
5. Is fit to be tied
6. Delivery letters
7. Its capital was Susa
8. Have "Us" continue
9. It's near the base
10. Show family of the late '70s
11. Paar catchphrase
12. Role for Leslie Caron
13. What some houses are built on
18. Event for Carl Lewis
22. "Warmer," e.g.
24. Stood up
26. Baja abodes
27. Night spot for the Marxes
28. *Laugh-In* catchphrase
29. OB's and ENT's
30. Run a meeting
32. *Wings* got the first one
33. All systems go
36. Bow-shaped
39. Wide view
40. Dept. of the Treasury division
42. Johnnycake
43. Tetley rival
45. "Masochism Tango" singer
47. Lassie
49. Goes ballistic
51. NASDAQ debuts
52. Poor dog's portion
53. Trevi tosser's thought
55. Go backpacking
56. Comparable
57. Nucleus
58. Snake "talk"
61. Oscar-winning title film role for Jamie Foxx

Catchphrases

solution on page 316

ACROSS

1. Witticisms
6. Kachina doll maker
10. St. Louis sight
14. Folk singer Hoyt
15. Bean in space
16. Michael's *Mr. Mom* costar
17. Ben's mother Anne
18. She worked with Alice and Flo
19. Couturier Cassini
20. Albums
22. Mash preceder
23. Snapshot, for short
24. Hand-picks
26. Parking lot desirables
30. It keeps things rolling
31. Type of sportscar
35. The whole thing
39. Look like
40. Famous
42. Jodie Foster's alma mater
43. Ate through with teeth
45. Middle-of-the-road sorts
47. First word of many church names
49. Wall Street woes
50. Wyatt Earp, e.g.
54. Giant of baseball
55. Reached Dulles
56. Conked out
62. Kosovo force
63. Tempo
64. 1982 film with Kevin Bacon
65. Peck film, with "The"
66. Legalese phrase
67. Mulcahy, for one
68. Title role for Bette
69. Loser of 1917
70. The Bard's theater

DOWN

1. Plays jazz
2. Suit
3. Dallas Cowboys emblem
4. ⅓ of a WWII movie
5. Large turtle
6. What brats wreak
7. Sub in a tub
8. Picnic places
9. Shortly
10. *The Sweet Hereafter* director
11. Souvenir
12. Wave part
13. Euphoric moments
21. Animal on a nickel
25. It has many spots
26. Pert blurt
27. No contest, e.g.
28. Small number
29. Jewelry store purchase
32. *Doctor Detroit* foe
33. Region for DDE
34. Big Brit. bk.
36. M. Hulot portrayer
37. Fish sauce
38. Sometimes it's more
41. Profundity
44. "How stupid of me!"
46. Suitable for most movie audiences
48. Racetrack automaton
50. Bruce Wayne's home, e.g.
51. Hertz rival
52. Baptism and Bar Mitzvah
53. Legal claims
54. Playful swimmer
57. Leaping Lipinski
58. Camay rival
59. Get rid of a knot
60. Sarajevo citizen
61. Shoe holder

Nothing Much

solution on page 316

ACROSS

1. Clay fighter of legend
6. Silverstein's light place
11. Z3 maker
14. Amtrak's bullet train
15. Lobster claw
16. Wide-shoe width
17. Past fresh
18. Senator Hatch
19. Road-map abbr.
20. French peace accord?
22. It makes towels plushy
23. Rocker with a family
24. Nettle
26. Oola's Alley
27. Salad dressing liquid
29. Mountain lakes
32. Eight days, in a Beatle song
34. Tropical starch
35. UN labor gp.
36. Wiped out
39. Ideology
40. Hit for Bowie or Cara
42. Latin lover?
43. *It's a Wonderful Life* cabbie
45. *Hart to Hart* pooch
47. Draft choice
48. In a tizzy
49. Name of nine popes
54. Chow catcher
55. Irish backgammon items
57. Hope provider?
58. Juan Gonzalez's son
59. Ready to hit
60. Fitting nickname for a chef
61. Role played with fake ears
62. Torment
63. "The buck stops here" monogram
64. Things to do
65. Slalom curves

DOWN

1. Horror-film reactions
2. Relating to eight
3. Stand-up comic Dennis
4. *Invisible Man* author
5. Regally, in music
6. Squirrel stash
7. Pang
8. She plays a klutzy Desperate Housewife
9. Presidential slogan
10. Promised Land
11. Rediscovered European?
12. Long toe bones
13. Have tears
21. It may be blown
25. Hanoi holiday
27. Docs for crocs
28. Trevi Fountain site
29. Quarrel
30. Mountain-out-of-molehill sorts
31. Mosey around Italy
32. Lean and sinewy
33. SHAEF zone
37. "Sorry!"
38. Fragile
41. Velvet finish?
44. Questions authority
46. Most sprawling
47. Governor Richards
49. Longtime Supreme Court name
50. Sounds from a pen
51. Eastern bishops
52. Suspend
53. Park in the Colorado Rockies
54. Ford CIA head
56. Life stories

Capital Idea

solution on page 316

ACROSS

1. Get lit
5. Quaint hostel
10. Leave a mark
14. Ore door
15. Licorice herb
16. "Hey, sailor!"
17. Tiny millionaire?
19. Musical Horne
20. Leafstalks
21. They go with fishes
23. Like The Citadel, now
24. Transparent
25. Poisonous gas
28. Golf concern
31. Inebriated
32. Pouts
33. *Curb Your Enthusiasm* airer
34. Fluish feeling
35. Doesn't raise
36. Talk like crazy?
37. Green hole
38. Susan Saradon's *Rocky Horror Picture Show* role
39. Throw a tantrum
40. A janitor may have many
42. Becomes serious
43. Non-PC kid's character
44. Jeff Bridges' brother
45. Blue Beatle foe
47. Landing place
51. Woody's boy
52. They'd be hidden on Santa's suit
54. Place
55. Bailiwick
56. Freeman Gosden role
57. Emergency Broadcast System event
58. Range sizes
59. Mardi Gras follower

DOWN

1. It's saved for a rainy day
2. Big-tongued dog
3. Early Scot
4. Try to beat morally
5. Dry cleaner or repairman, say
6. Wagered
7. Picky people pick them
8. One way to the Net
9. Direct routes
10. Spiced meat
11. Action movie scene?
12. Best-rated
13. Showy rugs
18. Daft
22. Mercury rival
24. Tennis or seismology term
25. One way to be taken
26. Knave
27. Concern of *Seinfeld's* "Nazi"
28. Eagles end up there
29. Capp lad
30. *Ghostbusters* actress
32. Juicy fruit
35. Capital of Australia
36. Comeback
38. Guitarist Hendrix
39. Talk big
41. Was used up
42. Antitoxins
44. Kind of belt
45. Drive-in order
46. Border lake
47. Sixth month, in Jerusalem
48. Palatine Hill site
49. Part of
50. Clandestine signal
53. ECU issuer

Who Was That?

solution on page 316

10. Really Big

ACROSS

1. Tip off
5. Put safely away
9. Swell illness?
14. Creative spark
15. Kachina doll maker
16. Like Abie's Rose
17. Hit hard
18. Iron and Bronze
19. A&M student, familiarly
20. Unsturdy weapon
23. Fraidy-cats
24. Charles Foster Kane's estate
28. Muscles to crunch
29. "Big" burger
31. "Enterprise" journey
32. Come to
35. *The Crucible* setting
37. Genome stuff
38. Orbs that last half a decade
41. Rhoda's mom
42. Immigration island
43. No rocket scientist
44. Silence between notes
46. Paris when it sizzles
47. Like some blankets?
48. Repute
50. Inept GI
54. Piano tuner
57. Milton's muse
60. In the thick of
61. Super-duper
62. Take over land
63. Little brat
64. First-year cadet
65. Cronyn's frequent costar
66. Museo display
67. Yesteryears

DOWN

1. Small amounts of smoke
2. Loser to Dwight
3. Realizes
4. Junior, for one
5. Humiliates
6. Forum wear
7. Cartel since 1960
8. Trevi tosser's thought
9. Sporty Mazda
10. Can't-wait
11. Russian-made jet
12. Air-pump abbr.
13. "__ sells seashells . . ."
21. Steakhouse offering
22. Perform well
25. She played Miss Brooks
26. Lasting impressions
27. Czar's decree
29. Donny's sis
30. Heidi's home
32. Raring to go
33. Some shoes
34. "Halt, salt!"
35. Ice melter
36. Coped
39. Varnish resin
40. IE alternative
45. Did lab work
47. Duck's gait
49. Adhesive
50. Wooden walker
51. Bikini, e.g.
52. Shaped like a tornado
53. German biochemist
55. Auto parts company
56. Arab prince
57. Dig in
58. Gen. material
59. Massachusetts cape

Alien Invasion!!!

solution on page 317

ACROSS

1. Addendum conjunction
5. It goes downhill fast
9. Salad green
14. 1984 Peace Nobelist
15. Godiva's title
16. Squiggy's pal
17. Ever so much
18. Participant's comment
19. Like most people
20. It's up for bids
23. Filled up on
24. Come to the rescue
25. Ailment sung about by Ted Nugent
34. Archie's "dingbat"
35. Full of substance
36. Derisive cry
37. Daily records
38. Part of a suit
39. Japanese soup
40. ". . . __ he drove out of sight . . ."
41. Receiver, in law
42. Gave an edge to
43. Atlantic menace?
46. Fifi's friend
47. Like a hit show
48. DJ's next task
57. "I surrender!"
58. Battle song?
59. Hideaway
60. Old anesthetic
61. Abhorrent
62. Ides rebuke
63. They swing in saloons
64. Call out
65. Pillow cover

DOWN

1. Just slightly
2. Humdinger
3. Eight-sided sign
4. *Survivor* verb
5. Deli clerk, at times
6. Man of the mantra
7. Change one's story?
8. Force unit
9. Make plain
10. Hang one's hat
11. City near Tulsa
12. Hitch in plans
13. 1/1 song ender
21. Calamine target
22. Coins in Bangkok
25. Supermarket tabloid subject
26. Admire greatly
27. Woods on the links
28. Iowa commune
29. Basic belief
30. Feed en masse
31. In a contest
32. S45
33. __ Island Red
38. Daises
39. Glasses not worn by the masses
41. Garbagemen
42. Tortoise's foe
44. Vicious person
45. Bibi's nation
48. Jogged one's memory
49. "Do __ others ..."
50. Off-the-wall reply?
51. Kind of bean
52. Cherokee's kin
53. Volition
54. Courtroom ritual
55. Comic Rudner
56. Oil barrel

A Game of Pool

solution on page 317

ACROSS

1. Ferber work
6. *M*A*S*H* actor's middle name
11. He upset T.E.D.
14. Analyze
15. Lady with a train, often
16. Tax mo.
17. Rapper's skill
18. Patriarch who saw a ladder
19. Whom Uncle Sam wanted
20. *Westworld* or *King and I* actor, familiarly
21. Nimble
22. Opened a latch
24. "I dropped my toothpaste," said Tom ___
28. Wide receiver?
30. Flint org.
31. Bungling
32. "I lost my toothpaste," said Tom ___
38. Kind of soda
39. Rice dish: var.
40. Flightless bird
41. "I'm stuck in the classifieds," said Tom __
43. Paine's creed
44. *Gidget* star
45. Experts
46. "I'm a missionary," said Tom __
52. Hangman's need
53. Skelton forte
54. Chowderhead
57. Title for an atty.
58. Abu __
60. Come to terms
62. Bucharest coin
63. Leaked
64. Word with card or finger
65. Prior to
66. One cubic meter
67. Dark

DOWN

1. Nimble
2. Aloha Bowl setting
3. You just need a dab of it
4. Belief
5. Kin of "Golly!"
6. Etagere piece
7. Ender's commander
8. Commands
9. Old Tokyo
10. Galaxies
11. Father of the String Quartet
12. Give in too much
13. Monk's beloved
21. Reserved Net connection
23. Movietone item
25. Undertow causes
26. "Mangia!"
27. Ripsnorter
28. Verdi's slave girl
29. *Camelot* role
32. Provide help
33. Kind of will or wind
34. Indy 500 month
35. Liner builders
36. "__ we forget"
37. Orange food
39. Hammer head
42. Altar screen
43. JFK's predecessor
45. "Hail!," to Caesar
46. Anoint, once
47. Also-ran
48. Chef's hat
49. Dazzle
50. Roman river
51. Ammonia compound
55. Ferret out
56. Alluring
59. Spicy
60. Provide help
61. Stocky antelope

Swifties of 13 and 9

solution on page 317

ACROSS

1. Ad-hoc cowboy committee
6. Palomino's pace
10. Makes like
14. Touch-screen user, sometimes
15. Lunch time?
16. Type type
17. Puerto Rican vampire
19. It often has a twist
20. United
21. Suitably
23. Encompass
26. Store helper
27. Hole punches, of sorts
28. Klinger's hometown
29. Lose ground?
30. It can be tall
31. Snort
34. He's on the outs
35. Doodyville opener
38. Heston's grp.
39. Peace talks result
41. Risked a ticket
42. Crystal does him
44. Van Gogh title
46. Papal envoy
47. Comes from
49. Mille __
50. Sam and Remus
51. Infernal author?
52. Agnew's plea, for short
53. Calendar, perhaps
58. Horsefly
59. Made do, with "out"
60. Phillips of *Benson*
61. It's big in Louisi-anna
62. Fruit of the rowan
63. Valley girls?

DOWN

1. Pipe type
2. La la lead-in
3. VW predecessors
4. Leafed
5. Wipe outs
6. Macbeth title
7. Get-the-paper outfit
8. Court center
9. Trod upon
10. Sticks on
11. Anthropological fraud
12. Sedan school
13. Pan, for one
18. Fish and chips fish, often
22. Wide wingtip
23. What winter roads do
24. Kevin's mom on *The Wonder Years*
25. UFO art, to some
26. *The __ Gold Cadillac*
28. Helps oneself to
30. Pounds the keyboard
32. P.O.'d
33. They're pumped
36. Rates
37. Did a tec's job
40. Type of book deal
43. Accept
45. "__ Gotta Be Me"
46. Wolf or star
47. Kind of cap
48. Name in WWII flight
49. Inn, informally
51. Go-getter
54. WBA stat
55. Org. for Orr
56. Maiden
57. Annapolis grad.

More Mysteries

solution on page 317

ACROSS

1. Experiences
5. Musical Knife?
9. You might have a green one
14. De novo
15. Splash
16. Artist Rousseau
17. "Let my people go," e.g.
18. Doubtful story
19. "Take Me Out to the Ball Game" is one
20. 1975 LaBelle song
23. Carries on
24. Some fins
27. Recent opening?
28. Send off
31. Containing element 39
32. Mouth warmer of sorts
34. Grandma Moses
35. "Black Bottom Stomp" performer
40. He directed Marlon in '54
41. R and R spot
42. Bach specialty
45. Sub station
46. Imogene's partner
49. Railroad employee
51. He lost his tail
53. Famed medical hospital
56. Sharp
58. Colleague of Scotty and Spock
59. Japanese instrument
60. Less sullied
61. Tiny coat
62. Desert wheel
63. Tavern round, maybe
64. Forgetful actor's request
65. Show disrespect

DOWN

1. He played a frizzy-haired teacher
2. Bind up
3. Must
4. Rocks
5. Poetic tool
6. Banned apple spray
7. Reassure
8. Massage
9. Block
10. Advantage
11. Not yet picked up
12. Mohawked muscleman
13. Trade, slangily
21. Like some attics
22. Powell's screen wife
25. Type of type
26. Examine
29. Role for Marty Feldman
30. In heaps
32. He worked with Miss Richards
33. If not
35. Akbar's toon pal
36. Av successor
37. Tourniquet
38. Smallest part
39. Bay window
43. Desert bigwigs
44. Muppet eagle
46. California wine center
47. Eye malady
48. Interior designs
50. Snoot-y
52. "Yeow!"
54. Pol Andropov
55. *Havana* actress
56. *Jurassic Park* ore
57. Kind of ball or card

Quite a Spread

solution on page 317

ACROSS

1. Uncle __ (rice brand)
5. Stevedores do it
9. Is in cahoots
14. Domain
15. Improve
16. Outrigger
17. Society fish?
19. Steak choice
20. Record highlight
21. Common Market letters
23. Netizen
24. Unimagined
27. Salzburg vista
29. Fishy author?
34. April VIP
36. Dreamcast maker
37. Danish creator
38. Not just mine
40. Stipulations
42. Spanish conqueror of all
43. It's visible on cold days
45. Says softly
47. American species of alligator
48. Fishy musician?
51. Capra title starter
52. Asian weight
53. Sibilant summons
56. TV sked abbr.
58. LEM component
62. Nerdy
64. Fishy TV actor
67. Hooch
68. Pollster Roper
69. Singer Simone
70. Win every game
71. Viscous
72. Draft picks

DOWN

1. It's south of San Diego
2. A friend of Antony
3. Radar's quaff
4. Justice O'Connor
5. Any ship
6. Rocky rise
7. Formerly
8. Subject to rumor
9. False show
10. Woman's head scarf
11. Hazzard deputy
12. Muscular fitness
13. Omen observer
18. Strips
22. Cocktail component, at times
25. February stone
26. Theater area
28. Free TV spot
29. Ranee's garb
30. Word form for "sleep"
31. Wicked person
32. Type of will
33. Rochester's love
34. Salad name
35. Reverse knit
39. Cleanse
41. No longer an issue
44. It's a blast!
46. Common sense
49. Rapid talker
50. Wellesley grad
53. Places for pints
54. Bush spokesman
55. Pump or clog
57. Woody's boy
59. Tire ruiner
60. Trouble spots?
61. Showy rugs
63. Vim
65. Urchin
66. Powell's screen wife

Fishy

solution on page 317

ACROSS

1. For this purpose only
6. Modeling wood
11. Pipe type
14. Wampum
15. Maven
16. Game cry
17. Curry seller?
19. It's near Miss.
20. Acid rain org.
21. Item in a French cafe
23. Oft-seen spots
26. Tactic
28. Scrubs hard
29. Job's lot
30. Prominent boy of 2000
32. It's used at groundbreaking events
33. TV role for Polly Holliday
34. He had people shooting at water towers
36. Crossword cutter
39. Howl
41. Casino patrons
43. End of "Miss Mary Mack"
44. Bolt down
46. Boom-bah preceder
47. W.C. Fields persona
49. The Man Without a Country
50. People talk when it's broken
51. Like digestive juices
54. Valley with a wine train
55. Kenny G plays it
56. For the left hand on the piano, often
58. Eighty-six
60. Circus routine
61. Middle East rocks?
66. He's messed up
67. Eradicate
68. Overact
69. TV knob abbr.
70. Hit with a laser
71. Do a Hamelin job

DOWN

1. Ritalin is a common Rx for it
2. Cooper role of 1941
3. "Whazzat?"
4. Girl-watch
5. Another name for Ojibwa
6. Cote cry
7. Important gland
8. Albanian coins
9. Glasses
10. Affix
11. Russian outlook?
12. Courage
13. Chews the fat
18. Xylophone need
22. Biddy's bed
23. Horrible
24. Camera carriage
25. Lack of the Five Chinese Brothers?
27. Oscar role for Charlize
31. Crab or Horsehead
35. Mexican wraps
37. Author Jong
38. New Jersey county
40. French city
42. Lived in
45. Mix up
48. Heart
51. Embarrass
52. Hardly wimpy
53. The "It" Girl
57. The "it" ad place
59. Igloo shape
62. Took control
63. Choice word
64. H, to Homer
65. Collector's goal

Citywide

solution on page 318

ACROSS

1. Slatted shade
6. Nettles
10. Chatters
14. "Fibber McGee" medium
15. Wyle of *ER*
16. Be a lookout, perhaps
17. In the midst of
18. *Mon Oncle* star
19. Shaman's wisdom
20. Mr. Mooney and Mr. Wilson
22. Angler's bait
23. Marriage vow
24. Awfully cruel
26. Simulated
30. Hang low
32. Roman robes
33. Nana's spouse
37. First victim of fratricide
38. Act badly?
39. Blues singer Redding
40. Sheets, etc.
42. Bela of the banjo
43. Ryan who played Granny
44. Saucy dances
45. Arachne, for example
48. Tennis cry
49. *Same Time, Next Year* actor
50. Wingding
57. Androcles' friend
58. Garbage can, on a PC
59. Meet the day
60. Blowgun missile
61. Film lioness
62. Tom's *Jerry Maguire* costar
63. Fin components
64. Brings to Wapner
65. Rationed (out)

DOWN

1. Blow one's horn
2. Buddhist monk
3. Golden calf, e.g.
4. Lives a cat has
5. Woof-woofs
6. Opening bars
7. Hope and Crosby byway
8. O.J. witness Kaelin
9. Tibia
10. Opinion gager
11. Give or take
12. Quotable catcher
13. Bethlehem product
21. Peculiar
25. Gangster's gun
26. Shot in the dark
27. Soliloquy starter
28. Made mellow
29. Wanders
30. He bee
31. Ship deserters
33. Some Feds
34. Old-time actor Roscoe
35. 12-point type
36. Interrogates
38. Potencies
41. Dander
42. Loser's spot
44. Blue expanse
45. Hiker of kiddie lit
46. Name in millennial news
47. Really fancy
48. Pram pushers
51. Rights gp. that leans left
52. Meet defeat
53. Part of NAFTA
54. Isn't on the street
55. Gotcha!
56. Clarinet need

Gal Time

solution on page 318

ACROSS

1. Sawing logs
7. Bank transactions
15. Large prawns
16. Caruso rendition
17. Party talker
19. Little role?
20. Schlep
21. 1981 Julie Andrews film
22. Answer to popped question
23. Thomas of *Love and War*
24. Depressing sounds for doctors?
25. It might need to be cleaned up
28. Something to tote
29. Mail HQ
30. One in the hole
31. Puccini work
36. Grape pits, e.g.
37. Engine additive
38. Handles roughly
39. Florida 2000 newsmaker
42. March 15 words
43. A lot, to a poet
44. Ad trailer
45. Matthew's role in *The Producers*
46. Blood-typing syst.
47. Bottom in Bayonne
48. Mountain pass
51. Census query
52. Before, before
53. Kind of ranch
54. Cut seafood
59. Kind of rug
60. Eucalyptus lovers
61. Stannic ore
62. Sana native

DOWN

1. Put a value on
2. Sub viewer
3. Ray Finkle's career undoing
4. Bedouin bigwig
5. MPG raters
6. Marauder's verb
7. A McKenzie Brother in *Strange Brew*
8. Dianetics spin-off
9. Casual criticism
10. Cheap spreads
11. Kosovo native
12. Phelps's org.
13. Up to, in ads
14. Versatile bean
18. Broker's advice
23. Helen, on *Mad About You*
24. In a befitting way
25. Dire
26. Yo-Yo string?
27. Rendezvous
28. African tongue
29. Self-reproach
30. Dental brand
31. Gravel-voiced singer Mercer
32. Like some accents or angles
33. Love remark in *Ghost*
34. Popular
35. Spam you might can
40. Benigni of *Life is Beautiful*
41. Type of thinking
46. Smiley or Smart
47. Blubber
48. Cunning
49. Fellow who sells space
50. Soda seller
51. Roscoe of old flicks
52. Palindromic magazine name
53. Drop, so to speak
54. Plant sci.
55. William Tell's home
56. Kind of badge or horn
57. Geisha's accessory
58. Ready the soil

Lepidoptera

solution on page 318

ACROSS

1. All clear signals?
6. Tap word
10. No big thing
14. Fastball measurer
15. Palmist's words
16. Rafter's hangout
17. Ice cream vendor
20. Snitched
21. Notch shape
22. They might be in temples or torsos
23. Hams it up
26. Hot tub chemical
29. Ask for more Samoa's, say
34. Twiki player's other role
35. Cavity with a filling
38. Nudge forward
39. Matthau/O'Neal film of '76
43. He played Grace's ex on *Will & Grace*
44. Sample
45. Type of bar or blanket
46. Car by Hyundai
49. Feelings of dread
51. A new one is a cub
54. Where Belgrade is
58. Luau loop
59. Mrs. Victor Laszlo
63. Gritty tale for kids
66. Plenty of time
67. Driving items
68. Finley's Dinsmore
69. Stimulate
70. Nimble
71. Lowest high tides

DOWN

1. They might be fine or liberal
2. LOL, in person
3. She played Jeannie's evil twin
4. Fly-to-be
5. Capacity-crowd letters
6. It may be hard
7. *Barbarella* actor
8. Bread in Bucharest
9. Take a stripe from
10. "Lulu" composer
11. Nash's "one-L" priest
12. A Karamazov
13. Stockades
18. Passed the baton by CB
19. Thereabouts
24. She wrote "Tom's Diner"
25. Shell teams
26. Challenger's quest
27. Antiknock additive
28. Inscribed pillar (not yelled by Stanley Kowalski)
30. Word in a Poe title
31. Some chess endings
32. Sanibel Island sight
33. Squiggly music symbols
36. In reserve
37. It's known for impressive busts
40. Gentle bear
41. Sticky balloon phenomena
42. "Stand by Me" singer King
47. SOHCAHTOA subj.
48. There's lots to it
50. Edsel feature
52. Firstborn
53. Earth Day verb
54. Hobo fare
55. Teletubby greeting
56. Clint's *In the Line of Fire* costar
57. Blackjack blowout
60. Apple II component
61. Prune
62. Many a moon
64. "Verily!"
65. Barbie's guy, once again

Spaghetti Feast

solution on page 318

ACROSS

1. Jessica Fletcher's friend
5. Onion or tulip, e.g.
9. Halt, salt!
14. Carrot on a stick
15. China setting
16. Rumble
17. Land measures
18. Sub station
19. Revealed, as an identity
20. MATCH
23. There are five per foot
24. "Where the Boys __"
25. Damage
28. Record number?
30. It's down the drain
34. All things great and small
35. Ryder rival
37. Dublin draft
38. MATCH
41. Indiana Jones searched for it
42. Wings have them
43. Small lizard
44. Capone nemesis
46. Cry of triumph
47. Spates
48. Verb before "for" or "out"
50. Savoir-faire
51. MATCH
59. Shower time
60. Berlin-born Sommer
61. Blamed one
62. Irked
63. Seasonal air
64. Soiree
65. Soup servings
66. End of "For He's a Jolly Good Fellow"
67. Undress

DOWN

1. Quincy's table
2. Disney leader
3. *Jurassic Park* terror
4. Reluctant
5. Nag or hound
6. Narc's quarry
7. __ Marlene
8. He played Mr. Drummond
9. *Jurassic Park* rock
10. Plush fabric
11. Plant treatment?
12. Darned
13. Circus item
21. Squeals of delight, e.g.
22. It might be run
25. Llama herder, once
26. *Ghost* star
27. Hoodlums
28. Aesop animal
29. What a 49er does
31. Dressing type
32. Analogous
33. Pennies for Pedro
35. Where Jews are "gentiles"
36. Jr. at the frathouse
39. What ladybugs and leopards have
40. Rainy-day funds
45. Tea
47. Hardly ever
49. Hides and hairs
50. Bus fare
51. Allied target of 7/7/44
52. Until
53. Scull squad
54. Transmit
55. Arctic floater
56. Danny Kaye role
57. Folk item
58. Slightly

3 on a Match

solution on page 318

1	2	3	4		5	6	7	8		9	10	11	12	13
14					15					16				
17					18					19				
20				21					22					
			23						24					
25	26	27					28	29			30	31	32	33
34					35				36			37		
38				39							40			
41				42						43				
44			45		46				47					
			48	49				50						
51	52	53				54	55					56	57	58
59						60					61			
62						63					64			
65						66					67			

11. Think Big

ACROSS

1. D-Day beach
6. Guy
11. GI mess-hall crews
14. Hot flows
15. Donut, mathwise
16. Looky here!
17. Nerve-cell conduits
18. Stalactite shape
19. Beau, to Lloyd
20. KFC ad words
23. Nancy Drew's boyfriend
24. Easy start
25. Brylcreem ad words
34. Show a Danish toon, to some
35. Bacon bits
36. Model-train layout
37. *The Maltese Falcon* sleuth
38. Butter cup
41. Feminine force
42. __ go again!
45. MS enclosure
46. Hercules had twelve
47. Aglet's target
49. FTD ad words
53. Not even close
54. Rod Hull's bird
55. Loreal ad words
65. That's the spot!
66. Maury's wife
67. Children's song refrain
68. Seuss title character
69. Hook's partner
70. Radio-studio sign
71. Some ER cases
72. Heated offense?
73. Big name at the '76 Olympics

DOWN

1. King of crosswords?
2. Long skirt
3. Commerical caller
4. Install, as drapes
5. Agrees
6. Central points
7. Leif's dad
8. Wrestling or canal term
9. Caron film of '53
10. Yemeni port
11. Siege site of 1998
12. Yuk!
13. She played Mick in *The Heart is a Lonely Hunter*
15. Spanish squiggle
21. Depend
22. Certain Olympians
25. Gob's greeting
26. Big name in jeans
27. Abadan's country
28. Address book abbr.
29. Hot spot
30. Damaging
31. Tenderfoot's org.
32. Shaver
33. Pipe cleaner?
38. Load of bunk
39. Computer devotee
40. Track transactions
42. Magician's item
43. *Charlotte's Web* author's monogram
44. Bourbon ruler
45. Darn
46. Italian bread
47. *Blondie* or *Sesame Street* role
48. Dare acceptor's words
49. TV's __ *Gigante*
50. Scared, colloquially
51. Regatta craft
52. Easier to count
56. Pac-10 school
57. Skyrocket
58. Means justifiers
59. Introduction to Chinese?
60. Disposition
61. Ginger of *Gilligan's Island*
62. Brewski topper
63. Sundial numeral
64. When tripled, a WWII film

Old Ads

solution on page 319

ACROSS

1. Kind of history
5. *What's My Line?* wit
9. Henry's son
14. Tropical nut
15. Feet feat, on ice
16. Kind of accent
17. Most common Hebrew crossword month
18. Artist's inspiration
19. Big blows
20. Was a miser
23. Near the coast
24. They're charged
25. Highway activity
28. '60s Andress film
31. Rice dish: var.
35. PFC's addr.
36. *A Clockwork Orange* lead role
37. Immediate halting
41. Trouble spots?
42. CEO's deg.
43. Big name in baseball cards
44. Tea, in Tours
45. Pauper
48. Coin for Fellini
50. Burns creature
55. Domicile
58. Kid song refrain
59. Eject
60. Billfold items
61. Stun gun
62. Cambodia moola
63. *Who's the Boss?* mom
64. Pretentious
65. Christian Science founder
66. Easy mark

DOWN

1. African ruminant
2. *The Thinker* creator
3. Rachins and Arkin
4. Tough-wooded tree
5. Tourist's tote
6. Oozes
7. Ans.
8. Head for the hills
9. Xmas drink
10. Place for a snake
11. Store receipt
12. Times to call, in ads
13. Defense Secretary Aspin
21. Stimulate, slangily
22. It's curtains for this
26. *Beowulf*, et al.
27. NYSE debut
29. Pot material
30. They have split ends
31. Exam for jrs.
32. Restless desire
33. Most in need of companionship
34. Big galoot
36. Flap
38. "In other words ..."
39. Jazz org.
40. It makes scents
45. Religious retreat, perhaps
46. Mistreated
47. With finesse
49. Princeton and Yale
51. Dance at the Savoy, in song
52. Doo-wop group member
53. "Goodnight" girl
54. Op-ed piece
55. Whopper server
56. "It's My Party" singer
57. One pound sterling
58. Flight deck guess

Time for a Change

solution on page 319

ACROSS

1. Non-stick coating for pans
4. Primary strategy
9. Creator of the sisters Olga, Masha, and Irina
14. Litigator's org.
15. Frost-covered
16. Bar mitzvah pre-sider
17. Type of infection
19. Use
20. Name in a leak probe
22. Bit of color
23. Abscam role
26. Feeling of dread
30. Leopard look-alike
32. Up to, in ads
35. Least dotty
37. Apple treatment, once
38. Lives dangerously
41. Freud's daughter
42. Drove
43. Lacking
44. Granny's chair
46. Shakespearean manuscript
48. Cotton pest
50. '20s song
54. Poker standard
58. Lavender hue
61. Brings together again
62. Construct
63. *It's a Wonderful Life* cabbie
64. "The Whiffenpoof Song" ender
65. Rolltops
66. Burpee buys
67. Full of guile

DOWN

1. Coors competitor
2. Old adders
3. Georgia city
4. Masquerade
5. Bologna bread
6. Mideast mogul
7. *Hud* actress
8. Comic comeback
9. Iraqi language
10. Type of soup
11. *TV Guide* abbr.
12. Osaka sash
13. It's nothing at all
18. Dress for Caesar
21. Where tricks are performed
24. Immigrants' island
25. Pest or dance
27. Kind of juices
28. Author Wilson
29. Fifty past
31. Canasta card
32. Former ruler
33. Confidante's words
34. Light cavalry weapon
36. Manche capital
39. Rescind
40. Mad doings
45. Kicks out
47. Any one of five Norwegian kings
49. Ancient harps
51. __ and drabs
52. Archetype
53. Literary piece
55. Canary's nose
56. French moon
57. Sir Geraint's lady
58. Took by the hand
59. High dudgeon
60. Bandleader Brown

Kid Rides

solution on page 319

ACROSS

1. Knock silly
5. Foul mood
9. Quick looks
14. Harbinger
15. Lattice part
16. Eye color
17. Chem rooms
18. Jobless
19. Side with
20. Site of a 1979 accident weeks after *The China Syndrome* hit theaters
23. Clink
24. *Gidget* star
25. Auction action
26. MADD target
28. Suburb
32. For any reason
35. Type of pool
37. Former Communist leader
38. Saying about such a coincidence
41. Be, for we
42. Inheritance of the meek
43. He "found" Nemo
44. Kid in *Aliens*
46. Singer Orbison
47. Gerbil or hamster
48. "Rope-a-dope" boxer
50. Mrs. Calabash's well-wisher
54. *China Syndrome* concern
59. Honshu industrial center
60. Barks shrilly
61. Aid in evildoing
62. Sticky stuff
63. Emollient source
64. Wedding cake layer
65. Pallid
66. Hair holders
67. Air current

DOWN

1. Blockheads
2. Menotti hero
3. Kid's alphabet book critter
4. Musical group
5. Assaulted, a la *Ghostbusters*
6. Rock bottom
7. "__ be a cold day ..."
8. Quaker's pronoun
9. Full moon, e.g.
10. Aerie baby
11. Pound of poetry
12. Sharp as a tack
13. Coaster
21. A Dionne quint
22. Dimwit
26. Touched
27. Jazz home
29. Barbra's *Funny Girl* guy
30. Put on guard
31. Middle C, for one
32. Attorney Dershowitz
33. Get pooped
34. __ *Good Men*
35. "Catalan Landscape" painter
36. Go back to old habits
39. *Sound of Music* or *West Side Story* song
40. Do more than get engaged
45. *The Jazz Singer*, notably
47. Throbs
49. Country star Rimes
50. Porter's domain
51. Like some government contracts
52. "Boss" caricatured by Nast
53. A password provides it
54. Nick Charles's wife
55. Makes a patsy of
56. *Walk the Line* role
57. Ford role in *Clear and Present Danger*
58. Drake or stag

Coincidence? I Think Not!

solution on page 319

ACROSS

1. Jimmy the Greek's forte
5. Bridge bow
10. Analogous
14. His head is full of fluff
15. Prep a plane
16. Monaco's neighbor
17. Looking-glass land denizen
19. Summer pest
20. Chicken style
21. Plans
23. Tacked on
27. Tore
28. Shopping spots
29. Brute address
31. Offbeat
34. They're the tops
35. Annoy
37. Singer Eartha __ Kitt
38. Powell's screen wife
39. Get back, as a skill
40. Camp aide
41. Cotton-picking name
42. Picks out
43. Go down
44. Haunt
45. It might thicken
46. Fun partner
47. Like ER, at times
49. Least populated
52. Codger
55. "Un bel di," e.g.
56. David's predecessor
57. Breath freshener since 1870
62. Vitamin C source
63. Triceratops trio
64. Snowman's carrot
65. Peepers
66. Degauss
67. Dickens's Magwitch

DOWN

1. Take your pick
2. Wally Cleaver portrayer
3. Hart mate
4. Bazaar bread
5. Loitered
6. Beef
7. Lend a hand
8. Patriot target
9. School times
10. 1973 Rolling Stones hit
11. Heaven, idiomatically
12. Engine's thought
13. Wallenda omissions
18. Cacophonies
22. Turn down
23. Sauntered
24. It may shorten a sentence
25. Not showing all one's cards
26. Emulates Holmes
30. "__ was no lady ..."
32. Platforms
33. Abominate
35. Complain
36. Buttery sub
39. Copy, briefly
43. Trattoria treat
46. Cheshire Cat feature
48. Rubbernecks
50. Lowly pieces
51. Greet the day
52. Kon-Tiki Museum site
53. Sanctum
54. *Adventures in Babysitting* deity
58. Fab competitor
59. Dollop
60. Profit by
61. Alice's boss

Um?

solution on page 319

ACROSS

1. Roll out of bed
6. Modernize
10. Marina space
14. Rueing
16. It might be struck
17. 1962 Polanski film
19. Enraptured
20. Beetle juice?
21. Photo closeup
22. Anderson of Jethro Tull
24. Minute monkey
26. Too-late situation
34. Loan-ad stat.
35. Anon
36. Plumb crazy
37. *Rocky* character
39. New Deal org.
40. Ain't right?
41. Zen riddle
42. Paintball need
44. Get a move on
45. Oscar-winning Brando movie
48. Bellicose god
49. Gunk
50. Islam follower
53. It needs refinement
55. Hands at sea
59. Oscar ballot managers
63. Atlas dot
64. Misanthropic, often
65. Cold War news agency
66. "Runaround Sue" singer
67. It's often dunked

DOWN

1. Noah's neighbors' needs
2. Lacoste of tennis
3. Anteing words
4. Sentimental sort
5. Poetic preposition
6. Sofer of *General Hospital*
7. Young newts
8. "That's obvious!" in teen talk
9. Bullring "bravo!"
10. Silky-coated dogs
11. They're often drawn
12. Cousin of uh-huh
13. Fresh-mouthed
15. Join up
18. Including
23. Parched
24. Medical sorting
25. High-pitched role for Silla
26. Off-the-wall
27. It has strings attached
28. Grab the tab
29. Olios
30. His book has "Hate Hate Hate" in the title
31. Island crooner
32. Flip __
33. Bach art form
38. Makes more valuable
40. Inside stuff
42. Blow away
43. They implore
46. *that thing you do!* setting
47. Baroque style
50. Dinner holder, at times
51. Bear up?
52. Guitarist Lofgren
53. Camp Swampy dog
54. Bit puller
56. Bankrupt
57. Rebekah's oldest son
58. Bruise
60. High roller's roll
61. *The Phantom Menace* kid, for short
62. Mason's aid

Drip, Drip, Drip

solution on page 319

1	2	3	4	5		6	7	8	9		10	11	12	13
14					15						16			
17									18					
19					20				21					
			22	23				24	25					
26	27	28				29	30				31	32	33	
34				35						36				
37		38			39				40					
41				42				43			44			
45			46							47				
			48					49						
50	51	52				53	54			55	56	57	58	
59				60	61			62						
63				64										
65				66				67						

ACROSS

1. Cavort
5. Racetrack town
10. Ginger cookie
14. Last name in baseball
15. Papal hat
16. Where Timbuktu is
17. RHO
20. African country
21. Harangue
22. "... __ it Memorex?"
23. Down under birds
25. Sanford of *The Jeffersons*
28. Place just for sleeping
32. Opposite/hypotenuse
33. Greenstreet's frequent co-star
34. Cell letters
35. ROW
39. Anecdote collection
40. Kind of society or roll
41. "Don't tread __"
42. Oldest city in Ohio
44. Winter wear
46. Bento box liquid
47. Babysit
48. Barely talks
51. Disney film of 1940
55. ROE
58. Bustle
59. Liberace's forte
60. Otherwise
61. Like diaries or some wives
62. De Mille of dance
63. Match parts

DOWN

1. Absorbed
2. Blend
3. Blanc, for one
4. Settle with finality
5. Nolo contender
6. Organ accouterments
7. Have the lead
8. "Bobby Hockey"
9. Strawberry or Darling
10. Enemy in 007 novels
11. *Peter Pan* pooch
12. Oodles
13. Knotty wood
18. Buck's stopping point?
19. Monopoly buys
23. Misstep
24. Film comedy brothers
25. Musician Jones
26. City in Tuscany
27. Close by
28. Chocolate drink
29. Mischief Night act
30. Jungian self
31. Grendel annoyers
33. Slow in music
36. Religious belief
37. Some water lines
38. Phraseologies
43. Bestow
44. Calico horses
45. "Nay!" sayer
47. State in many King novels
48. Kennedy's Secretary of State
49. Buy a hand
50. Cut short
51. Eggy dessert
52. Dealer's deal
53. Part of M.I.T.
54. Eliza dislikes
56. Ecol. monitors
57. "Savvy?"

... Your Boat?

solution on page 320

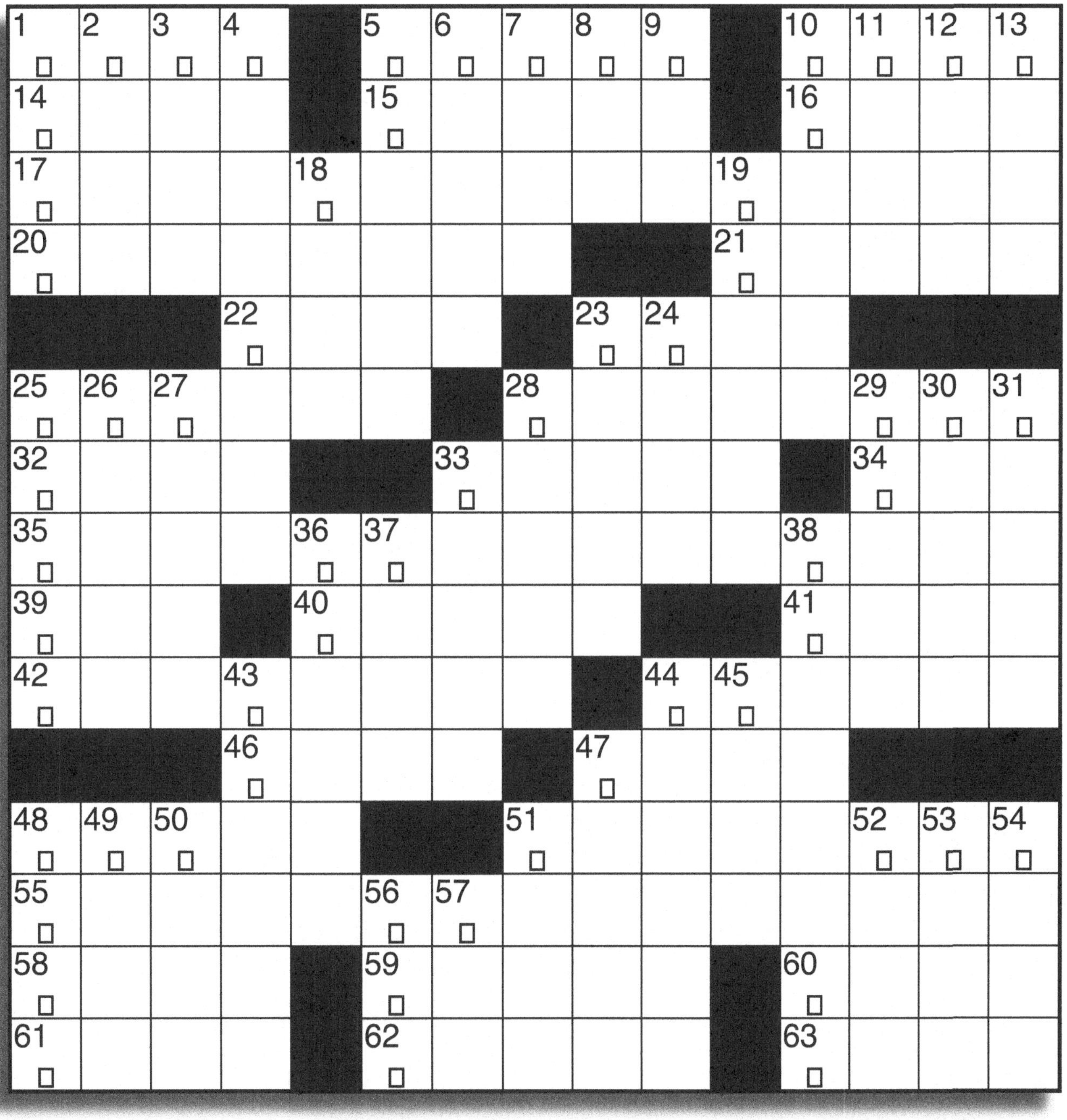

ACROSS

1. Wedges left by wedges
7. Young newts
11. Word of contempt
14. Poignantly contrary
15. Cleveland Indian?
16. MS-DOS popularizer
17. TIME
19. Excessively
20. Begrudging
21. Shower item
23. "Runaround Sue" singer
24. Confirm, in a way
26. Not appropriate
28. Lawn enhancers
30. Planet of Ming the Merciless
31. Part of L.A.
34. Claudius's adopted son
35. Luke Skywalker's sister
36. *Rigoletto*, for one
38. Rugged hill
40. Some bowling areas
41. "Stand by Me" singer King
42. Ration
44. Bullheaded
45. *As You Like It* locale
47. Embark
49. Kid's entertainer
50. Dutch treat
51. Masseur's target
55. Throws lightly
57. Eave's droppers
59. Dedicated to
60. MITE
62. Atelier output
63. Live shot
64. Baseballer Agee or Olympian Smith
65. Certain Wednesday
66. Refusenik's refusal
67. Harry Potter foe and others

DOWN

1. Cut into cubes
2. Rial spender
3. Saab rival
4. Type of chat
5. One of the Jackson 5
6. Bane
7. Rhyme time?
8. Dowdy people
9. Famous Father
10. It may be deviated
11. ITEM
12. Native
13. Patient-care gp.
18. Make a claim
22. Gay leader?
25. Gunned the engine
27. Salute
29. Crick's study
31. Of a lung or ear part
32. Bell workers
33. EMIT
37. Marine hazards
39. Kind of price
40. You can spend it in Romania
43. Male mousers
46. Maxima maker
47. "Open" closer
48. Seattle neighbor
52. Cluster
53. '30s skating star
54. Adlai's running mate
56. Oscar's girlfriend?
58. "__ a roll"
59. DOT org.
61. Paramount workplace

Double Double Time

solution on page 320

ACROSS

1. Slender-waisted insect
5. They're not true
9. Not shy about one's opinion
14. GI gone
15. "Vidi"
16. Where the fat lady sings
17. Verboten variant
18. High-fashion mag
19. Weighted down
20. Minty liqueur
23. Type of tea
24. Princess perturber
25. First name in country music
28. Patience, for one
33. Morale
36. Josip Broz
38. Ike's domain
39. Crammer's concern
40. Tour de France end spot
45. Polite response at the luau
46. Summer of *A Different World*
47. Rub the wrong way
49. Did penance
54. Latino boxing great
58. *My Cousin Vinny* star
60. Quattro maker
61. At the center of
62. Doff
63. Prom night woe
64. *Atlas Shrugged* author
65. Peter and Paul
66. *Sanford and Son* producer
67. Impatient

DOWN

1. Fob item
2. Mindful
3. On the wagon
4. Weight that sounds like a fruit
5. Boston Pops conductor
6. Dot in the ocean
7. Healing ointment
8. Win without losing
9. Charged
10. Colorful fish
11. Formally yield
12. Live and breathe
13. Office PC linkup
21. O.K. Corral shooter
22. Campbell of *Scream*
26. Berliner's quaff
27. Room at the top
29. Kind of IRA
30. Christmas centerpiece
31. Alternative to FedEx
32. Guinness suffix
33. Draw on glass
34. Jerk's offering
35. *Let's Make a Deal* choice
36. Skye cap
37. George's lyricist
41. Brings forth
42. One-third of a 1970 film title
43. More like powder
44. Anti-fur org.
48. African cattle pen
50. Midway alternative
51. Footloose one
52. Giving the once-over
53. Danny Thomas title role
54. Govt. watchdog group
55. *The Lion King* baddie
56. Il __ (Mussolini)
57. Mrs. Garrett
58. Type of stock option
59. Mr. Pulver's rank

Of 13

solution on page 320

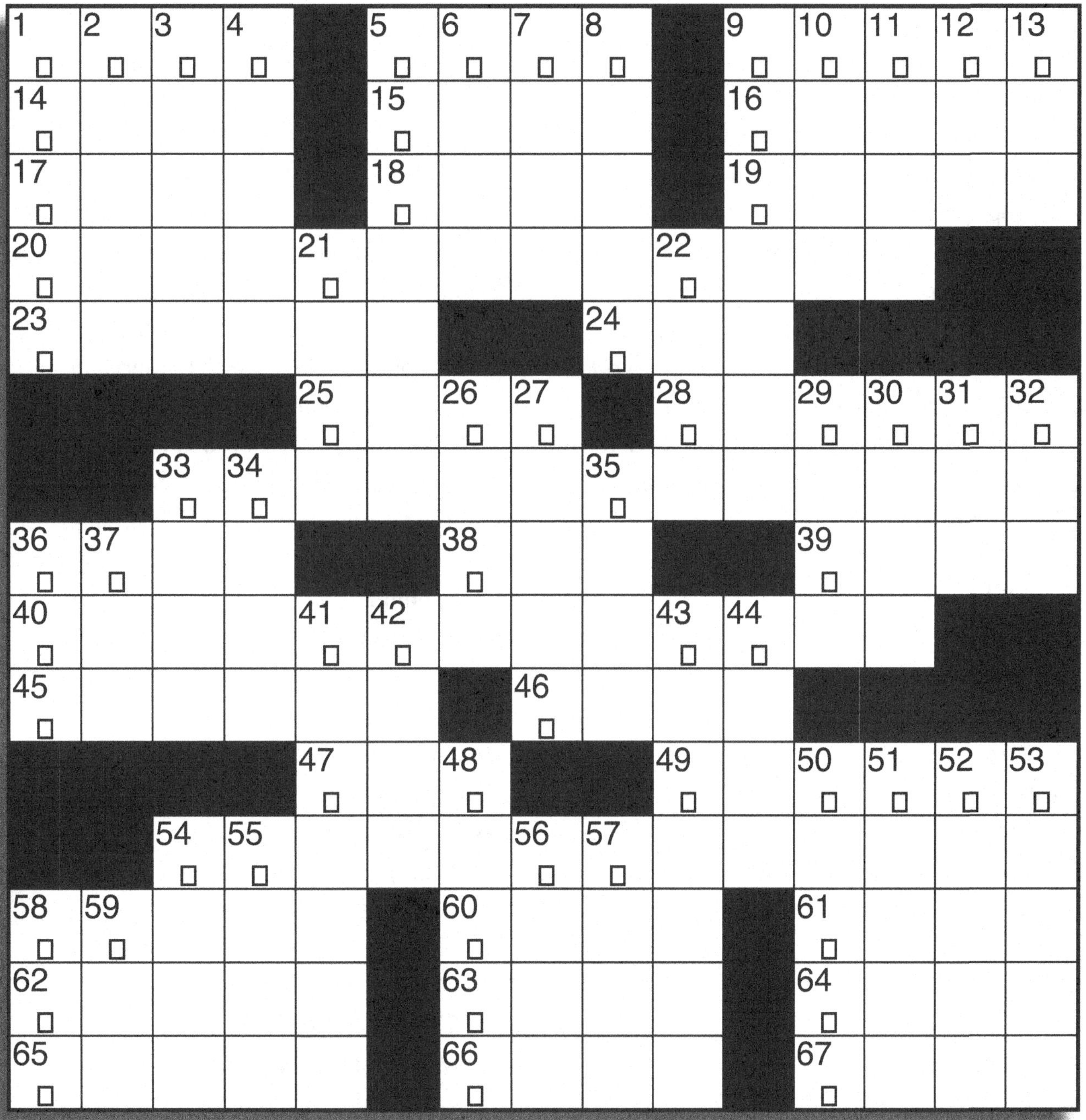

ACROSS

1. Bow of the screen
6. Marshall, for one
10. They're often not reported
14. Friend in need
15. Super-duper
16. Alice's chronicler
17. PLAY
20. Educational meetings
21. Faithful
22. It's often held
23. Stroller
24. "Riders of the Purple __"
27. A Yalta conferee
29. Some laughs
32. 007, e.g.
34. Name of nine popes
36. PLAY
39. Build up one's confidence
40. A 007 of film
41. D.C. zone
42. Sacred beetle
45. Johnny Tremaine had one
46. Boxer's signal
47. "Confound it!"
49. Duds
52. Make thin
56. PLAY
58. Pop singer Brickell
59. "__ Old Black Magic"
60. __ Park, CO
61. *Let's Make a Deal* choice
62. Llama's have two
63. Mall tenant

DOWN

1. Big Mama
2. Bar sign
3. Doc Bricker of *The Love Boat*
4. Army units
5. Fight site
6. Imitate
7. *Gigi* playwright
8. "Your point being ...?"
9. Elementary particle
10. Ryan's daughter
11. Blooming bulb
12. Scheme
13. PlayStation 2 maker
18. Erases debt
19. Noodle holder
23. Stratagem
24. Cavalry sword
25. Fevers
26. Insinuate
28. Capp lad
29. Mayhem
30. Ghana's capital
31. More desert like
33. Catapults
35. Least warm
37. What a soda bubble does
38. Kind of history
43. Lets in
44. Prankster
46. Harley dude
48. Sore spots
49. Wowed
50. Much fuss
51. Kingston, e.g.
52. And others
53. Anent
54. Stratum
55. Latin life
57. Gp. opposed to sticking

Playtime

solution on page 320

ACROSS

1. Valley
5. Clemency
10. Seuss' *McElligot's* __
14. Measure up
15. Sentence type not found in crosswords
16. Grease job
17. Greek myth re: Trojan War roots
20. It might be common
21. Author McEwan
22. Car ad abbr.
25. Do lunch
26. Sun. chat
27. Part of UCLA
30. Shoulder flashers
34. Elegant affair
35. Arabian lute
36. Mourned
37. Dubbed one
38. Hingis hit
39. Ballad ending
40. Prepare to be shot
42. A foot wide?
43. Breakfast dish
46. Chicano gang film of '79
49. Cow or sow
50. Escorted
51. Clio nominees
52. Senate vote
53. Billy Budd, e.g.
54. Sang out
56. Bing's "That __ in Athlone"
63. Nairobi Trio members
64. Baseball bigwig Bud
65. *Village Voice* award
66. Car ad abbr.
67. New voters
68. Introduce to solid food

DOWN

1. Hoopster Erving
2. *Mer* contents
3. Old Ford model
4. Staying power
5. It's calm with a pin
6. Seeks solace from
7. Buy a hand
8. Bill's mate
9. Edmonton neighbor
10. __ *9 from Outer Space*
11. Start of many church names
12. Kobe robe tie
13. Bandleader Brown
18. More timid
19. Mutuel leader
22. Belly muscles
23. For
24. Distribute again
26. Cold-shoulder
27. Papal, perhaps
28. Dug in
29. U.K. money, as the clean clue
31. *Tempest* spirit
32. Swain
33. N.H. Senator
38. Cop's clue
39. Patronages
40. *Barney* broadcaster
41. Cry of delight
42. Hillary's hill
43. They close
44. ATV kin
45. Bicentennial Minute, e.g.
47. JFK regular
48. His theory was aped
53. Cook's meas.
54. "Merry old" king
55. Arab vessel
56. Flat hat
57. Elevator buttons
58. Cousteau's milieu
59. Part of a *Song of the South* song title
60. Justice Fortas
61. "The Company"
62. Knowledge

Repeat, No Repeats

solution on page 320

ACROSS

1. When Earth Day is celebrated
6. Boom or gaff
10. Code with a checksum char.
14. Bird feather
15. It may be belted
16. It's often nautical
17. Essentials
19. __ fours
20. Barney cohort under Mr. Phelps
21. Verifies
23. Completely wrecked
26. Mary Richards player
27. Dryly
28. Troubadour
31. She played Nurse Betty
32. Cares or resents
33. Flock sound
34. Lagniappes
35. Backs off
36. Sharks' foes
37. Nabokov work
38. Sweetened the pot
39. It comes from the heart
40. Followed fastly
42. Nab
43. Deck out
44. Supreme being believers
45. Up-river swimmer
47. V cast
48. Woodstock name
49. Oddjob's boss
54. Coworker
55. Movers get this out
56. *Waterworld* role
57. Iterates
58. Jacuzzi action
59. Take hold

DOWN

1. Dragnet letters
2. By order of
3. Cytoplasm stuff
4. Considerably
5. Bunkers' old auto
6. Laid-back
7. Paparazzi wares
8. Flood insurance?
9. Answers
10. Consequence
11. "Mary, Mary, Quite Contrary" prop
12. Eye shade
13. Costner or Stack role
18. *South Park* co-creator Parker
22. *Friends* role
23. Calculus kin
24. McCain foe
25. Composers' milieu
26. Like some fields
28. Tightwad
29. Nettles
30. SDI weapons
32. British buddy
35. Intertwine
36. Cooking verb
38. High top fade, for one
39. Wordsworth works
41. Mail items
42. Child or Puck
44. Lingerie item
45. Fall guys
46. 'Hood
47. Like some rags
50. Coleridge wk.
51. Came down with
52. He played Tuco
53. Kurosawa epic

Test Your Metal

solution on page 320

12. Hitting It Big

ACROSS

1. Intro
6. Slugger's slouch
11. ATM screen
14. Sitar side-player
15. *Frisco Kid* prop
16. Rte. planners
17. "I'm not changing gear," said Tom __
19. *Casino Royale* kidnap vehicle
20. It comes from the heart
21. Stays to the end
23. Rate
27. Got off the bus
28. He got things done by Friday
29. Stiffness
33. Bill tack-on
34. They might be tall
35. Corp. VIP
36. He wrote "To be loved, be lovable"
37. Simplifies, with "down"
38. *Cagney & Lacey* star
39. Brief time
40. Puts into pigeon-holes
41. Telephone greeting
42. Boy Scout's handiwork
44. It's north of Central Park
45. Oberlin locale
46. Zenobia was queen there
47. Ink source
49. Clear the bar, in a way
51. Como's "__ Impossible"
52. "It's peace-bonded," said Tom __
58. Diddly
59. Regarding
60. Way to go
61. Nathan Hale, e.g.
62. Prescribed amounts
63. They run on runners

DOWN

1. 6, for a TD
2. Ole's kin
3. Binder of sorts
4. Keebler crewman
5. Toro tempter
6. Cubic meter
7. Island castaway show
8. Major or Minor preceder
9. Trouble in France
10. Lars' gal
11. "I wound my watch," said Tom __
12. Gold coin flipper of film
13. Kit Carson's house is there
18. Ballpark section
22. Handouts
23. Unlike this clue
24. Nonsense
25. "This is a seder plate," said Tom __
26. Type of car
27. Improves, as wine
29. "Nick of Time" singer
30. Misfortunes
31. One who does windows
32. French-born cellist
34. Mower maker
37. Chastity's last name
38. Skinny form?
40. Area used for handling tests
41. Summer tops
43. It's after upsilon
44. *Let's Make a Deal* host
46. Tries to make a hole
47. Transgresses
48. Wax remover
49. Goes for the gold
50. Actress Archer
53. She had a Plastic Band
54. La preceder
55. Boy's name of song
56. Brit. corp. suffix
57. "Owner of a Lonely Heart" band

Swifties of 11

solution on page 321

1	2	3	4	5		6	7	8	9	10		11	12	13
14						15						16		
17					18							19		
				20						21	22			
23	24	25	26						27					
28						29	30					31	32	
33					34						35			
36				37						38				
39			40						41					
42			43					44						
	45					46								
47	48				49	50								
51			52	53					54	55	56	57		
58			59					60						
61			62					63						

ACROSS

1. Tourist's need-to-know word in Hawaii
7. Cain raiser
11. Jack Horner's last words
14. Lost one's tail?
15. Basilica feature
16. Early riser
17. Peter Pan portrayer
19. Cock and bull
20. Carpenter or soldier
21. Camp aide
22. Estimator's words
23. *Shining* actress
29. U.N. member since 1992
31. *The Man from __* (Stewart film)
32. Sandpaper grade
33. Luigi's lucre
34. Mortise filler
35. *Night Court* role
36. Safecracker's soup
41. Alamo rival
43. Actor Stevens
44. Common pill
48. Rolled-meat dish
49. Comic who plays the dad on *Curb Your Enthusiasm*
51. Deck wood
52. Not be 100%
53. Green parrot
56. Hooray!
57. Dodger and a pitcher
62. Ancient greeting
63. Falco of *The Sopranos*
64. Steep
65. Appetite
66. Fowl males
67. Put in a kitty

DOWN

1. Phoenix suburb
2. Adam Arkin's dad
3. Large, non-lethal spider
4. Throw in
5. Rocket writer
6. Like a single sock
7. Ado __ of *Oklahoma!*
8. Phalangeal
9. Frank's second ex
10. Big boys
11. Hindu retreat
12. Breakfast choice
13. Shoe lining
18. Bruins' sch.
22. Biologist's eggs
24. Sub
25. Tangle up
26. Blip on a polygraph
27. Patriotic org.
28. Heavy metal
29. Do something
30. Name in a 1973 decision
33. Sol followers
35. Religious quorums
37. "La __ Bonita" (Madonna song)
38. Appreciative
39. Carmine or cerise
40. Galena or bauxite
42. Do battle
43. Dedicated to
44. Off course
45. Bundle barley
46. Female fowl
47. Variety
48. Bank (on)
50. Tarries
54. Let up on
55. Let go
57. All ready
58. Bedlam
59. Singer Addotta
60. Hawaiian food fish
61. E.T.'s craft

Back to the Beach

solution on page 321

ACROSS

1. "Doggone it!"
5. Radius partner
9. Bewilder
14. Fox's *X-Files* partner
15. Cambodia moola
16. Less tentative
17. Modern war weapon
19. Stain or smudge
20. They have more keys than a janitor
21. Belittle
22. Its known for ham and bull-fighting
25. Teased
26. Netman Lendl
27. *Fantasticks* role
30. It fits a thole
31. Cider girl
32. They're used when making zombies
36. Merciless dynasty?
38. Stage part
40. Each
41. Threat ender
42. Dirty addressee of film
43. Giant's third word
44. Grows incisors
48. Links alert
49. Big name in small planes
52. Handled the helm
54. Loses weight
55. Number on a pump
57. Rice dish: var.
58. Doesn't let on
62. Love to pieces
63. Dorothy Gale's dog
64. Bowed deity
65. Fits like Russian dolls
66. Tommy's tommy-gun
67. Dancer Moreno

DOWN

1. Calculus deg.?
2. Butter
3. Literary olio
4. Large game fish
5. Suave
6. Son on *The Jeffersons*
7. Nautilus captain
8. Church robes
9. Excoriate
10. Popular *Match Game* joke topic
11. Foreboding
12. Car dealer's offering
13. Muffed
18. 10th anniversary gift
22. Ecological community
23. Profit
24. "The one that got away" and others
25. Group foiled by Superman on radio
28. Circumference
29. Oklahoma's Annie
33. __ grabs
34. A 007 player
35. Runaway-bus movie
37. Show with the cone of silence
38. Type of code or rug
39. Host Sajak
45. Follows
46. Heir-splitting subject
47. Linger
48. Bird attraction
49. D.C. airer
50. Omit, as a vowel
51. Grain or missile holders
53. Tennessee has two
55. Chooses
56. Platelet goal
59. Home to Tell
60. Word from the Oise
61. Merit badge grp.

Intelligence

solution on page 321

ACROSS

1. Elizabeth I's family
6. Hoofed it
10. Do some circus work
14. Practical
15. Mock words of understanding
16. Word to Yorick
17. Small one-crop nations
20. It's blown in a synagogue
21. First star to be paid $1M/year
22. Rosemary's portrayer
24. "Twilight" gp.
25. Rhyme time?
26. Term of affection
32. Sundial numeral
33. Celebes, e.g.
34. Do the full monty
38. Where the cheese stands alone
39. Dog tag datum
42. Skin
43. Precincts
45. "Liftoff" preceder
46. Man, e.g.
47. Crane kin
51. Pierce Arrow competitor
54. Author Foley
55. CTRL-__-DEL
56. Like sidewalk dining
59. Take for granted
64. Reason to meet at seven
66. Uncle Pinky
67. Unfit for highborn Brits
68. Big dos
69. La Boheme updated
70. Pirate's punch
71. Add one's two cents

DOWN

1. Clumsy crafts at sea
2. Deseret today
3. Rat Pack name
4. King of crosswords?
5. Supply a new identity
6. Billy Budd, e.g.
7. Zeus' mom
8. Bird of prey
9. Bar order
10. Soft rock
11. Of the same stripe
12. Twinned crystal
13. Ruhr city
18. Melodic passage
19. Water bobber
23. One or two
26. Radames' love
27. Buttress of sorts
28. Rug factor
29. Whitman bloomer
30. Lord's home
31. Principle
35. Insurance factor
36. "Wink wink nudge nudge" guy
37. Stare
40. Clannad member
41. Make new blueprints
44. Petruchio's Katherina
48. Mitigating
49. Parish head
50. Opposite of "Abort! Abort!"
51. Red October feature
52. Perk up
53. Time and again
57. Conclude one's case
58. Mr. Bill's shriek
60. Easy job
61. Citrus hybrid
62. It's in the middle
63. It can come after no one or someone
65. Dog days mo.

Strange Fruit

solution on page 321

ACROSS

1. "Son of the Sun"
5. Make a no-go
10. White-water car-rier
14. Apted flick of '94
15. Fuss
16. Big do
17. Completely
20. Like some favorites
21. It's next to cleanli-ness
22. Chicago T-man
25. Leaping group of ten
26. Spoonfuls of sugar, say
30. Mugs, say
33. He lost to Dwight, twice
34. A Darling dog
35. *Little Red Book* author
38. Strip-in-a-strip hero
42. ⅙ fl. oz.
43. Radar's quaff
44. Background for Wile E.
45. It can be associ-ated with bad luck

47. Roly-poly
48. Six Degrees guy
51. Marker that might be erasable
53. Resilient
56. When mammoths roamed
61. The Truman show
64. At any time
65. Kind of bull
66. Brown meat
67. Melanie, in *Work-ing Girl*
68. Plunges into
69. Far from exciting

DOWN

1. Dope, shortly
2. That Urkel kid, for one
3. He's boorish
4. Pauper's cry
5. Lit
6. One of the Village People
7. Fall to ruin
8. "Whoops"
9. Coddle
10. Formula concept
11. Intro to math?
12. Fern leaf
13. Heavy reading?
18. Dangler atop a pipe
19. Eyeball
23. Could tell
24. Wiped out
26. A little off
27. Hugo works
28. Hockey shot
29. Hammer site
31. Jazzed up
32. Oriental way
35. PC operators?
36. Doesn't just sit there
37. Ma or Pa Joad

39. Heel
40. Soda mix-in
41. Globlet
45. They weep
46. Stay in
48. Sire
49. Andes film
50. Where Morlocks live
52. They go up for votes
54. Pranksters
55. Fireside talk
57. Sunrise direction
58. Code word?
59. Measure of a mole
60. Rochester's love
62. *A Civil Action* org.
63. Big dog, for short

Tom, Dick, and Harry

solution on page 321

ACROSS

1. Hubbubs
6. Is down with
9. George Bailey's bailiwick
14. *South Pacific* role
15. Feminine force
16. Superior's title
17. Phileas Fogg portrayer
18. Noir classic
19. Inelegant
20. Bush insider
23. Gets it wrong
24. Having excess at the opening
25. Tuck's partner
28. One of Snow White's seven
29. Chicken follower
30. Funny fellow
32. Relative crony?
36. Taverns
37. Sulked and skulked
40. Rink leap
42. Raised
44. Kind of farmer
47. Gullet
48. Salt to Sartre
50. Ballpark fig.
51. Full-scale
54. "Sweet 16" org.
55. They're popular in poker
57. Tongue neighbor
60. Office VIP
61. Lift up
62. Brought on board
63. Vichy water
64. Encourage
65. Discoveries
66. Mensans have two
67. Imaginative Thurber role

DOWN

1. Became taut
2. Greek vowel
3. Separation
4. Bread spreads
5. E-mailed
6. Most of water
7. Garlicky sauce
8. Mobile home dweller?
9. Kappa follower
10. Controversial wedding vow word
11. Sit-up targets
12. Uh-unh and nuh-uh
13. It's fit for swine
21. Play to the balcony
22. Grovel
25. Nothing special
26. It's not free of charge
27. Pub orders for short
29. How the weasel goes
31. Schmutz
33. Actress Negri
34. Maglie, of the Dodgers
35. Resonating
38. Humpty Dumpty-shaped
39. Motown org.
40. Absorbed, as a cost
41. Marks a box
43. Fanatically
45. Water nymphs
46. Hosp. attention
49. In conclusion
52. French school
53. It has depth
54. Ruth's ma-in-law
55. Practiced blackmail
56. Word in a *Mary Poppins* song
57. Weird Al's movie
58. Caesar's seven
59. Ode inspirer

Let It Ride

solution on page 321

ACROSS

1. Restraint at some restaurants
6. Manhandles
10. Snapper's snack
14. Hold
15. Loser of 1917
16. Machias Seal Island sight
17. PETER
20. Leaked slowly
21. Transferee, in law
22. Comb creation
25. They're history
26. Old drag racing injection
30. Sumatran swingers
32. It often gets a blessing
33. Second Gospel
34. Retain
37. PAUL
41. Brilliant Pebbles letters
42. Greek salad item
43. Da-dums
44. Unsusceptible to rumor
46. Loon-like bird
47. Homage
50. WB show
52. Embodiments
54. " ... but fear __"
59. MARY
62. Wind catcher
63. PBS series
64. Green
65. Author __ Frank
66. *Tiger Beat* audience member
67. *Memento*, for one

DOWN

1. Auction actions
2. Early '60s TV kid role
3. Untalkative type
4. Pins up
5. A small one may lead to extinction
6. WWII craft
7. Ember, later
8. Etna output
9. Sufferer at the end of 2004
10. Sparta's rival
11. Woman's name meaning "lion-like"
12. Soft food
13. Pre-deal payments
18. Eddie Cantor's better half
19. Triangle tone
23. *Patton* role
24. County fair puller
26. Runs in
27. Cooled down
28. Siamese, today
29. Tommy follower
31. Not well-known
34. Free, in a way
35. Actor associated with "Dum-da-dum-dum"
36. Wall St. workplace
38. Kind of nerve that sends outward
39. Tubular pasta
40. Eurasian frame drum
44. Fictional *M*A*S*H* captain
45. The little people
47. Style for Gloria Estefan
48. Flu type
49. Mr. Chips' subject
51. Chest protector
53. Sour fruit
55. The Ugly Duckling, eventually
56. It's an OK place
57. Matchmaker Dolly
58. Part of R.F.D.
60. NY's Madison, e.g.
61. "Oh __!" (Swiper saying)

Peter, Paul, and Mary

solution on page 322

1	2	3	4	5		6	7	8	9		10	11	12	13
14						15					16			
17				18					19					
20							21							
			22		23	24		25						
26	27	28	29		30		31							
32					33						34	35	36	
37				38					39	40				
41					42				43					
		44	45					46						
47	48	49				50		51						
52					53			54		55	56	57	58	
59						60	61							
62				63					64					
65				66					67					

ACROSS

1. It might be tossed
6. It has threads and a head
11. Proof letters
14. Bakery lure
15. Name on the Tara deed
16. Reuters rival
17. What fruitflies do?
19. Item always charged
20. Savvy
21. What Abner really isn't
22. Sideways ess
24. Artist amphibians?
28. Attacked
31. Days before
32. Series of disasters
33. Type of photography
38. Sub human?
39. Saint Pete neighbor
40. Heavy metal
41. Turnoffs
43. Kind of water
44. She played Mrs. Mr. Mom
45. Wear
46. Agents out in the cold?
51. Island or pants style
52. It's mushy
53. It might need to be cleaned up
56. Nutrient stat.
57. Fish market barter?
62. It may be footed
63. Sheer fabric
64. Fly off the handle
65. She played Maude
66. Gratifies to the max
67. "Nine-day-old" veggies

DOWN

1. It takes panes
2. "Verrrrrrry interesting" comedian's first name
3. You might be knocked for one
4. Mosh pit item
5. Just a bit
6. Video-game hedgehog
7. Soft limestone
8. Headed up
9. Clemens stat.
10. Profligate spender
11. John Hancock implement
12. Lyric verse
13. Eats well
18. Bunches
23. Cry of Dr. Frankenstein
24. Aquatic mammal
25. Magazine since 1952
26. Those who fill in
27. The eyes have it
28. Movies, to Fellini
29. First name in answer questioning
30. She's "got me sad and dreamy"
33. Dravidian tongue
34. Devilkin
35. Sleight-of-foot artist
36. Palm starch
37. '50s Prime Minister
39. King of The Avengers
42. Stands firm
43. Like Big Leroy Brown
45. Lion tamer's accessory
46. Stunted tree
47. Father Mulcahy, for one
48. Bucky Beaver's toothpaste
49. Nimble-footed
50. Ways
53. Water color
54. Tarot suit
55. Pledge drive gift
58. As
59. Final form
60. One of 435, for short
61. Bank deposit

O Gee, Ogee!

solution on page 322

ACROSS

1. Dribble
7. Eris's twin
11. Ben in *Ben*
14. Join the party
15. Bruce's ex
16. Judge with many hourglasses
17. "She Works Hard for the Money" singer
19. Devitalize
20. Hamlet's weapon
21. Eliel's son
22. Former Turkish title
26. One way to get the message across
28. Purina rival
29. Ashcan School artist
30. Dumbbell moves
32. Post-op room
34. Called it a day
37. He inspired *Cats*
38. Tarnish
39. *60 Minutes* regular
40. Home site?
41. Pipe cleaner?
42. Blank look
43. Hellenic
45. Lamb in hiding
46. It's sworn
50. Like some coalitions
51. Marian, e.g.
52. Foresight
54. High dudgeon
55. LifeSaver flavor
60. Harden
61. Get-out-of-jail fee
62. Looks after
63. Do sum work
64. Comedian on a trike Johnson
65. Silver-tongued one

DOWN

1. Part of B&B
2. Plastic __ Band
3. Ode inspirer
4. Parisian put-down
5. David Copperfield's mother
6. Designer Schiaparelli
7. Those in charge
8. What to do before you "cut once"
9. "Bam!" cook
10. Poitier title role
11. Full circle, with success in the middle
12. Nintendo's precursor
13. Filmdom's Tevye
18. Prosperous times
21. Issues forth
22. Lead car in a race
23. "Be-Bop-__"
24. *Simpsons* or *Father Knows Best* setting
25. *Star Trek: TN6* technology for a pretend room
27. Soil deposit
31. Mrs. Peel's partner
32. McDonald's catchphrase
33. Small island
35. Goosebump-inducing
36. Apprehension
44. Expensive eggs
46. Early personal computer
47. Got along
48. Cordage fiber
49. Backgammon impossibility
50. He maddened Madison
53. Ballpark figure follower
55. Pugilists' org.
56. New Yorker cartoonist
57. Ballpark fig.
58. Region for DDE
59. Easter lead-in

The Four Seasons

solution on page 322

ACROSS

1. Ray on the screen
5. Like some tones
11. Vit. suggestion
14. Wound
15. She had a cow
16. Spinner in space
17. Rough holiday for singles
20. Chicago hub
21. What snobs put on
22. Draws a bead
23. 1936 Summer Olympics star
25. Talking birds
26. Be the boss
30. The one here
32. Disco-era suffix
33. Contribute
35. Meringue need
38. Ultimate football?
41. Call, in poker
42. *The Mixed-Up Chameleon* author
43. British bike
44. Fuzzy Wuzzy was one
45. Silver and gold
46. Powerless
49. Religion where the deity is not to be drawn
52. He played a Section 8 seeker
53. Major force behind *Spamalot*
54. Zero
59. When the President pardons a turkey
62. Chunk of eternity
63. Made a note of
64. Warmonger
65. Unlucky Star Trek shirt color
66. Stumpers
67. January 1 song ending

DOWN

1. Reply to "Are not!"
2. Thin slat
3. 1982 movie thriller
4. Epps of *The Mod Squad*
5. Tool shed item
6. Arm bones
7. Become established
8. Coiffure
9. Sea birds
10. Paint the town red?
11. *The Thinker* creator
12. Serious theater
13. Gaping hole
18. One of the Bowery Boys
19. Emulates Simon
24. You and me
25. Colonial type
26. Type of transit
27. Big chill
28. Uh-uh
29. AARP membership determinant
31. Part of H.R.H.
33. Bear breakfasts
34. It makes a fine point
35. Novelist Ferber
36. Caesar's France
37. Swindles
39. Herd word
40. Wayne's word
44. Square-dance site
45. Barker of note
46. Fairy tale closer
47. Chevy SUV
48. Cattle mark
50. Snail trail
51. Voting-machine part
53. :
55. Cries of disgust
56. Sheila's hi
57. Laugher on *Laugh-In*
58. Little kid
60. TV role for Tom Hanks
61. Does a security job

Those Were the Days

solution on page 322

13. Extreme Theming

ACROSS

1. King
5. Find
9. To-do
13. Foil
14. Thus
15. Hoar
16. Chap
17. Gael
18. Soon
19. Jibe
21. Date
22. Geek
23. Call
25. Firm
27. Post
30. Aped
34. Aura
35. Quip
36. Tame
37. Cuts
39. Spot
40. Fled
41. Soil
42. Part
44. Dump
46. Just
47. Slap
50. Stun
52. Odor
56. Fail
57. Clue
59. Down
60. Avow
61. Upon
62. Serf
63. Head
64. Balm
65. Back

DOWN

1. Gams
2. Ajar
3. Coty
4. Pawl
5. Jiff
6. Here
7. Gawk
8. Lugs
9. Wild
10. Rope
11. Eros
12. Hang
20. Duds
24. Lows
26. Hams
27. Razz
28. Lean
29. Song
31. Muck
32. Dash
33. Ding
36. Mete
38. Tank
39. Kook
43. Part
45. Boor
47. Hunk
48. Spun
49. Lost
51. Turn
53. Lest
54. Moth
55. Ogle
58. Peak

4-Letter Words

solution on page 323

1	2	3	4		5	6	7	8		9	10	11	12
13					14					15			
16					17					18			
19				20		21				22			
			23		24			25	26				
27	28	29							30		31	32	33
34				35				36					
37			38				39				40		
41							42			43			
			44		45		46						
47	48	49			50	51			52		53	54	55
56					57			58		59			
60					61					62			
63					64					65			

ACROSS

1. Ergo
5. Wilt
8. Haul
12. Kiln
13. Like
14. Buff
15. Runs
17. Foil
18. Fury
19. Poem
21. Mean
24. Blew
28. Sped
29. Mesh
30. Till
31. Eggs
32. Stag
33. Talk
34. Soak
35. Flog
36. Tale
37. Part
39. Fees
40. Bend
41. Mutt
42. Kind
45. Airy
50. Some
51. Stun
52. Thus
53. Hour
54. Pull
55. Gait

DOWN

1. Also
2. Luck
3. Hire
4. Pace
5. Glut
6. Brew
7. Fuel
8. Wimp
9. Tear
10. Goon
11. Gosh
16. Live
20. Chap
21. Keep
22. Book
23. Sore
24. Fore
25. Sire
26. Undo
27. Dues
29. Look
32. Yarn
36. Loft
38. Dull
39. Herb
41. Gnaw
42. Pose
43. Sash
44. Edge
46. Pair
47. Flub
48. Past
49. Fate

4-Letter Words 2

solution on page 323

ACROSS

1. Wise
5. Defy
9. Bows
13. Ajar
14. Lily
15. Kick
16. Asea
17. Duct
18. Rail
19. Best
21. Sway
23. Crag
24. Rent
25. Yarn
29. Heap
33. Reed
34. Curt
36. Ecru
37. Like
38. Core
39. Best
40. Slow
42. Eden
44. Bulk
46. Goal
47. Curt
50. Clad
54. Lack
55. Rest
57. Rend
58. Bite
59. Rapt
60. Foil
61. Cost
62. Dare
63. Tear

DOWN

1. Aria
2. Each
3. Tale
4. Name
5. Soak
6. Grad
7. Bawl
8. Tend
9. Away
10. Base
11. Gist
12. Lead
20. Quip
22. Celt
24. Land
25. Bufo
26. Deft
27. Lend
28. Hops
30. Molt
31. Axes
32. Genu
35. Plan
38. Load
39. Beau
41. Blur
43. Isle
45. Lieu
47. Pier
48. Head
49. Hire
50. From
51. Aged
52. Fair
53. Feat
56. Grow

4-letter Words 3

solution on page 323

1
2
3
4
5
6
7
8
9
10
11
12
13
14
15
16
17
18
19
20
21
22
23
24
25
26
27
28
29
30
31
32
33
34
35
36
37
38
39
40
41
42
43
44
45
46
47
48
49
50
51
52
53
54
55
56
57
58
59
60
61
62
63

ACROSS

1. Dad
5. Casa clay
10. Grad. class
13. Catch
14. Grand
15. Spank
16. __ trap
17. Cash and __
18. TV brand
19. "48 __"
21. Warrant
22. Wharf
23. Nap
26. Pass
28. Knack
29. Garb
32. Garland
33. Sway
34. La Paz pal
38. Fat cravat
40. Placard
42. Carp
43. Bank
45. Map abbr.
46. Pranks
49. Can't stand
51. Lackaday!
52. Chap
55. Madras man
56. Gab

57. Attack
59. Grandma
62. __-la-la
63. Saw
64. Small part
65. Bad __ (spa)
66. Backs
67. Nada

DOWN

1. NBA stats
2. PAC-10 sch.
3. Sad
4. Yards
5. Ball's path
6. Pact
7. Bad man
8. Swap
9. TV Tarzan
10. Small mall
11. Big A events
12. Catch
20. Car part
22. Hand part
23. Casa part
24. Wraths
25. Tarzan pal
27. Shacks
30. La Paz cash
31. MacGraw and
     Baba
35. Start
36. Slash
37. Gawk
39. Ballads
41. __ *Blas*
44. Sham
46. A la __
47. Warn
48. Dads

50. Ball's man
53. Snarl
54. Pranks
57. Phat
58. Grass
60. Scand. land
61. __, amas, amat

A lot 1

solution on page 323

1	2	3	4		5	6	7	8	9		10	11	12
13					14						15		
16					17						18		
		19		20		21				22			
23	24			25			26	27					
28				29		30	31						
32				33				34		35	36	37	
38		39			40		41			42			
		43		44						45			
46	47	48					49		50				
51					52	53	54		55				
56			57				58		59		60	61	
62			63						64				
65			66						67				

ACROSS

1. Warm
4. Jam-pack
8. Path at Panama
13. a.k.a. Clay
14. Harm
15. Casa clay
16. __ Galahad
17. Aardvark snacks
18. Drab
19. Thwarts
21. Frat cask
22. Assay
23. NAACP part
26. Lat. math wd.
30. Grand lands and casas
33. TV Tarzan
34. "Halt, salt!"
37. Sway
38. Atlas chart
39. *Adam's* __
40. A way's away
42. Sans a match
44. __ Schwarz
45. Hats
47. Yaw
49. Aka CCCP
50. Brad
54. MP pt.
56. Draw back
58. Grand Am part
61. Catchall abbr.
63. Watch
64. Blab
65. Rack part
66. Santa part, at a mall
67. Sharp
68. Play's last part
69. Nav. rank

DOWN

1. Attacks
2. Salad "ball"
3. Car parts
4. Yak
5. Attacks
6. Craft
7. Ararat and Alps
8. Java at a plaza, say
9. Saw
10. Wag
11. Bart's grandpa
12. Ran
20. Blvds. and rds.
21. Pants part
24. Wraps
25. Yacht backs
27. San __
28. *M*A*S*H* star Alda
29. Class
31. Take a __ at
32. Lath
34. Barks
35. Flask
36. __ Hassan
41. __ ball
43. D-Day craft
46. Wayward
48. Act badly
51. Gangway, e.g.
52. Wash
53. Has
55. Mad
57. Alt.
58. Car stat., a la radar
59. Plata pal?
60. Spank
61. Qantas stat.
62. Small spasm

A Lot 2

solution on page 323

ACROSS

1. "__ a man ..."
5. __ wrap
10. Pan spray
13. Facts
14. Class A
15. Map abbr.
16. Yadda-yadda
17. Sandglass
18. Canard
19. Say
21. Grassland
23. NaCl
25. Ran
26. Map abbrs.
29. Salts away
31. Talks
35. Part
37. Claptrap
38. Bad
39. Latch __
40. MLB stat
41. Away
42. Band
43. Art stand
45. Darn
46. "Pshaw!"
48. Halts
50. __ salts
53. Marsh plant
57. Slash
58. Macaw
62. Dart
63. PAC-10 sch.
64. Grandmas
65. Wraths
66. Brand-__
67. Saw
68. __ and pans

DOWN

1. Plan
2. Small pads
3. LAX data
4. Sagas
5. Calm
6. MacGraw that acts
7. Glass part
8. Had a shank
9. Brass
10. __ Mall
11. Rah-rah
12. Track __
20. Cad
22. Banks
24. Land
25. D-Day craft
26. Ad
27. Sharp part
28. __ trap
30. Gang
32. Rara __
33. Stay
34. Scads
36. Jazz band
40. Say what?
41. *M*A*S*H* star
44. Wrap
47. "__ plan, a canal,
    ..."
49. Small mall
50. MBA class
51. 24-karat
52. Jambalaya
54. NZ plant
55. Rap star
56. Stack part
59. Phat
60. Santa __, CA
61. Scrap

solution on page 323

1	2	3	4		5	6	7	8	9		10	11	12
13					14						15		
16					17						18		
19			20					21	22				
		23			24		25						
26	27	28		29			30			31	32	33	34
35		36			37				38				
39				40				41					
42				43			44			45			
		46	47			48			49				
50	51	52					53				54	55	56
57				58	59	60	61			62			
63				64						65			
66				67						68			

ACROSS

1. "Wish __, wish . . ."
5. Smirk
10. Mississippi-Islip dir.
13. Clip
14. NL MVP in '71
15. Dig in
16. This: Sp.
17. Dins
18. Liq.
19. 1984 sci-fi film
21. Dirt
23. Chill
24. Ski lifts
26. Wild shindig
29. Criticism
30. This: Sp.
34. Slim fish
35. Pick
37. "Ship __"
38. Nigh
40. Tilting
42. Dig this
43. First 007 film
44. Didn't stir
45. Mix flick
47. Ill
49. R.N.'s skill
50. Skin
53. Likings
57. Shin finish?
58. Sprints
61. Pink
62. Glib
63. Shill
64. __ dixit
65. Thin printing widths
66. Instinct
67. __-dish

DOWN

1. Ill wills
2. Sprit
3. "__ girl!"
4. Thirsts
5. Binding
6. High __
7. Distinct time
8. Slip
9. Fix stitching
10. Grill
11. It stings
12. Imprint
20. Tidbit
22. Drifting
24. Implicit
25. Picks
26. Twist
27. Smirk
28. King with biting wit
29. Sprint in shifts
31. BB firing
32. Split
33. Flirt
36. Hitch
39. Drift
41. Ring
46. Tick
48. Nitpicks
49. Sip
50. Nitwit
51. High spirit
52. Finks
53. Ink sticks
54. Binding strip
55. Irish
56. Drip
59. Inn drink
60. British "tin"

1 □	2 □	3 □	4 □	■	5 □	6 □	7 □	8 □	9 □	■	10 □	11 □	12 □
13 □				■	14 □					■	15 □		
16 □				■	17 □					■	18 □		
19 □			20 □				■	21 □	22 □				
■			23 □			■	24 □	25 □			■		
26 □	27 □	28 □			■	29 □			■	30 □	31 □	32 □	33 □
34 □			■	35 □	36 □				■	37 □			
38 □			39 □	■	40 □				41 □	■	42 □		
43 □				■	44 □		■	45 □	46 □				
■			47 □	48 □			■	49 □			■		
50 □	51 □	52 □			■		53 □				54 □	55 □	56 □
57 □			■	58 □	59 □	60 □			■	61 □			
62 □			■	63 □					■	64 □			
65 □			■	66 □					■	67 □			

ACROSS

1. Dig finding
4. Pink
8. Wind dir.
11. Bliss
12. Kilns
14. Spring
16. Fish dish
17. Rigid
18. Wingding
19. Bi + 1
20. Kiln
21. Lifts
23. Climb
25. Firm
27. Smirk
29. Witch bird
30. Stifling thing
33. First victim
36. Instincts
38. Dipstick slick
39. Insist
41. Stick
42. Skirt
44. 'Til
45. Diving birds
48. __ dixit
49. Nitwit
50. __ cit.
51. Fill
53. Wins
55. Grim
59. Striving
62. Did
64. __ king
65. Din
66. Diminish
68. Digits
69. Rich find
70. Snitch
71. Flight bd. listings
72. "__ Miz"
73. GI dining district
74. It's with "pick"

DOWN

1. Stinks
2. Dig find
3. Wind dir.
4. Spins
5. Birds
6. Schisms
7. Slim printing widths
8. Impish
9. Visits
10. Diminish
11. This: Sp.
13. Mild
15. Divs.
20. Till bill
22. Spring
24. Wright wings
26. Sips
28. Dismiss
30. Climb
31. Chips in
32. Mirth
33. Drifting
34. Gin mills
35. Sight things
37. Gist
40. Flirt
43. Big fibs
46. List
47. Dispirits
52. Bind
53. Drills
54. Did in
56. Kiwi
57. With it
58. Li'l miss
59. __ king
60. Buffoon
61. Diminish
63. Big stirs
67. It's in MB's
68. Whip

I Spy 2

solution on page 324

ACROSS

1. Ms. Hogg
4. "Oops!"
8. Old pro
11. Snow toy
12. Snoot-y
14. World org. for Kosovo
16. Bonds
17. Loom
18. Go down
19. __ loss
20. Brood
21. OK nod
23. Folk song
25. Cowboy show
27. Follow
29. Born
30. Son of __
33. School prom tot
36. Hot spot
38. __ roll
39. "__ of God"
41. Boost
42. Mork's boss
44. Boy
45. Mongol
48. Top-notch
49. Mormons' gp.
50. Control
51. Dog's hoot
53. Gob's "Stop!"
55. Thrown
59. Go-__
62. Strong __ ox
64. Ford or Cord
65. Nos. for Nomo
66. Block
68. Prom cohort
69. Gold cloth
70. Golf pro
71. Took off
72. Oolong for 4 o'clock
73. Goofs
74. Grown boy

DOWN

1. "__ song go ..."
2. __ of Honor
3. Spots
4. Solo
5. Not soft
6. Dogwood
7. Owns
8. So-__
9. Show TLC
10. Bond's school
11. Mop
13. Honcho
15. Go (for)
20. Cop
22. Do
24. Solo
26. "Soon ..."
28. Longs
30. Not too hot
31. Soon
32. Locks
33. Not short
34. Horrors!
35. Knocks off
37. Roost
40. Hot spot
43. Knocks or blows
46. Honors
47. Slows
52. Horror show pro
53. Lost
54. __ tots
56. Scot's __ Flow
57. Moth-__
58. __ Scott
59. Clot
60. Proof word
61. Control
63. Scorch
67. Opp. of WSW
68. Flood control

OOOOO! 1

solution on page 324

ACROSS

1. Crops
6. Box top
9. Pt. or qt.
12. "No __, Bob!"
13. __ tot
15. TV room
16. Door: Fr.
17. Root rot
18. Common vow
19. Scoop
21. Troops
22. Chow down
23. Photo __
26. Fox cop show on CBS
27. Knot
29. "So!"
30. Comfort
31. __ cost
32. Strong
34. Not con
35. Mr. Tolstoy
38. Rock
39. Block
40. Tots' toys
42. Stock gp.
43. "__ Town"
44. Scoff
45. __ ho!
47. Dollop
48. Bond
49. Hold
52. Gold por otros
53. "Horrors!"
54. Oolong
55. __ roll
57. Boy toy?
58. Do wrong
59. Row
61. Solo
66. Pod for Mork
67. Dolts
68. Sot
69. Sol.
70. Mom's boy
71. Door word

DOWN

1. Cookbook's ⅙ oz.
2. __ Lobo
3. Not std.
4. Got to know
5. Pod
6. Boy
7. Scoop
8. Kook
9. So long
10. __ of Honor
11. Gov. bond
13. Not too hot
14. Took too long
20. "Who __?"
23. Rows
24. Shot
25. Clog, of sorts
28. Sorrow
31. Offshoot
33. Mom's bro
34. Golf norm
36. Top
37. '20s song
39. Flop
40. Go off
41. Look for
43. Concord
44. Confront
46. Odor
47. Prods
49. Lost
50. Stoop
51. Droops
56. To boot
60. Tho'
62. __ Nol
63. Go (for)
64. Born
65. Botch

OOOOO! 2

solution on page 324

ACROSS

1. To's mate
4. One from Kuwait
8. Stable mate
12. Lubricate
13. O'Hara estate
14. Initiate
15. Manipulate
16. Mideast potentate
17. Necessitate
18. Live's mate
20. Go up to the plate
22. Yes, to the first mate
24. It might apparate
28. Wait
31. Pierre's date
34. One who does calculate
35. Great weight
36. Posed for a portrait
37. Hardly an Oscar candidate
38. Lennon's mate
39. Renovate
40. Sit for a portrait
41. Nina's sea mate
43. Bolt's mate
45. USNA graduate
47. Hesitate
51. One of equal weight
54. Fateful date
57. License plate
58. Commensurate
59. Exasperate
60. CSA state
61. Chip's cartoon mate
62. Radiate
63. Rooster's mate

DOWN

1. Contaminate
2. Escalate
3. Socialist presidential candidate
4. __ rate
5. Ewe's mate
6. Jackie's mate
7. One that does lacerate
8. Part of a date
9. Imitate
10. Ruff's mate
11. Terminate
19. Skate
21. What a ring count might indicate
23. Ameliorate
25. Pedro's eight
26. Places to rejuvenate
27. Subjugate
28. Deactivate
29. The Captain's mate
30. As of late
32. Irate
33. Pour __ (exaggerate)
39. Was on the slate
40. Sch. affiliate
42. Metal-coated plate
44. Agitate
46. Originate
48. Brigham Young's state
49. Event with a rebate
50. *A Summer Place* actor
51. Natural soil aggregate
52. Che's mate
53. Shark bait
55. Opacate
56. New Haven collegiate

8 Sounds Good to Me

solution on page 324

ACROSS

1. Soy product
5. Recipe amt.
8. Baste
11. Their tails are used in soup
12. Pacific tuna
13. What kneading dough removes
14. Mixer with vodka
16. What lean meat lacks
17. What an apple grows on
18. Folic, for one
20. Salty sauce
21. __ goong
22. Not go bad
24. Pot-au-__ (boiled meat and veggie dish)
25. Beer top
26. Turkish liqueur
29. Sauteed butter, in France
35. *Chocolat* actress
36. Fruit quaff
37. Potatoes __ (baked in butter in sealed cookware)
38. Toffee base not to be overdone
42. Snort glass
43. Fries or slaw
44. Gp. that may comment on heart-healthy diets
46. Form of broccoli
47. GI pouch
48. Taro treat
49. They're useful in rotisserie oven
50. Indian butter
52. Lentil dish
53. Kind of nut
58. Absorb, as gravy
59. Edible tuber
60. Sour fruit
61. Gnawed at
62. Arroz __ pollo
63. New Orleans harbor with great food

DOWN

1. Quick drink
2. Cooking tool maker
3. Place for cranberries
4. Sea urchin, to sushi fans
5. Haitian rum
6. Roe source
7. Peach seed
8. __ Sue Milliken (one of the Too Hot Tamales)
9. Goose
10. __-cook
15. Place to eat cod?
17. Preferred muffin part
19. Type of sandwich
20. Italian for seed, as in "__ di melone"
22. Where kim chee comes from
23. Corn unit
24. Mickey __
25. Soft candy
26. __ roy (drink type)
27. Indian potato
28. Aperitif of white wine
30. __ vie (kirsch or framboise, say)
31. Wine valley
32. Hawaiian food fish
33. B and B
34. Rachael of cooking fame
39. Ming of cooking fame
40. Imbibe slowly
41. Steak order
45. Cheese cloth
46. Caviar base
47. Where to find Leonardo's "The Last Supper"
48. Acini de __
49. Tex-Mex fare
50. Cookie gp.
51. Like Szechuan food
52. Italian wine standard
54. *Happy Days* diner
55. Claret relative, for short
56. Aussie delicacy
57. Drumstick

solution on page 324

ACROSS

1. Improve wine (but not champagne)
4. Bar offering
7. Nuoc __ (Vietnamese seafood sauce)
10. __ Equis
11. __ purpose flour
12. "Fashioned like" on a menu
13. Chinese food direction?
15. __ en place (prepped for cooking use)
16. Genuine Dutch article
17. Black-and-white treat
20. Wine center near Turin
23. Hush __
26. Dutch oven cooker Dub
27. Romans' caviar
28. Sandwich with mayo
29. Joyce of cookware, or an Iron Chef
30. Spanish munchies
32. They back the safety of food irradiation
34. Prep *Iron Chef* for American TV
36. Champagne word
37. Daiquiri base
38. Something for the waitress
40. __ Roy
42. French __ (sandwich au jus)
43. __ Slim (herbal tea maker)
45. Sugo __ (pink sauce)
47. Had some chow
49. Hawaiian food fish that means "delicious"
50. Italian wine standard
51. __ leber (chopped liver)
53. Octopus for sushi
54. Keg tapper
55. Vert-__ (greenish herb sauce)
57. Drink too much
60. Wrinkly Jamaican fruit
64. Large cask
65. Oldest chef school in the US
66. One way to get the gravy
67. Fondue __
68. Egg source
69. Hawaiian kava

DOWN

1. Fruit drink suffix
2. Its cuisine is an Indo-Portuguese mix
3. Food processor blade shape, often
4. Mai __ (rum drink)
5. Diner visited by the Fonz
6. Prep food starch, sometimes
7. When doubled, a fish
8. Andy Capp's drink
9. With a paddle, it's used when making sushi
14. Place for meringue
15. __ di Cremona (fruity chutney)
18. BBQ order
19. Sushi fish
21. Kernel
22. __ San Guido (wine maker)
23. Soup cooker
24. Grapes
25. Deli wrap
29. Pain de __ (country bread)
31. Bread soup
33. Li hing __
35. Russian meat patties
39. Indent on a wine bottle base
41. *The Joy of Cooking*, e.g.
43. Radar's drink
44. Caviar source
46. Part of a 40 Across
48. 4 o'clock drink
52. Indian potato
53. Place to eat a smore
55. Qt. divs.
56. Bitter herb
58. Goose
59. Place for sauteing
61. Samoa sellers
62. __ carb
63. Beer choice, for short

Food, Wonderful Food 2

solution on page 325

ACROSS

1. Pooh's has honey
4. Hawaiian kava
7. DDT banner
10. Hawaiian food fish
11. Chicken choice
12. Emeril's exclamation
13. Conform to the mold
14. Beverage ending
15. __ colada
16. Sally __ (sweet bread)
20. Jelly fruit
23. French beef-with-red-wine dish
25. Shad delicacy
26. __ ayam (Indonesian chicken in coconut milk)
27. __-in-one method
28. Vitamin-regulating org.
31. French chive
37. Monkfish
40. Indian bread
41. Cream cookies
42. Food fish

45. Picnic pest who tastes good in chocolate
46. Diner slang for milk
47. Pierre's breakfast choice
50. Hawaiian victor-fish
51. Stop for the drive-in
52. Bottle size
54. Dip a donut
56. Eating "gait"
59. Americanize *Tampopo*, say
61. Tuna type
64. __ paratha (potato-filled bread)
65. Draft drink
66. Shred with one's hands, as lettuce
67. Child's meas.
68. Diner boss on *Alice*
69. Edible tuber

DOWN

1. Milk bottle top
2. Pits in an avocado
3. __ House cookie
4. Menu phrase
5. Grinder
6. Ripening agent
7. Sushi shrimp
8. Omelet maker
9. Org. for Weil and Atkins
15. Potato skinner
17. Asparagus-like veggie
18. Cover with sauce without hiding the food's shape
19. __-mam (Vietnamese fish dish)
21. *Like Water for Chocolate* director
22. Food with arroz
24. Pickle juice
28. *Alice* waitress
29. Italian wine standard
30. Gobbled up
32. Cheers or Phil's
33. Hungry-Man rival
34. Brewed drink

35. Won __ soup
36. A wine, when tripled
38. Lunch in a husk
39. Japanese mushroom
43. Food fish eaten by cod
44. Lettuce unit
48. Grey snapper
49. Where to pick cranberries
51. Burnt, in cooking
53. Red-waxed cheese
55. Corn syrup brand
56. Butter bit
57. *Happy Days* diner
58. Half a pint
60. __ Paese cheese
62. Sot's sound
63. Beer type, briefly

ACROSS

1. Kind of oil
5. Faux cough
9. Showing lots of guts?
14. Bargain spread
15. Heir to the Carsonian throne
16. Majorca seaport
17. Furrow
18. Bator lead-in
19. Comb-using?
20. Richard Bachman, for one
22. Hold the deed to
24. "It's clear now!"
25. Divers info
26. Break the tape
27. __ Dee River
28. Eugene's daughter
29. Customizer who ships PC's, say
30. Friend of Dora the Explorer
33. Old Chevy model
36. Baseball player or battery type
38. Sculpture by Michelangelo
39. See red?
40. It's near a radius
41. Shed some light on
44. Concerning a snoring cause
46. Ginger __
47. Nice donkey
48. Insect wings
49. *The Matrix* moniker
50. Dogpatch sobriquet
51. Where many vets served
54. It might be laid down
57. Baby sitter?
58. Like a lion
60. An affair to remember?
62. Forthright
64. Matching
65. Solution ratio
66. Kind of green
67. Seuss's *McElligot's* __
68. Tea room selection
69. Dirk's kin
70. Cato's year

DOWN

1. Daddy
2. *Zelig* director
3. First name in hotels
4. Trimmed
5. Bauxite component
6. Western capital
7. Spain's last queen
8. Type of radio antenna
9. Girl's place
10. Luxury's locale
11. He directed some of Tennessee's works
12. Nanking nanny
13. WWII pinup's first name
21. Baseless?
23. Pay period, often
28. Luau locale
30. Miss's equivalent
31. I, in *The King and I*
32. Ring out
33. Pelvic bones
34. "Miss Peach" cartoonist Lazarus
35. Fair-skinned
36. Overwhelm
37. Crescent-shaped figure
39. Like a game of HORSE
42. Ed Norton's entrance
43. Arrow poison
44. Property receiver
45. Alto opening
48. Cause of hereditary variation
51. Pentax rival
52. It's a little bit negative
53. Edison's park
54. Diogenes carried one
55. First-aid plant
56. Beat the rap
59. Chinese cabbage
61. Big Red?
63. Dickens character

ACROSS

1. Pardon me!
5. Easy gait
9. *The Divine Comedy* locale
13. Timbuktu's country
14. Bucky Beaver's toothpaste
16. "Roast Pig" dissertator
17. Style
18. It's curtains for this
19. "Stop pouring!"
20. Candidate
22. Kingly
24. Pizazz
25. Michelle Phillips, once
26. Tom Hanks TV role
29. Request
31. Giraffe kin
35. TV actress Graff
37. Involved
39. Reader's aid
41. Vinyl tile, for short
42. Doddering
43. Purina rival
44. *Clair de __*
45. Lap pup
46. Copy, in a way
47. Brouhaha
49. Captain Kirk grew up there
51. Lofty peak
52. "Birth of a Nation" group
54. Mrs. Romano of *One Day at a Time*
56. Where the Angels play
60. Patella
64. He follows the news
65. Russian coin
67. Rug factor
68. Part of a Marilyn Monroe title
69. Go to Gretna Green
70. Samoa's capital
71. Pair on a angelus
72. Olympian Zatopek
73. Use a bungee

DOWN

1. "I'll say!"
2. Overhead lighting?
3. *Easy Street* actor
4. About a drop
5. Hereditary
6. Aunt Bee's charge
7. Move the camera sideways
8. Name in WWII flight
9. Felled
10. Kind of school
11. Mortgage
12. Fixed route
15. Showy flower
21. Uh-uh
23. Ribboned tree of song
25. Fashion dummy
26. Dispatch
27. Pelvic bone
28. Tube pasta
30. One abroad
32. Bean's brother, in *Ender's Game*
33. Majorca's capital
34. Motivate
36. Coward, of comedies
38. Dairy case item
40. Exhaust
42. Simian
46. Lion's pride?
48. Stretch out
50. Rotary engine name
53. Soap plant
55. Kathmandu's land
56. Mrs. Colin Powell or Mrs. Alfred Hitchcock
57. Apollo 11 name
58. Actress Paquin
59. Phoney it up
60. Military cap
61. King Cole's request
62. Others, to Ovid
63. Spring opposite
66. Lap dog, for short

Go Hawaiian 2

solution on page 325

ACROSS

1. It might hold water
5. Electric unit
8. She played Jennifer Marlowe
12. Jesus in the outfield
13. An *American Idol* judge
15. Safe from the storm
16. Mute effect
17. First *Tonight Show* host
18. Part of a Poirot title
19. One of Matlock's daughters
21. Lawyer's quest
23. It means nothing
24. Princess perturber
25. He played the VP of KAOS
28. Karl Malone nickname
32. 9000, in *2001*
33. Of layers
35. It's watered down
37. Most-wanted poster letters
38. "Society's Child" singer
39. Mystery-story pioneer
40. Role for Whoopi Goldberg or Eric Idle
41. Boxer Joe
45. Koop's gp.
46. His singing helped Murphy Brown's baby sleep
48. Poisonous chemical used in manufacturing
50. Comics caveman
51. Darlin'
52. Monte Cornu for one
57. Stop steering a boat
61. Magician's verb
62. Sheer fabric
64. Others, to Ovid
65. Pelvic bones
66. It dropped Little Boy and Fat Man
67. Observe
68. Author Milne's first name
69. Girl on a ranch
70. One in Bonn

DOWN

1. Ratchet engager
2. Corolla petals on legumes
3. *The Music Man* setting
4. *King of the Hill* daughter
5. Bad start?
6. Ship's frame
7. Butterine
8. Author of *The Hipster Handbook*
9. Crazy quilt
10. 1994 Jodie Foster film
11. Tech. org.
13. Saffron-flavored dish
14. Blindness
20. Not to wish
22. Grant name
25. *Star Trek II* villain
26. Jute fiber
27. Primary strategy
28. Tabby's plaint
29. Cornerstone word
30. Horrify
31. Wynonna's mom
34. "Bloom County" character
36. Heraldic fur
41. Subatomic particle
42. Like the Matterhorn
43. Hawaiian medicine man
44. At any moment
47. Female, say
49. Suck up
52. Upolu port
53. Dark cloud
54. Charles Lamb's pen name
55. Half a golf course
56. Ample, once
58. Wells race
59. Friend of Androcles
60. Construct
63. Arena cry

Go Hawaiian 3

solution on page 325

14. Head Games

ACROSS

1. Economize
6. Snare
9. Kitchen gadget
13. More perilous
15. *Jungle Book* boy
16. It might be a slippery one
17. Idle chat
18. Made a slight difference
20. Identity
21. Durango direction
22. Arrow poison
23. *Mask* star
25. Choice word
28. Certain jackets
29. Item often knitted
30. Rich dessert
34. "We'll __ cup ..."
35. Practical
37. Pizza part
39. Plagiarizes
41. he makes you happy
42. Game of chance
43. Cads
44. Noodles
45. Shakespearean king
46. Ridges
48. Hawaiian goose
50. Cargo box
51. Parched
53. Reign
54. McCaffery's world
57. Nabokov novel
58. Act
60. Evasion
63. Microsoft's headquarters
67. Volkswagen model
68. Culture medium
69. Repo hirer, often
70. Destroy
71. Cape fox
72. Scatters

DOWN

1. Harry Potter has one
2. It's belted out
3. Dixieland trumpeter
4. They kill
5. Be in a bee
6. Stuff
7. Indiana river
8. Cranky engine, say
9. Nuclear reactor
10. Seed for a great tree
11. Home on the range
12. Noted conductor
14. Favor
19. *SNL* star
23. Tighter around the neck
24. Viable
26. All forms of life
27. Agog
28. Gawk
31. Big do
32. Some muscles
33. Develop slowly
36. Accumulates
38. Stash
40. Verbal nudge
41. Price reductions
47. Met Life rival
49. CT town
50. One with a beat
52. Poet Kudirka
54. Cut
55. Jotted down
56. Singer Baker
59. Past one's limit
61. First man
62. In this place
64. Not here
65. Understood
66. Middle time

Head Games 1

solution on page 326

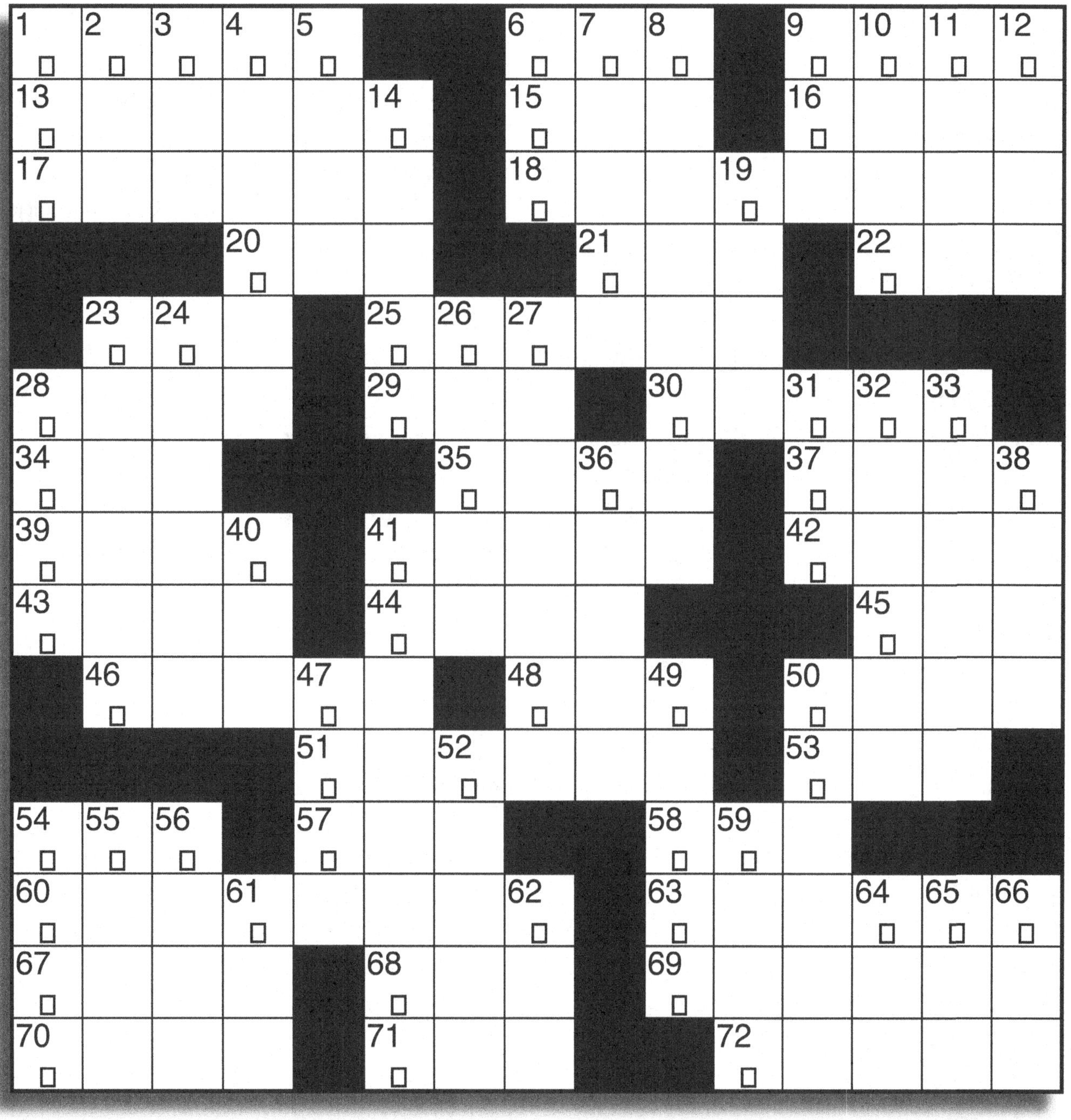

ACROSS

1. Nimble
6. Name in Dolphin football
10. Stumble
13. Job security
14. Entertained
15. Diva ditty
16. Defeated
17. Fix again
18. Follow
19. Sloped steeply
21. Ice cream holder
22. Wild pig
25. Pub crawl chant
26. Telar
29. A-Team role
30. Rain dancer, to friends
31. Reprimand
32. One more likely to say "Gesundheit"?
34. Jeopardy
35. Engulf
36. French state
37. German model
41. More agile
44. Goaded
46. Side by side
48. Gossip
49. Long ago
50. Pedestrian
51. Gordian item
52. Whirl
53. Drawer of Homer and Apu
54. Insulted
58. Italian noble family
59. Bundle wheat
60. Handle up front
64. Jury member, they say
65. Less warm
66. Fool (oneself)
67. Throws in
68. Smart associates
69. Doctrines

DOWN

1. French notion
2. Writer Bontemps
3. Boxing event
4. Hidden mikes
5. Big stinks
6. Fall guy
7. Signal flare
8. Mixing together
9. Gp. for not mixing beer with veer
10. Bal __, FL
11. He gets it in the end
12. Acted as
14. Come out
20. Tease
22. Reluctant
23. Secret supply
24. Bass basket
27. Latin being
28. Shylock, for one
31. Time without
33. Hobbled
34. '50s late-night host
36. Return it as it was
38. Give an edge
39. Egg sites
40. Gulf War name
42. Scottish hillside
43. Gladstone rival
44. Splatter safeguard
45. Arte, to Ruth
46. Helped out
47. Kitchen gadgets
48. *Gilligan's Island* castaway
50. Got rid of
55. Title role for Snipes
56. Donates
57. Fred's sis
59. Cut
61. Kid's ball game
62. Groove
63. Blinkers

Head Games 2

solution on page 326

ACROSS

1. "Rubaiyat" name
4. Actor Hawke
8. Small hooter
13. Basic block name
14. Duvall's __ *Tale Theatre*
16. Shocked, SHOCKED!
17. Strategy
18. Swindles
19. Krikey!
20. Channels
22. Lower
24. Mil. aide
25. Slope a caber might roll down
26. Take a powder?
29. Actor Jannings
31. Celeb
33. Harrison Ford has one
35. Tenet
38. Minotaur's home
39. Yoda's pupil
40. "The __ Love"
41. Lost air privileges
43. Run away
44. Adjutant
45. Letter turner
46. Blarney stone's locale
48. Honorary poem
49. Aural
50. Gen-__ (bommers' kids)
51. "Vissi d'__"
53. Not VHS
55. FDR's pooch
57. __ de corps
59. Treat like a hero in Britain
63. Take five
66. Aaron had 755
68. Killer whale
69. Like a gun in a Bond film
70. Roues
71. Yuletide
72. Darn again
73. Elementary?
74. Item for hair or an actor

DOWN

1. Refine
2. Snert is his dog
3. Swedish coin
4. Begins
5. Believer
6. Handleless teacup
7. Not a divider
8. Scottish imp
9. Twirling
10. Dollar
11. Mobutu __ Seko
12. LL.D. holder
15. Carried a child
21. Cotton thread
23. Play place
27. Joking
28. Gets up
29. Fixer
30. Least sure
32. Conductor Alberto
34. Have offspring
35. Plait
36. He ate no fat
37. More unfeeling
38. Soprano Berger
42. Seam
47. Tidy
52. Abate
54. West role
55. More equal
56. Type of picture
58. Turn over
60. Terra __
61. Film award
62. It helps get a rise
63. Siouan
64. Steer
65. Green gem
67. Leningrad's river

ACROSS

1. On fire
6. Gestation stations
10. Dies follower
13. Kid's colorer
14. In a panic
15. She worked with Flo and Alice
16. Hallways
17. Contact lens solution
18. Used item condition
19. Faltered
21. Bridge ancestor
22. Bird sound
25. Lou Grant's paper
26. Harangues
28. Melville book
29. Depend
30. Family members
31. Man from the Boot
33. Frank alternative
34. *Star Trek II* director
35. Newsman Marvin
36. "Azucar!" singer
40. Roof of the mouth
43. Reproving
45. Come before
47. Hurry
48. Type of test
49. Fished, in a way
50. Use a microwave oven
51. Space chimp
52. Role for Bea
53. Mr. Simpson's neighbor
57. Direccion del sol de la dia
58. One behind the other
59. Skimpy top
63. Kind of crossing
64. "Password?" person
65. Relax
66. Throws in
67. Summoned
68. Jammed in

DOWN

1. Bushy do
2. It's easily molded
3. *Court Jester* star
4. Writeoff, briefly
5. Official tsk tsker
6. Carrel
7. Penthouse
8. Popcorn concern
9. Vast
10. Be in charge
11. Hilton and Latsis who hang together
12. Critters
14. Showing signs of healing
20. Cheshire Cat showing
21. Ran a committee, say
22. Ike's wife
23. Study suffix
24. Replicant
27. Louvre displays
30. Restrain
32. Small boat of old
33. Drug carrier
35. Turnstile
37. Foreigner
38. Kind of bean or horse
39. Epics
41. Joy
42. Prepping a horse
43. Fail under pressure
44. Unlike Miss Daisy's driver
45. Put in the tiles
46. They put the metal to the metal
47. Awful
49. Rubbed out
54. *Gremlins* director
55. McCarthy's sidekick
56. Like some coalitions
58. Jumping insect
60. Dateless
61. __ majeste
62. Raised

solution on page 326

ACROSS

1. Predicament
6. Eh
9. Bulkhead
12. Kilmer or Clooney role
13. Piece of leg armor
15. "Gotcha"
16. Principles
17. Went through the roof
18. Unseen *Will & Grace* role
19. Artist's inspiration
21. Titanic's undoing
22. Rolling stone's lack
23. Talents
26. Hock shop, perhaps
28. Hook-shaped architecture features
30. *Gaslight* star
31. Leash
32. Johnny Tremain had one
34. Bundled up
37. Head of France
38. Emma Peel's follower
39. Burns' hillside
41. Thomas' island
44. Hock a loogy
45. Ushers show you to them
47. Pilfer
49. They take them away
51. Cabbie's question
54. "The bacon"
55. Idiot
56. Cease
58. Hindu queen
59. Vittles
60. *L.A. Law* partner
62. Not at sea
67. Speed
68. Alpine features
69. Assassin
70. *Citizen Kane* prop
71. Thought for Truffaut
72. Bars, in law

DOWN

1. Whole bunch
2. He worked with Ruth
3. Mountain man?
4. Milky gem
5. One who gives lashes with a wet noodle?
6. Certain South African
7. Grammarian's concern
8. "Wouldn't It Be __?"
9. "For Your Eyes Only" singer
10. Magic word
11. De-blubber
13. Accurate
14. Like some maze gardens
20. Alley whisper
23. Soused
24. Stored
25. Hit the trail
27. Double Day word
28. Emancipate
29. Get away
30. Certain salt
33. Dehli wrap
35. More agile
36. Like van Gogh's night
40. Untouchable role
42. *Two and a Half Men* actor
43. Varmint
45. Beliefs in totality
46. New Zealand parrot
48. Like film, often
50. Mr. Drake, on *Cheers*
51. Sung by a group
52. What Holmes does
53. Investigated
57. Rash
58. Fathers
61. Dagger of old
63. Marker
64. Pooch in Oz
65. Get ready
66. Towel word

solution on page 326

ACROSS

1. One place to love from
4. Plunder
7. Vampires
12. Where to find a hero
13. Typing bar
15. Nothing-but-net shot
16. They might be calling
17. Om, etc.
18. Like a loose top
19. Not quite yet
21. Bone starter
23. It takes aim at Aim
24. Drools
27. Marathon
30. '97 title role for Jennifer Lopez
32. Stable keeper
34. *SNL* star
36. Stranded like Crusoe
38. Fetch
39. Capable of being put away
41. Gifts
43. *Rocky Horror ...* role
44. A holy book
46. Assents
47. Saviors of sorts
49. Special groups
51. Solidifies
52. More shaky about
54. High home
58. Lots of curls
59. Indy's first film
61. It's free
65. Scram!
68. Yuletide story starter
69. Tool for parmesan
70. Leaning
71. Big bash
72. Breaks apart
73. Sun. speeches
74. Saudi gulf

DOWN

1. "__ I See You Again"
2. *Cheers* owner, at first
3. Gnashes
4. Play with reverb
5. Agreement
6. Time, e.g.
7. She played Xena
8. Novel set on Tahiti
9. Network show of 1990
10. Bonnie one
11. Pallid
13. Bridge part
14. Rub out
20. Well-read
22. Took big steps
25. One of two of the Shangri-Las
26. Office shape
27. Like brine
28. Aromas
29. Shipping hazards
31. Smooth-talking
33. Under pressure
34. Off-key
35. They give a darn
37. Kopell who played Doc Bricker and Siegfried
39. Warehouse
40. Less distant
42. Words of understanding
45. Melting clock artist
48. Likes better
50. Uses a sieve
53. Cleaving tools
55. Made suds
56. User who takes
57. Ebb
60. *Knight Rider* car
61. *Fame* singer
62. General Bradley
63. Chooses
64. Skedaddle
66. *Wizard of Oz* surname
67. Magi leader

solution on page 326

ACROSS

1. Aloe __
4. Do without
8. G-rated
12. PC unit of time
13. Like loose mica
15. Room at the top
16. Arkin or Arden
17. It shows a point
18. __ drum
19. Repairs again
21. Developed slowly
23. Data-entered
25. It opens with a twist
26. Engine sound
28. Envelop
30. Whiten
34. Iota
35. Barbecue
37. Aligns
39. Was talented
41. Aft locales
42. Sci-fi pioneer
43. Jane Eyre's charge
44. Half a spa
45. *Jaws* vessel
46. Give a gun to
48. __ fixe
50. "... Grapevine" singer
51. Reindeer herder
53. Early President
55. One with nothing nice to say
59. Did TSA work
63. *Ab Fab* role
64. They're scared
67. Herb or weapon
68. Yankovic parody
69. Where there are wills, they're away
70. Avast
71. Greek isle
72. Popular news adjective since 9/11
73. Lady's man

DOWN

1. Beau __
2. King had one
3. Mother-of-pearl
4. More openly spaced
5. "Mighty __ Rose"
6. Blankie spot
7. Apple tool
8. Full assemblies
9. Do work in Hamelin
10. Laissez __
11. Knock-__
13. West Virginia town
14. Finds an early market for
20. Blood type, Earth's pull, or type of Shabbat
22. Certain Amerind
24. Jonathan/ Wagener hybrid
26. Nag
27. Useless
29. Spread one's seeds
31. Truth alternative
32. Run along
33. From where
34. It should be punched out
36. Went astray
38. Not landlubbing
40. Virginia willow
41. They have loud feet
47. Fruit juice prefix
49. Desired
50. Football bomb
52. Togther, they licked the platter clean
54. Not quite right
55. It has blips
56. High and mighty
57. Be victorious
58. Kind of marble
60. Make an eight?
61. Spy mission
62. Talented
65. Squushed circle
66. Singer Seeger

ACROSS

1. One who repents
6. Body fluids
9. Book for the Bard
13. Homer king for 27 years and others
15. Mighty mite
16. Singer O'Day
17. Check before it's necessary
18. De __, Illinois
19. Peggy Lee hit
20. Staff, for short
22. They tell a tale
24. Clean
27. Tongue waggers?
28. Suggest
29. He raised Cain
31. Prickly shrub
35. Breeding
36. Brave homes
38. Buffa alternative
39. Ration
40. Ship's wheel
41. Belly button schmutz
42. Fishhook leader
44. Vile-tasting oil
46. Protect a bet
47. Yuletide drink
49. Punta del __
50. "Like a Rock" singer
51. Kabobn thingama-bob
52. Henpecker
54. Less neat
58. Valhalla VIP
59. He played Young Frankenstein's monster
60. Luth. or Episc.
62. Official rebuke
67. Eeyore's mood
68. Akimbo
69. Janitor, at times
70. Sales sites
71. Early film screamer
72. Title role for Ahn-old

DOWN

1. Dipper part
2. Center
3. Troop group
4. __ majeste
5. Certain button
6. Greek salad item
7. Humble toiler
8. Casino patrons
9. Feature of an Earth slice
10. Andes film
11. Metric system measure
12. They're hog wild?
14. Spanning
21. Ways out
23. Festive
24. Acred homes
25. *Gorky Park* concerns
26. Selects
28. Tejana singer
30. Food fishes
32. Cut down to size
33. Remora, say
34. Gat
37. Lowered in rank
43. Remote controlled switches
44. One who stumbles
45. Look before you look
46. Banana slipper
48. Sundial number
53. Victor
54. Plantlife
55. Courtyard
56. Wet thud
57. Swedish coin
61. Bar memb.
63. Sailing
64. Tarot suit
65. A Desperate Housewife
66. German mister

Appendix A
Glossary

#:
Crosswords are called by the number of rows and columns they have, which tend to be the same in the crossword world (a newspaper's daily puzzle is usually a 15, and a newspaper's Sunday crossword is usually a 21; almost always a square puzzle and an odd number).

American-style:
See construction.

anagram:
Rearranging letters to spell something else; occasionally used in a theme

British-style:
See construction.

byline:
A constructor credit.

cheater:
A black square that maintains word count, making the grid easier to fill in.

construction/constructor:
In an American-style crossword, a constructor constructs using the art of construction. For British-style crosswords, setters set crossword puzzles. British-style puzzles DO NOT have cross-checking, and the clues have a straight half and a cryptic half (there are about a half dozen different styles of acceptable cryptic form).

cross-checking:
Having all white boxes used in both across and down entries, so that you can check a square against valid entries going in both directions.

crossword:
The first crossword, created by Arthur Wynn, appeared in the December 21, 1913, edition of New York World. Word squares go back at least to early Rome.

crosswordese:
Words that you rarely encounter outside the crossword world.
cruciverbalism:
The art/science of crosswords.

cruciverbalist:
Crossword constructor.

entry:
An across or down answer.

fill:
The entries stuffed into a grid.

grid:
A crossword's black/white square pattern.

interconnectedness:
Grid quality where black squares don't chop the puzzle into separate pieces.

isle of white:
Cut-off part of a grid that is not interconnected.

knothole:
A square that's hard to break open, because you have no clue about the across and down entries crossing there.

Margaret Farrar:
The world's first crossword editor (for the New York Times); she laid down the first ground rules, giving legitimacy to the field.
mirror-symmetry:
The feature of a grid where if you chop it in half, then spin it around on its center, it'll match up.
Monday:
Traditionally, an easy crossword in a daily newspaper.

new wave:
A construction style where entries go beyond your typical dictionary and atlas (more pop

culture, arts, business names, IT terms, very recent news, and clues apropos for Jeopardy and Trivial Pursuit).

open:
A dense concentration of white squares in a grid.

palindrome:
Something that is the same spelled forward and backward; occasionally used in a theme or clue.

partial:
A fill-in-the-blank where multiple words go in the blank.

patch:
A minor grid rework.

Ray Hamel:
Keeper of a great crossword reference list at www.primate.wisc.edu/people/hamel/cp.html

Saturday:
Traditionally, a tough-as-nails crossword in a daily newspaper; a Monday would be the easy puzzle.

Scrabble:
A word game where one can stack across and down words, forming a crude crossword puzzle. When I was a kid, I would jot down good open areas.

square:
A box in a grid.

stacking:
Putting long answers side by side.

Stephen Sondheim:
Lyricist credited for popularizing cryptic crosswords in the U.S.

sticky:
Adjective describing a square or section that's hard to break open.

tag:
A clue about an entry's form, such as ": 2 wds." or ": Fr." or ": var."

teardown:
A major grid rework.

theme:
Common concept that runs throughout a puzzle's long entries or even the whole puzzle; such a puzzle is said to be themed.

Tom Swifty:
Swapping the initial consonant sounds/blends on the starts of words; occasionally used in a theme.

Unch:
Short for "unchecked letter" (see cross-checking).

Will Shortz:
Current New York Times crossword editor (who added bylines and made the puzzles more new wave), host of NPR's "The Puzzler Presents," and someone who actually got a college degree in enigmatology (the study of puzzles).

Will Weng:
Former New York Times crossword editor.

word count:
The number of entries in a grid; some publishers specify word count limits.

word square:
A crossword variant (dating back at least to ancient Rome) where the downs and acrosses are the same. It may be well advised to attempt making these before tackling the construction of a whole puzzle. An example of a word square is as follows:

```
START
TABOO
ABOUT
ROUGE
TOTEM
```

Appendix B
Answers

1. The Big Intro

Addled

```
BOLT IRISH WMDS
ALEE FATHA EARP
BLEDMOVIES LINA
AIRLINES BALLOT
RESELLS CENSE
    WAY SUET DSL
UNPIN VERNE TAU
LOIS DEALS PANS
NAG LULLS WEIGH
AHS ENDS FIR
   TRACT PREFECT
UNYOKE TOILETRY
SOLO COWLEDCHIP
DUET ADAIR TAME
ANDS PESOS ONES
```

Word Wackies

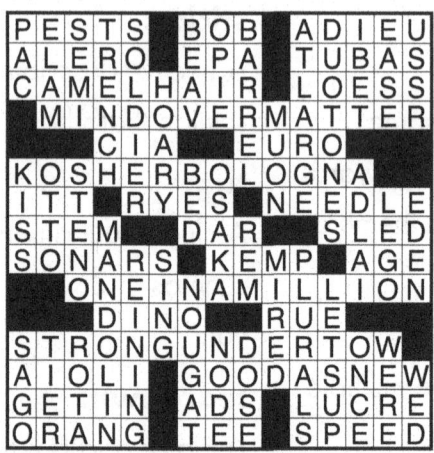

```
PESTS BOB ADIEU
ALERO EPA TUBAS
CAMELHAIR LOESS
 MINDOVERMATTER
   CIA EURO
KOSHERBOLOGNA
ITT RYES NEEDLE
STEM DAR SLED
SONARS KEMP AGE
  ONEINAMILLION
   DINO RUE
STRONGUNDERTOW
AIOLI GOODASNEW
GETIN ADS LUCRE
ORANG TEE SPEED
```

Swifties of 10

```
SPLAT ACED LAGS
LAUGH SLAW ULNA
INNER SAGA SLOT
DEGRADEDLY CAME
   SIR ENGINES
HIGHHATS ETO
ASEA LIPS OUTER
SEAN SNIPS SEMI
HERDS GEEK LAMP
   SOB DAISYMAE
DEPOSIT KEN
ELAM GRUESOMELY
TAPE TINA CURIE
ETAL OATS ALIEN
RELY PLOY TEENS
```

Scatter

```
LIARS DORM SODA
ONTAP ARIA APEX
ADOZE LEAN LILI
MOZZARELLA MULL
   KAY THOMAS
TUTTUT ATEIN
SCRAP EPHEMERAL
ALAR ARIAS LEIA
RAPARTIST FLANS
  NOTCH DEARTH
ODETTA BUY
FILE CITRONELLA
FALL HAHA EMAIL
ONEL EGAD SMITE
NANA SONY SAREE
```

Friends of Yoko Ono and Iggy Pop?

```
RIMS EXEMPT OFT
ELAL REMORA RIO
MONICASELES ERR
ANGEL RESTHOME
PAYROLL LEO
   GEORGESOROS
SLUGGISHLY DATA
MONEY TOE YOGIS
UPTO MIDASTOUCH
GEORGETENET
   GAS SCRAPIE
SORENSEN INEPT
OHO DARYLHANNAH
ONO EGISES ANNE
NOT RECENT SEAL
```

Something Fishy

```
ICHOR DOA MRED
HOOKA RULE IAGO
OWLET ESPY SMOG
PLAYINGTHEBASS
   DOES ABED
MALONE ABANDONS
AWAKE SUET POW
COMEDOWNTHEPIKE
EKE NETS MANIA
RESTATES RESEAT
   ALOT EARS
 WHIPPERSNAPPER
CHIC ONES LOOSE
POSH FEMA DROSS
ASTI ROY STROP
```

Casually

```
ARMED  ABCS  PREP
TIARA  TARP  ROBE
OPTIC  TREE  IDOS
PETERFONDA MINT
     OAR ORLANDO
ALIGNING  SAD
DESI  TERI GOTTA
DATA  HYENA NOEL
SHONE SEEN  NONO
   TAN KATMANDU
SCEPTER RIO
LAVA  CHINCHILLA
OMEN  TINE  ARIOT
WEND  ANTS  WOLFE
SOSA  ROOT  KNITS
```

I'm Just Wild about Saffron

```
BAEZ  FETID  ISBN
ALDA  BERNE  NCAA
SINGLIKEACANARY
STARE   ELEMENTS
    EGGS  LIAR
KABBALAH  THETAS
ALA  TOMES   ARGO
YELLOWBRICKROAD
AREA   ADDLE  TVA
KOSHER SEARCHES
    DRUB  SYNE
ASSIGNER   ELIDE
MEADOWLARKLEMON
ETNA  ALGAE  BANG
NASH  YOUNG  SCAR
```

O Ho!

```
HOHUM  DODO  GERM
IVANA  USES  ALOE
FATHERCHRISTMAS
ILSA  CHAMELEONS
    PRAY  ARIA
SCAPE     MULCT
TINYBUBBLES  OOH
ALT  PAIGE   ERE
III  CABCALLOWAY
DACHA     YIELD
   ATAD  WREN
APOSTROPHE  KRIS
JOLLYGREENGIANT
ALEE  OILY  SNIDE
REST  TATS  AGLOW
```

I'd Like to Thank the Little People

```
BAOBAB  SIR  BRA
INCOME  USES  LAG
NATRON  PAPA  IVE
  GRUMPYOLDMEN
SLA  MOO   ANENT
HAPPYBIRTHDAY
ATSEA   TVA
GHERKIN SLOTCAR
    REA   BOONE
  DOCSEVERINSEN
PARRY  ILO   TWO
SLEEPYHOLLOW
AGA  ROAN  LLAMAS
LED  UGHS  ELNINO
MRS  SAN   DADDYO
```

2. Big Deal

Um ...

```
ILIAD LOST GRAM
LITRE AUTO RULE
KETTLEDRUM OLLA
   FUMES OSTEAL
CAVESIN BRITONS
EMERIL HEREOF
DUNNO IAGO STEN
EST NOSHOWS HMO
DEUS FLAT EDUCE
   RUFFES ACUMEN
EVERETT BLOBBED
DOSIDO PLANA
IWON PALINDROME
FEMA IDOS ERWIN
YLEM CODS DYERS
```

It Comes Around

```
ASSET KOPS CLAP
HEAVE ABIT HERO
ALGER TITO EGOS
BLANKCHECK CASE
   ERA HECKLER
SAMPLERS SAP
OHIO WITH POKED
DELI SNOOP INTO
AMONG EMMA NEON
   TED PENITENT
WARBLER PIC
ABEL FULLCIRCLE
TINA AREA CURIO
EDEN MATT LEANN
REEK ELSE EDGES
```

Metal Meddle

```
SPLIT DICED MAC
ALICE AMOVE ADO
SIRES FACIA NOR
HEARTOFGOLD ORE
   FLOES SAFER
DAWDLED REUSES
UNARY INSTANT
INFO SLOPE TESS
   FOCUSER TIEUP
DOLLOP OPHELIA
OBESE VICAR
ELI QUICKSILVER
SIR ULNAE LEAVE
IGO AVERT LASES
TEN LADES SPENT
```

Swifties of 14

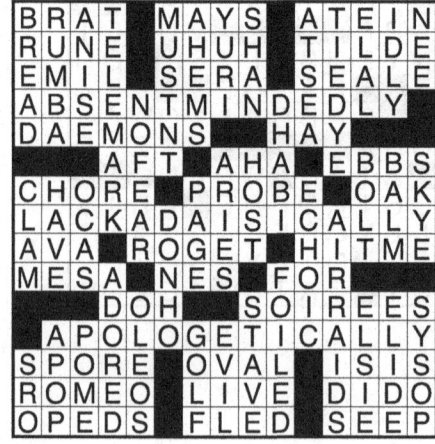

```
BRAT MAYS ATEIN
RUNE UHUH TILDE
EMIL SERA SEALE
ABSENTMINDEDLY
DAEMONS HAY
   AFT AHA EBBS
CHORE PROBE OAK
LACKADAISICALLY
AVA ROGET HITME
MESA NES FOR
   DOH SOIREES
APOLOGETICALLY
SPORE OVAL ISIS
ROMEO LIVE DIDO
OPEDS FLED SEEP
```

Ball Bearing

```
SASE SONY ATLAS
CENT KNEE SOAVE
ASIA ITLL COZEN
DODGEBALLCITY
SPEEDUP HISSES
   RIM POI YURI
OCTET CORNU SOS
PERSONALBALLADS
IRA ROVES CONEY
NINA FED WEB
EASTLA PARSECS
   FOOTBALLSTOOL
PRUNE ABUT ESSE
OASES ALTO RITE
WEEDS LEON SNAP
```

Civil Rights

```
REDS SPA USAIR
SUMAC POD NONCE
WEBDUBOIS MATED
UFO MAR TAR
MULE ITUNES FAT
LITTLEROCKNINE
REEDIT ASKS
PARADE AORTAS
ACED COGNAC
GREENSBOROFOUR
EEL BISHOP SNOB
COX SIS FOE
CAROM ROSAPARKS
PLUMB OWE EPEES
RITES END WEED
```

Going Down

I	N	A	P	T		I	N	T	R	O		T	L	C
S	E	N	O	R		S	E	R	I	F		O	A	R
M	A	K	E	A	N	O	T	E	O	F		P	R	E
S	T	A	T	U	E	S		A	T	I	S	S	U	E
			I	M	A	C		D	E	C	A	Y	E	D
R	O	D	C	A	R	E	W		D	E	B	T		
O	D	E		S	E	L	I	G		R	O	U	S	E
B	O	C	A		D	E	L	L	S		T	R	I	O
E	R	E	C	T		S	M	E	A	R		V	A	N
	L	U	R	E		A	N	T	O	N	Y	M	S	
E	V	E	R	E	T	T		N	O	S	E			
P	I	R	A	N	H	A		F	R	E	A	K	E	D
O	C	A		D	E	T	E	R	I	O	R	A	T	E
D	A	T		E	N	U	R	E		L	E	T	O	N
E	R	E		D	E	M	A	Y		A	R	E	N	T

Gotta Dash!

H	A	S	I	D		A	H	A		F	U	G	A	L
A	B	A	C	A		L	E	S		O	S	A	K	A
H	A	B	E	R	-	E	R	S		R	E	L	A	X
A	S	E	P	T	I	C		A	M	E	R			
S	H	R	I	E	K		I	M	A	G	I	N	E	D
			C	R	I	S	P		I	O	D	I	D	E
F	L	A	K		S	W	A	R	M		S	E	G	A
R	A	T			A	N	I					C	A	R
O	U	T	S		S	P	E	C	S		E	E	R	Y
T	R	I	P	L	E		M	E	L	D	S			
H	A	C	I	E	N	D	A		A	R	C	A	N	A
			T	A	T	A		O	P	I	A	T	E	D
W	H	I	T	S		V	O	N	-	E	P	A	R	D
A	M	B	L	E		I	L	L			S	E	R	V	E
D	O	M	E	S		D	E	Y		T	R	I	E	D

Deployment

D	I	L	L		P	O	S	T	O	P		S	O	D
A	R	I	A		E	M	E	R	I	L		W	R	Y
V	E	N	U	S	D	E	M	I	L	O		I	C	E
I	N	T	R	O		N	I	P		S	U	G	A	R
D	E	S	A	N	D		O	D	I	N				
				J	O	I	E	D	E	V	I	V	R	E
M	A	S	S	A	C	R	E		B	E	S	E	E	N
A	R	C	H		K	A	R	A	T		O	N	I	T
I	G	U	A	N	A		I	P	O	D	N	A	N	O
N	O	M	D	E	G	U	E	R	R	E				
			E	W	E	S		S	M	A	R	T	S	
B	A	N	D	S		H	E	P		U	B	O	A	T
U	S	O		I	L	E	D	E	F	R	A	N	C	E
S	I	R		E	A	R	N	E	R		S	C	O	T
Y	A	M		R	O	S	A	R	Y		H	O	S	S

3. Big Quotations

Wilde Quote

```
ABA ABOUND TADA
LOL CENSOR ARAB
FOB MEMORYISTHE
ABILENE MESSILY
LONE  HARM CIA
FOOTSTOOLS ALAN
ASS OVAL  CREST
   DIARYTHAT
NAVEL DIAL PAM
ICAN WEALLCARRY
ARM TINY  TESS
GOODEGG TRUMPET
ABOUTWITHUS ANI
RASE ANNALS RAF
ATES METIER ELY
```

Billboards

```
OCA  SKIDS  SOFT
RAM BMOVIE PILL
ANY EERIER ALEC
TATASWEETVERSE
OPALS ASSESS
RENDER   SETTO
  ALONGTHEROAD
ODE SEIKO  POD
WERESADTOSEE
LLANO   SIDLES
  GUMBOS FAINT
YOUREOUTOFMODE
DULL DOTAGE NOW
WAIF ITGIRL EWE
INNS ASONE LSD
```

Chanukah Greetings

```
DEFY SCARS LORE
SLOE CADET ARIL
LIRA ARENA RAGU
 SHARONEMAILED
TRY ICU EFFABLE
RUTHLESS OTT
ASHE AWARE XES
ITISPALINDROMIC
NSA ITSME DIDO
  TET SCREENER
AVERTER DAR URN
DELIAMENORAHS
DRIP PLATE IOTA
ENOL TETES GNAW
RETE SEEST HERE
```

Nietzsche Quote

```
SCRIM SLANG CAR
APACE PALER EVA
MANYAMANFAILSAS
   LAID  NESTS
AMOR ANORIGINAL
NAPALM ANO ARE
DRANO NOIR
 THINKERSIMPLY
   ARTE TROOP
ARI GOV IVANKA
BECAUSEHIS TEEN
OMEGA  ONTO
MEMORYISTOOGOOD
BEA DONNE ZONED
STN SNAIL EBERT
```

Humorous Observation

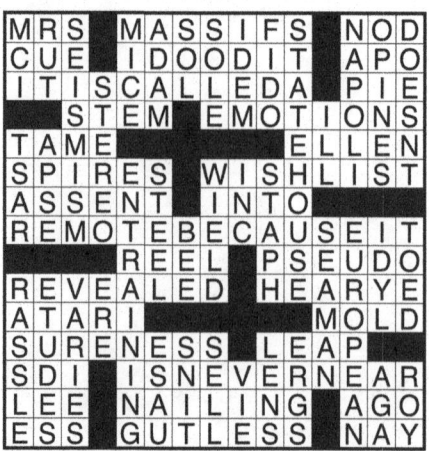

```
MRS MASSIFS NOD
CUE IDOODIT APO
ITISCALLEDA PIE
 STEM EMOTIONS
TAME    ELLEN
SPIRES WISHLIST
ASSENT INTO
REMOTEBECAUSEIT
   REEL PSEUDO
REVEALED HEARYE
ATARI    MOLD
SURENESS LEAP
SDI ISNEVERNEAR
LEE NAILING AGO
ESS GUTLESS NAY
```

4. Big Films

'50s Films

```
MALL ASIA MOTET
ALEE VEAL ALINE
SEAT ARGO SINGE
SUNSETBOULEVARD
ATTILA    ARE
    TIRAMISU SAD
SKIRT NODS GIGI
ANNIEGETYOURGUN
GOOP RAIL NINES
OWN EARFLAPS
    SDI  LITCHI
DESTINATIONMOON
ADLIB SASH ICES
INALL PLEA LORE
SABLE SEES LAST
```

The Year: 1951

```
MEDAL PLUS RAZE
OLIVE AONE OXEN
JULIUSROSENBERG
OLLA ETTU ARDOR
    TRAY LENO
CAVIAR ALLAYING
ODEON ARIA MIR
DENNISTHEMENACE
ELO ATAD BOGEY
DEMOCRAT LOSERS
    CHIC BONE
STATE HALO ELLA
THEAFRICANQUEEN
IRON INNS UMIAK
RUNE OGEE OSAKA
```

New in '52

```
MALTS LIEF CHAD
ATEUP ENTOURAGE
WAITINGFORGODOT
RDA TAME ELAINE
   ATTAR LITTER
RACCOON TIS
ACHOO LAM BOCA
THEINVISIBLEMAN
SEWN END ATILT
    CNN SHUTTLE
ABSURD SHIRE
TEEPEE CAFE TWA
ERNESTHEMINGWAY
IRONSTONE CAINE
NARD AWED EDGES
```

The Year: 1953

```
EPEES ASPCA JAB
DERMA SHORN ORY
DOUBLEHELIX NIT
INCLUDED TIRADE
ESTATES PIOUS
    ZEN BEQUESTS
DOJOS VIRUS AHA
IRAN PENCE GLEN
PAM SEEDY CAKES
SLEEPERS TUM
    SLIPS CAREENS
ROBOTS SUBABBOT
ILO THECRUCIBLE
FIN LOYAL ARETE
END EWERS ODDER
```

The Year: 1954

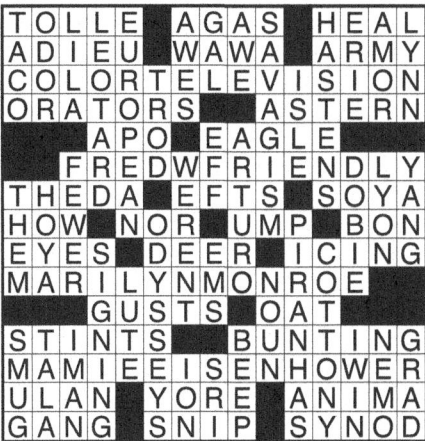

```
TOLLE AGAS HEAL
ADIEU WAWA ARMY
COLORTELEVISION
ORATORS ASTERN
    APO EAGLE
    FREDWFRIENDLY
THEDA EFTS SOYA
HOW NOR UMP BON
EYES DEER ICING
MARILYNMONROE
    GUSTS OAT
STINTS BUNTING
MAMIEEISENHOWER
ULAN YORE ANIMA
GANG SNIP SYNOD
```

New in '55

```
RASH SMASH JERK
ERIE HELIO AGUE
DISNEYLAND MANN
YEARNS NEEDEDTO
ELLIOTT SHES
    LEAD OLDHAT
EARMARKED LEAVE
ALEC SEGOS ALES
ROADS NASTINESS
LEMONS SEEM
    NAIL SWEDISH
DIMAGGIO PAELLA
EVIL HERMANWOUK
LAND TIEIN ANNE
INKS SNOBS RAGS
```

4. Big Films continued

Say What Songs of '56

```
ACHE  DINAR GEMS
LOAM  ECOLE ELUL
DORP  BEBOPALULA
OLDHAT STOLIDLY
    AGOG   IDEAS
QUESERASERA
OVOID LACES  BAA
PENS  GOULD BABU
HAS  ENOLA OOHED
    TUTTIFRUTTI
SLUSH    RAZZ
COMPADRE ROOKIE
ABBONDANZA URNS
NERO  AVOID KISS
TSAR  YELPS ISTO
```

Films of '57

```
EBBS  LUSTS PART
LOLL  ONEAL ODIE
FLOE  ULTRA NAVE
 TWELVEANGRYMEN
  SPIRALS OUSTS
STAIDER   IMP
HOWE   NACRE  TAP
AFAREWELLTOARMS
GUY RADII  NAPA
   FOR  ELITIST
STRAD TUNEDIN
THESEVENTHSEAL
ROUT ASTER TBAR
ESSE  STILE ALOE
WEED  TYLER MESA
```

Songs of '58

```
AGNEW SPIRE  APT
PESTO LEMUR DUE
BLACKPEPPER IMP
   APSE  EDIE
 CHANTILLYLACE
BLOUNT  BOISE
JOHNNYBGOODE
SON   OYS   BEA
 CHIPMUNKSONG
SNOUT  OOOOOO
JAILHOUSEROCK
ELSA  NCAA
SIS HABERDASHER
TVA ICANT IRONY
SAN PERTH DODGE
```

The Year: 1958

```
SCAB  BELA SQUAB
TORI  ETAL EUROS
ABUT  LURE VOILA
BOBBYFISCHER
SLAYERS  INURNS
  BAY CUT MAUI
CHAIR EOSIN ILL
YERTLETHETURTLE
NAM YATES BOTOX
ITOR TUN PBS
CHROME  FAIENCE
  VANALLENBELT
BATIK FOUL UHOH
ALONE ABEL DRNO
SLOGS ROSA SUES
```

TV of '59

```
SPEC  PASTA CITY
PARA  LITER ASHE
ITIS  ALARM NEON
THEHONEYMOONERS
   BRED  IPO
NABOBS SPRITZER
OLIO  ELLEN UTE
MICKEYMOUSECLUB
ABE  NUMBS AUDI
DIPLOMAS VERSED
   ELM  RENT
CAPTAINKANGAROO
UHOH EIEIO BERM
BARA SLEDS LACE
ABEL TENSE ELAN
```

5. Time Machine: The '50s

You're the Tops

```
GILD DECOR ELAL
ASIA ADOBE NAPA
MANHANDLED FRET
 WELLDIDYOUEVAH
   BEE  UPTAKE
HERDER DEBIT
OVOID MAUL EDIE
MISSOTISREGRETS
ELAM ECHO REARS
  ARRAY DADDYO
IRONER  LEV
CESTMAGNIFIQUE
OVAL IRENEDUNNE
NUKE NIVEN ITIS
SEAS SNERD PODS
```

Ready, Aim, Fire!

```
SLEET REN DIVAN
HINDU AMA ANIME
ALIGN NUMERATOR
HIDEANDSEEKWORD
   FAR PYLE
BIGWIG PLOY BSA
ALOES HEAR TAIL
TOOTHPASTEBRAND
ONUS ONCE LIEGE
NAT MIDI WOODEN
  SONS MAW
BRIMSTONEGOWITH
LADIESMAN VIDEO
EVERY ETS EPEES
DESKS REA REAMS
```

Cargo

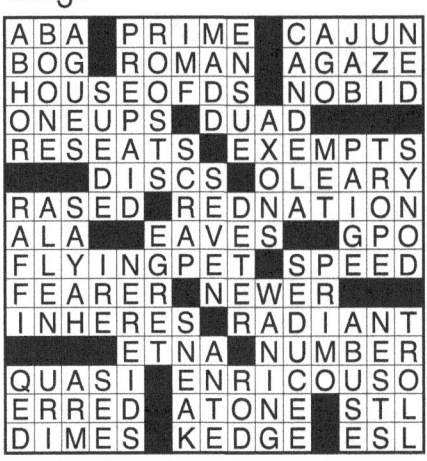

```
ABA PRIME CAJUN
BOG ROMAN AGAZE
HOUSEOFDS NOBID
ONEUPS DUAD
RESEATS EXEMPTS
  DISCS OLEARY
RASED REDNATION
ALA EAVES GPO
FLYINGPET SPEED
FEARER NEWER
INHERES RADIANT
 ETNA NUMBER
QUASI ENRICOUSO
ERRED ATONE STL
DIMES KEDGE ESL
```

Mysteries

```
RANIS ABEL TEEM
OPART TARA ONLY
BERMUDATRIANGLE
ESCAROLE DUELER
  GEL  IDLERS
AMUSES GENIE
BUNCO PELT SIVA
LOCHNESSMONSTER
ENOL MATS ELSIE
  EMITS ROYALS
AGAMAS  ION
LATINS INTAGLIO
ALIENABDUCTIONS
MOLL RAYS ENROL
OPTS YALE SAYNO
```

Crosses to Bear

```
URGE CISCO DAHL
ROAM ONION ABET
SOLEMNCROSSWORD
AMERICA PETE
  GLENN TASSEL
CAREER OUST AVI
AVON TANG OGDEN
REDCROSSHERRING
FREYA ILSA ESSE
USO THAI GLAMOR
LESSEE POLIS
  ARIL BENEFIT
CROSSFIREENGINE
OAFS EMILY ULNA
DEFY RAMIE NESS
```

Canines

```
AMEN BEANO FRAT
NANA ORLOP AIDE
DOGDAYAFTERNOON
  ILL AIRED
STARLET FALAFEL
HUSSY HAY INAWE
ENS LOU SEGUES
 AFTERTHEFOX
RAGBAG ROW PAR
AVAIL AYE IDAHO
JAIALAI DARESAY
 GORSE SAN
LONEWOLFMCQUADE
ANON METOO DUEL
PERT ASSET EGAD
```

5. Time Machine: The '50s continued

Anagram This!

```
EMMA  SHRED   MAC
LIAR  COURIC  ABE
MARTIANGASH   RID
   INRE  SEASIDE
PASSKEYS  ATONED
AGATES  EASTLA
TRIED DEWEY  GNP
HENS  BARES  WHOA
SET COMES  CHART
  GLOBES  BOOSTS
MORALS  STEALTHY
ENABLES  EASE
ASH AGAINSTHARM
REA REGRET  OMIT
ATM  RESTS  GAGA
```

Boo!

```
OTIS  TRALA  TIFF
LOOP  HOLES  OGRE
LOWERINGTHEBOOM
ANACONDA  NORMA
   IAGO  BOZO
ROSARY  PONYTAIL
ITLL  FORUM  SRO
PEEKABOOISEEYOU
ERE MALLS  RENT
RIPCORDS  ZLOTYS
   ARES  PIED
IWASA  ARRAIGNS
LITTLEBLACKBOOK
ENOL  SEETO  LOTI
TOME  STEEN  EDEN
```

Chas Did 'Em

```
JAPES  DAR  IPASS
OBESE  ERE  RALPH
VERSE  WEDNESDAY
ELF RISHI  HERE
  EATEN  OXCARTS
UNCLEFESTER  SAT
SATANIST  SUM
ABORT  SIM  SOFIA
  MAL  PAGANISH
TVS GOMEZADDAMS
HEAVEHO  EPEES
IRMA  ANELE  CPA
COUSINITT  QUOIT
KNEED  ETO  ERECT
SALSA  SUV  DISKS
```

Space Invaders

```
SHIV  SCREW  POPS
AUTO  TEETH  IDEA
WHOLLYINCONCERT
  CALLA  DON
ARCADES  PURITAN
LEONID  VENACAVA
FLUID  TORI  VIM
 INCAPACITATED
JET  RUES  MARIO
OVERTOPS  FEINTS
BEREAVE  PARLAYS
  FLO  TRUCE
ATTACKVIOLENTLY
ALEC  ECLAT  DAYO
ACNE  DRESS  SUES
```

This Car

```
AVESTA  PRATFALL
DISTAL  REROUTES
OCTOPI  ONEARMED
  AID  AMENDS
CABCALLOWAY  EPA
ALL  NOG  MRED
LEI  CLOD  CHAINS
  SHELLEYHACK
OTHERS  MAIN  EBB
OVEN  RND  SAY
PAD TAXIDOWNTHE
  MOTELS  OAR
MACARONI  AVIATE
EGOMANIA  MELDER
GETAHEAD  INSANE
```

Ads of 13

```
CHEW  APSE  AKITA
HONE  BETS  INNED
IOTA  BRET  NEEDS
DRIVERSWANTED
EATEN  ISTO  HIRE
SHY CPA  ENROBER
  PORNO  HOLLER
 WHERESTHEBEEF
DIODES  TAROS
OSMOSES  SOT  SUE
TEEM  LASS  INEPT
 BEALLYOUCANBE
FORTE  ARCS  DEER
CHEER  DIKE  ICAN
COWRY  SASS  RATE
```

6. Big Entertainment

Oz

Some Like It Hot

Mushrooms in the End

Film Villians

Doo-wop Hits

Funny Gals

6. Big Entertainment continued

Game Shows of 11

S	N	I	F	F		I	N	M	A	N		T	E	N
A	T	R	I	A		D	O	U	C	E		I	L	O
W	H	A	T	S	M	Y	L	I	N	E		C	A	L
			C	O	L	O	R	E	D		T	I	E	
H	A	T	P	I	N	S			L	E	A	N	S	
A	R	A	R	A	T		S	I	L	E	N	C	E	S
S	I	T	E	S		K	A	T	Y	D	I	D		
H	A	T	S		A	N	G	I	E		G	O	I	N
	L	E	S	S	E	E	S			A	M	U	S	E
S	T	E	N	C	H	E	S		I	M	A	G	E	S
L	O	T	T	E			S	M	A	S	H	E	S	
E	R	A		P	A	L	A	T	A	L				
E	E	L		T	H	E	G	O	N	G	S	H	O	W
P	R	E		R	A	N	U	P		A	L	O	N	E
S	O	S		E	S	S	E	S		M	A	T	E	D

Game Shows of 13

S	P	A	Y		A	R	R	A	S		A	D	A	M
T	U	N	E		L	E	A	S	H		L	U	R	E
A	R	I	A		M	E	N	S	A		D	E	F	T
L	E	T	S	M	A	K	E	A	D	E	A	L		
K	E	A	T	O	N		E	M	I	L				
			R	A	Y			E	L	A	P	S	E	
	C	O	N	C	E	N	T	R	A	T	I	O	N	
S	A	U	D		T	A	O		O	P	T	S		
T	H	E	D	A	T	I	N	G	G	A	M	E		
L	A	S	S	I	E		O	E	D					
			D	R	U	B		N	A	P	L	E	S	
	P	R	E	S	S	Y	O	U	R	L	U	C	K	
R	H	E	A		E	A	R	N	S		U	G	L	I
P	O	S	T		S	I	N	C	E		T	E	A	M
M	E	T	E		T	R	E	E	S		O	R	T	S

Game Shows of 14

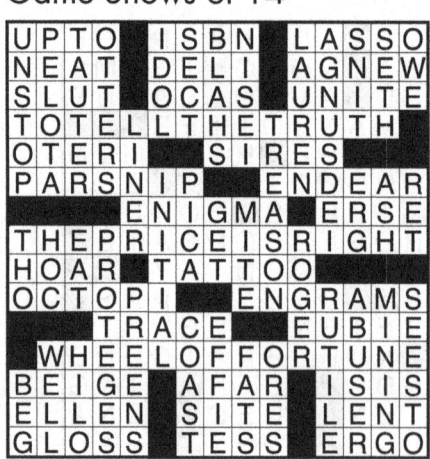

U	P	T	O		I	S	B	N		L	A	S	S	O
N	E	A	T		D	E	L	I		A	G	N	E	W
S	L	U	T		O	C	A	S		U	N	I	T	E
T	O	T	E	L	L	T	H	E	T	R	U	T	H	
O	T	E	R	I		S	I	R	E	S				
P	A	R	S	N	I	P			E	N	D	E	A	R
			E	N	I	G	M	A		E	R	S	E	
T	H	E	P	R	I	C	E	I	S	R	I	G	H	T
H	O	A	R		T	A	T	T	O	O				
O	C	T	O	P	I		E	N	G	R	A	M	S	
	T	R	A	C	E		E	U	B	I	E			
W	H	E	E	L	O	F	F	O	R	T	U	N	E	
B	E	I	G	E		A	F	A	R		I	S	I	S
E	L	L	E	N		S	I	T	E		L	E	N	T
G	L	O	S	S		T	E	S	S		E	R	G	O

Harlem G.

M	A	C	R	A	M	E		C	I	T	A	T	O	R
A	D	R	E	N	A	L		A	N	I	L	I	N	E
M	E	A	D	O	W	L	A	R	K	L	E	M	O	N
A	L	V	I	N		S	H	I	E	S				
S	E	E	R		P	E	K	O	E		P	O	P	
		E	V	I	L		P	R	O	C	U	R	E	
A	B	S	C	I	S	S	A		R	E	P	R	O	
W	I	L	T	C	H	A	M	B	E	R	L	A	I	N
A	P	E	E	K		P	I	T	I	L	E	S	S	
R	E	D	D	I	S	H		A	N	N	O			
D	D	S		M	E	N	S	A		P	E	E	L	
	S	N	O	R	E		S	H	A	R	I			
R	E	E	C	E	G	O	O	S	E	T	A	T	U	M
A	T	L	A	R	G	E		O	R	I	N	O	C	O
T	O	M	B	O	Y	S		P	A	R	E	N	T	S

7. Time Machine

Songs of '29

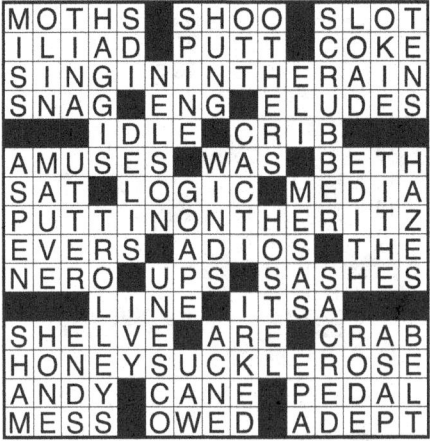

Songs of '39

The Great Race

Fad Toys

Fads

More Fads

7. Time Machine continued

Born on the 4th of July

```
MOSS SLATS SPAR
ACME HIRAM ORCA
STIR UNSHELLING
CALVINCOOLIDGE
ONION NELL
TEN RNA ABODE
GEORGEMCOHAN
IDOL NIOBE ROBS
RUBEGOLDBERG
ADIEU SKI AGA
NILE OWNER
LOUISARMSTRONG
SUBSTATION ARTY
ALEE ACCRA PALL
GUYS CHANG SKYE
```

On February 29th

```
SETS GLASS ASTO
ATIT LETUP RHEA
NATIVEAMERICANS
GLORIA SYNAPSE
OMAR KNEES
STAHL DEPOSE
ISSUE HULA CPA
SAINTPETERSBURG
IRA AREA EUBIE
DICERS TRAMS
LEWIS SEAT
OREGANO BEANIE
GONEWITHTHEWIND
ODDS CAMEO ONCE
NEST KYSER LEAN
```

American Pie

```
STEP GLAD MCGEE
LIAR RILE YANKS
OTTO IMPS SPUES
THEBIGBOPPER
HERONRY ILLICIT
SDI ASIF ASH
ABACI ERIC LUTE
MARIAELENAHOLLY
AMIS TING YOKED
HBO CHAT NES
LITCHIS BENEFIT
RICHIEVALENS
SHLEP OKRA ELLA
HAITI WORD ALAR
ELLEN ENYA FAYS
```

8. Big Time

Lock, Stock, and Barrel

```
OPEL MYEYE TARA
OLLA EARLS AMOR
HOLDINWRESTLING
STAYSUP MOROCCO
SASSY UNION
MASHY ADAMS
ANTI ERRATA BUR
KEEPININVENTORY
OWN CITIES OLGA
SEDAN SOLES
DACHA GSPOT
ENRAGES YESHIVA
WOODENCONTAINER
ALOE DODGE EDIT
REND STEER ROLE
```

Swifties of 15

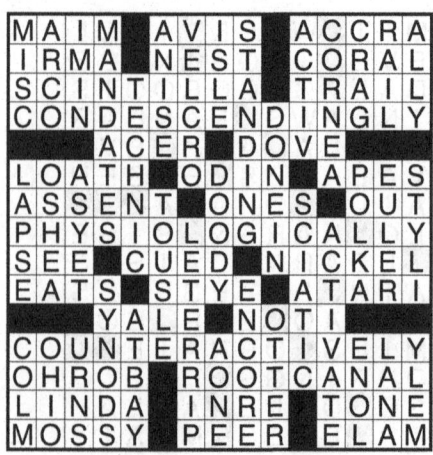

```
MAIM AVIS ACCRA
IRMA NEST CORAL
SCINTILLA TRAIL
CONDESCENDINGLY
ACER DOVE
LOATH ODIN APES
ASSENT ONES OUT
PHYSIOLOGICALLY
SEE CUED NICKEL
EATS STYE ATARI
YALE NOTI
COUNTERACTIVELY
OHROB ROOTCANAL
LINDA INRE TONE
MOSSY PEER ELAM
```

Yeggs Over Easy

L	S	T	S		C	R	E	D		I	C	A	R	E
A	P	S	O		O	O	Z	E		N	O	B	E	L
B	Y	H	O	O	K	O	R	B	Y	C	R	O	O	K
R	E	I	N	V	I	T	A	T	I	O	N			
E	R	R		E	E	L		E	N	G		P	R	O
A	S	T	E	R		I	R	E		C	O	E	D	
			S	E	I	K	O		O	C	H	R	E	D
	I	T	T	A	K	E	S	A	T	H	I	E	F	
G	A	M	E	T	E		I	N	C	A	N			
A	G	A	R		A	N	N		G	A	S	P	S	
S	O	N		T	I	N		A	I	R		E	E	E
			S	U	B	S	E	R	V	I	E	N	C	E
O	N	E	A	R	M	E	D	B	A	N	D	I	T	S
H	A	Y	D	N		L	I	O	N		D	O	I	T
O	G	E	E	S		S	E	R	A		A	R	N	O

Can Can

M	I	D	S	T		P	O	L	O		C	A	T	S
I	D	A	H	O		A	R	U	M		A	B	I	T
S	E	M	I	C	I	R	C	L	E		N	O	T	I
C	A	N	N	O	N	B	A	L	L		O	M	A	N
			M	A	O		S	E	A	P	I	N	K	
P	E	A	C	E	N	I	K		T	H	E	N		
A	L	M	A		E	L	I	A		S	N	A	P	E
I	S	B	N		R	E	N	D	S		E	T	O	N
L	A	U	D	S		D	E	V	O		R	E	N	D
	L	Y	R	A		R	E	C	E	S	S	E	S	
T	E	A	C	O	S	Y		R	I	O				
R	I	T	A		C	A	N	T	A	L	O	U	P	E
A	E	O	N		E	Q	U	I	L	I	B	R	I	A
M	I	R	E		N	U	N	S		T	I	L	E	S
S	O	Y	S		T	I	N	E		H	E	S	S	E

Double Trouble

T	A	R	T		B	M	W		A	F	G	H	A	N
A	L	O	E		L	E	A		S	L	E	I	G	H
C	O	A	X	C	O	A	X		P	A	T	R	O	L
O	U	R	T	O	W	N		S	I	N	G	E		
			B	O	U	D	O	I	R		O	S	L	O
S	T	L	O		P	E	W	T	E	R		H	I	D
T	R	O	O	P		R	E	E	S	E		I	N	D
R	I	C	K	Y					P	U	R	E	E	
E	P	A		L	E	A	P	S		O	P	E	N	S
A	L	L		E	M	M	E	T	T		P	S	S	T
M	E	L	T		A	P	P	E	A	S	E			
		O	A	S	I	S		P	L	U	R	A	L	S
S	O	C	I	A	L		C	O	O	P	C	O	O	P
O	R	A	N	G	E		H	U	N		U	N	T	O
B	E	L	T	E	D		I	T	S		T	E	S	T

Fishy Fish of 11

B	I	O		A	C	H	I	E	R		R	A	T	A
O	O	P		D	O	O	D	L	E		A	M	E	S
M	T	A		M	O	R	A	Y	P	O	V	I	C	H
B	A	H	R	A	I	N		U	R	I				
	W	Y	N	N		W	E	L	C	O	M	E	D	
E	D	I	E		G	N	A	R	S		L	I	L	I
L	E	N			I	N	R	E		I	N	N	S	
P	U	F	F		O	C	T	A	D		S	N	I	P
A	C	R	E		B	E	E	T		O	N	E		
S	E	E	S		S	T	R	A	P		A	W	O	L
O	D	Y	S	S	E	Y	S		H	T	T	P		
			E	U	R		B	O	O	M	E	R	S	
S	H	A	D	E	V	E	R	E	T	T		A	U	K
R	A	G	U		E	M	I	L	I	E		R	D	A
I	H	O	P		S	U	M	A	C	S		L	E	T

The Parent Trap

O	P	E	R	A		A	N	T	E		I	L	L	S
H	E	L	E	N		R	E	E	L		S	E	A	T
M	A	L	A	D	Y	M	A	R	M	A	L	A	D	E
S	T	A	G		E	Y	R	E		N	A	D	I	R
			A	S	S		S	E	T		I	D	O	
P	A	I	N	T	E	R	N	A	T	I	O	N	A	L
A	P	B		A	S	I	A		O	P	T			
N	O	M	S	G		M	C	I		O	C	E	A	N
			D	E	E		R	A	I	D		E	V	E
M	A	K	I	N	G	W	E	N	C	E	S	L	A	S
A	B	E		A	G	O		A	S	P				
G	O	Y	I	M		O	P	A	H		A	B	B	A
P	A	S	T	E	J	E	A	N	N	E	D	A	R	C
I	R	I	S		E	R	I	N		E	E	R	I	E
E	D	N	A		U	S	D	A		E	S	T	E	R

Be It Ever So 'Umble

A	N	I	S	E		A	L	A	S		D	O	T	S
G	O	T	T	A		P	A	L	E		U	H	U	H
A	N	E	A	R		O	M	I	T		M	A	R	E
R	U	M	B	L	E	S	E	A	T		B	R	I	E
			D	A	T		S	E	A	L	A	N	T	
S	U	M	T	O	T	A	L		E	V	E			
P	N	E	U	M	A	T	I	C		A	D	O	P	T
E	D	A	M		T	E	N	O	R		O	P	I	E
D	O	L	B	Y		S	A	L	E	S	R	E	P	S
			L	E	G		C	O	N	C	E	D	E	S
A	M	N	E	S	I	C		M	A	R				
M	E	O	W		B	U	M	B	L	E	B	E	E	S
E	R	I	E		E	T	U	I		E	L	A	T	E
N	Y	S	E		R	I	T	A		N	A	S	A	L
S	L	E	D		S	E	E	N		S	H	E	L	F

8. Big Time continued

Who Makes House Calls

```
A B Y S S   A S P C A   I M P
G O O U T   B A L E S   N O R
E A G L E   A M E N S   D O A
D R I L L A T E A S E   I N N
      E L L E   U N M A S K
S I G N A L   W A S T E D
O N O   R O T O R   S O R E R
A R I D   T O R A H   W I S E
R E N E W   M R B I G   N A P
      G L O S S Y   R U C K U S
M E D L E Y     T E A R
O U R   I N N E R D R E A R S
T B A   S T A R E   D O B I E
H I P   M A N I A   E L U D E
S E E   E X A C T   D E T E R
```

No Repeats

```
A V I D   R A M P S   A B U T
L E N A   I D E A L   S O N Y
D E R M A T O G L Y P H I C S
O P E N S U P     H E L L O
      L A T E   L E S S E N
C H A P E L   C R E W
L O R R E   E L I A   P A C T
U N C O P Y R I G H T A B L E
B E S S   O O P S   O N C U E
      M U S S   K I S S E S
L A R D E R   E T A L
I D I O M   I R E P E A T
M I S C O N J U G A T E D L Y
P E E K   R E S E T   S E E K
S U N S   A W A R E   O N C E
```

All in the Family

```
D A B   A R B O R S   G A I T
I R E   D E A D O N   A N K A
S L A   J U N E C O L L Y E R
C O M B U S T   S B A
      U S E U P   S W A B S
S P U R T S   R E S T A R E A
E A S T S   D E V O   L E T T
C R E W   L O S E S   L O T I
U S D A   E R A S   C Y L O N
R E T R Y I N G   M A C E R S
E R O D E   E R A T O
      A I R   I N E X A C T
E A G E R B E A V E R   T O W
G D A Y   E N G A G E   A L I
G O R E   T O O L E D   D A N
```

Keeping in Shape

```
T O M B   C L A M S   S P O T
I D E A   B O R I C   T I D E
C I R C L E O F F R I E N D S
S E E K E R S   F A R E A S T
      R A S E D   M A R C
H A S O N   N I P   S O R E
A R I O S O   S O H O   L I L
D I A M O N D J I M B R A D Y
I S M   N O N O   S L I D E S
T E E M   A I D   I C A R E
      S A P S   N E I G H
A M E R I C A   B R E N D A N
B A C K T O S Q U A R E O N E
B R A E   T A U N T   S I N S
R I T T   S P O K E   S T E T
```

9. So Big

Just Vegging

```
E M A I L   G L E N   D I E S
M A R C O   E I R E   I S L E
O K R A W I N F R E Y S H O W
T E A R   S U E   D U H
I S S U E R S   S T R E T T I
O D E S S A   B L O T S O U T
N O S   S E E Y A   U P T O
      C E L E R Y C A P
B A B A   R O S I E   E S T
M A I N T A I N   T R A N C E
W A N N A B E   G R Y P H O N
      I R S   A L I   P A N T
G I V E P E A S A C H A N C E
O L E S   N Y P D   U L C E R
P O E T   T E S S   B L E S S
```

Paging Reverend Spooner

```
S P R Y   S A T   P A S T A
E R I E   W B A   S I N K E R
S O P S T E I N   P A T E N T
A B E   O A T   F I N E D
M E N T O R   D E T O U R E D
E D S E L   F E D   S P A R E
      E S C A P E E   R O B
Z A P S   A C O R N   N E S T
E P A   L A S A G N A
R O L E S   D E L   O P A R T
O P E R A T E D   A R E T O O
      T A L E S   P B S   E L I
P A Y S I N   C O N E F A L L
A P P E N D   O R E   I S E E
R E E S E   P E R   B E R T
```

My Fill

```
  S A M S P A D E   A M P L E
S H O E L A C E S   D A R I N
A I R S I R E N S   O R E A D
I N T A C T   T E M P T E R S
L E A   E N S   S A T I N
      C R E P T   Y E A G E R
S A L E S R O O M   E L A T E
O L I N   S O D A S   A G U E
N E S T S   N O N P A R E I L
S C A R C E   S T R U T
      B I R T H   A U G   S T U
T W O F A C E D   C U S T E R
O W N U P   A R R E S T I N G
S I E G E   D E B U T A N T E
S I T E S   S K I P A N T S
```

Strings Attached

```
J A V A   A L A N S   M A Z E
A S I S   S I C E M   A R I D
M O N T I C E L L O   R E N D
E N C O D E   U L T I M A C Y
S E E P I N G   E R A
      O D I U M   A D A P T
W I G H T   J L O   Q U E R Y
I N R E   O T T   K O O P
S T E R N   E R E   S E N S E
C O S B Y   S A L V E
      V E R   S U R F E R S
H E S I T A T E   L I E N E E
E X P O   M A G I C F L U T E
R E A L   B I O T A   T R I M
O C T A   O L S O N   S E E S
```

Cats and Mice

```
D R A P E   O H G O D   F I B
D A V I D   V E R N E   E R A
S N A G G L E P U S S   L A D
      L A I R   B E E P I N G
I N T E R N   T R I X I E
R O O T   E Y E S   T E T
A T M   A I R E R   C H A I
T E A S   G E N I E   E E L S
E D N A   E L I Z A   C A L
      D V D   D E E P   L A M E
M A J O R S   P H O T O S
O V E R A T E   S L U G
M I R   M I G H T Y M O U S E
M A R   A L G A E   P U P I L
A N Y   S T O M P   S T I N K
```

Begone!

```
M O T I F   F R O S T   S E T
O H A R E   L O E W E   P R O
M O O S E H E A D E R   I N D
      B O A R   A M E L I A
S T R O L L S   B R I M L E Y
P O O P E D   P O S T I T
E R O S   I W O N   E T H A N
N A T   S T A N Z A S   E L I
T H E F T   I D O S   G A I N
      R O O S T S   T R A N C E
I N F A N T S   D R E S S E S
V A L L E E   B I A S
B I O   A V E R C L E A V E R
A V A   G E N I E   T R I P E
G E T   E N T E R   S T E A M
```

9. So Big continued

I'm Still Just Wild About Saffron

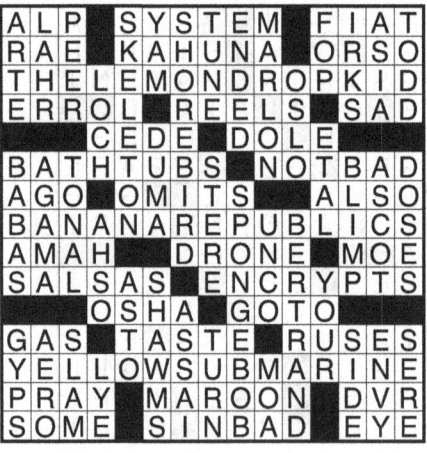

```
ALP  SYSTEM  FIAT
RAE  KAHUNA  ORSO
THELEMONDROPKID
ERROL  REELS  SAD
     CEDE  DOLE
BATHTUBS  NOTBAD
AGO  OMITS   ALSO
BANANAREPUBLICS
AMAH   DRONE   MOE
SALSAS  ENCRYPTS
     OSHA  GOTO
GAS  TASTE  RUSES
YELLOWSUBMARINE
PRAY  MAROON  DVR
SOME  SINBAD  EYE
```

WW4

```
ASWELL  SOSO  OCT
STEREO  TBAR  SOY
WEARYWILLIE  OAR
INNS  BROIL  ALTO
ROE  ELO  GOOBER
LSD  WONDERWOMAN
   FEWER  ERICA
RIAL  DAR  TOKE
ANDOR   MEALS
WHERESWALDO  LIZ
ELIXIR  IDO  ICE
FRAN  MAUVE  FLIP
LEI  WICKEDWITCH
END  ELKE  LONELY
ATE  NESS  YONDER
```

Catchphrases

```
GALAS  CERF  OILS
ALONE  OLEO  SKIP
BOOKEMDANO  MILE
SENATE  METHODIC
   HER  WHINY
COSMETIC  INDOOR
APODS  SHALT  USE
SECS  PEARL  INCA
ARK  PANIC  BROAD
SAILON  REGISTRY
   TENOR  DIG
INTHERAW  REHASH
POOR  AGIRLLIKEI
ONME  MESA  OKIES
SEER  ASHY  WENDS
```

Nothing Much

```
JESTS  HOPI  ARCH
AXTON  ALAN  TERI
MEARA  VERA  OLEG
SCRAPBOOKS  MISH
   PIC  SELECTS
SPACES   COG
ALFAROMEO  TOTAL
SEEM  NOTED  YALE
SAWED  MODERATES
   OUR  PANICS
MARSHAL  OTT
ALIT  BITTHEDUST
NATO  BEAT  DINER
OMEN  INRE  PADRE
ROSE  TSAR  GLOBE
```

Capital Idea

```
GOLEM  ATTIC  BMW
ACELA  CHELA  EEE
STALE  ORRIN  RTE
PARISTROIKA  NAP
SLYSTONE  EATAT
   OOP  VINEGAR
TARNS  WEEK  TARO
ILO  OMITTED  ISM
FAME  EROS  ERNIE
FREEWAY   ALE
MANIC  BONIFACE
BIB  DUBLINCUBES
USO  ELIAN  ATBAT
STU  SPOCK  TEASE
HST  TASKS  ESSES
```

Who Was That?

```
TOPE  BANDB  SCAR
ADIT  ANISE  AHOY
RICHLITTLE  LENA
PETIOLES  LOAVES
   COED  FILMY
ARSINE  HANDICAP
BOOZY  MOUES  HBO
AGUE  CALLS  RANT
CUP  JANET  BESET
KEYRINGS  SOBERS
   SAMBO  BEAU
MEANIE  AIRSTRIP
ARLO  REDBUTTONS
LIEU  REALM  AMOS
TEST  ACRES  LENT
```

10. Really Big

Alien Invasion!!!

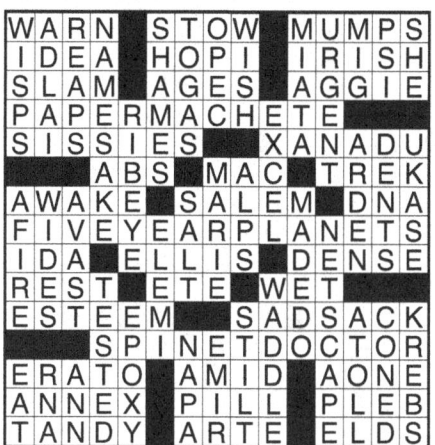

```
WARN  STOW  MUMPS
IDEA  HOPI  IRISH
SLAM  AGES  AGGIE
PAPERMACHETE
SISSIES   XANADU
   ABS  MAC  TREK
AWAKE  SALEM  DNA
FIVEYEARPLANETS
IDA  ELLIS  DENSE
REST  ETE  WET
ESTEEM   SADSACK
  SPINETDOCTOR
ERATO  AMID  AONE
ANNEX  PILL  PLEB
TANDY  ARTE  ELDS
```

A Game of Pool

```
ALSO  SLED  CRESS
TUTU  LADY  LENNY
ALOT  IMIN  ASIAN
DUPLICATEBRIDGE
   ATE      AID
CATSCRATCHFEVER
EDITH  MEATY  YAH
LOGS  PANTS  MISO
ERE  DONEE  HONED
BERMUDATRIANGLE
   AMI      SRO
CUEUPANEWRECORD
UNCLE  ARIA  LAIR
ETHER  VILE  ETTU
DOORS  YELL  SHAM
```

Swifties of 13 and 9

```
SOBIG  OGDEN  HST
PARSE  BRIDE  APR
RHYME  JACOB  YOU
YUL  DEFT  UNDID
  CRESTFALLENLY
AERIAL     UAW
INEPT  AIMLESSLY
DIET  PILAU  RHEA
ADMIREDLY  DEISM
  DEE    ADEPTS
  ALTERNATIVELY
NOOSE  MIME   ASS
ESQ  DHABI  AGREE
LEU  OOZED  INDEX
ERE  STERE  DUSKY
```

More Mysteries

```
POSSE  TROT  APES
VOTER  HOUR  PICA
CHUPACABRA  PLOT
  ASONE  MEETLY
INCLUDE  SPENDER
CORERS  TOLEDO
ERODE  TALE  SWIG
UMP  SAYKIDS  NRA
PACT  SPED  LAMAS
  IRISES  LEGATE
DERIVES  BOURNES
UNCLES  DANTE
NOLO  STONEHENGE
CLEG  EKED  ETHAN
EASY  SORB  DOLLS
```

Quite a Spread

```
KENS  MACK  THUMB
ANEW  ELAN  HENRI
PLEA  TALE  WALTZ
LADYMARMALADE
ACTSUP   DORSALS
NEO  SHIP  YTTRIC
  STOGIE   ANNA
JELLYROLLMORTON
ELIA   RESORT
FUGUES  DELI  SID
FLAGMAN  EEYORE
  THEMAYOCLINIC
ACUTE  SULU  KOTO
PURER  ARIL  EMIR
BEERS  LINE  SASS
```

Fishy

```
BENS  STOW  ABETS
AREA  HONE  CANOE
JOHNPERCH  TBONE
ASIDE  EEC  USER
   REAL  ALPS
  SALMONRUSHDIE
CPA  SEGA  BAKERY
OURS  TERMS  AMOR
BREATH  COOS  ONE
BLENNYGOODMAN
   ITSA  TAEL
PSST  TBA  LUNAR
UNHIP  BRILLMACY
BOOZE  ELMO  NINA
SWEEP  ROPY  ALES
```

10. Really Big continued

Citywide

```
ADHOC BALSA PVC
DOUGH ADEPT RAH
DEHLI MARKET ALA
    EPA ESCARGOT
ADS PLAN SCOURS
WOE ELIAN HOE
FLO WELLES SNEE
ULULATE BETTORS
LYLY SECURE SIS
  SOT NOLAN ICE
AMINIC NAPA SAX
BASSCLEF END
ACT KABULSTONES
SHE ERASE EMOTE
HOR RAYED DERAT
```

Gal Time

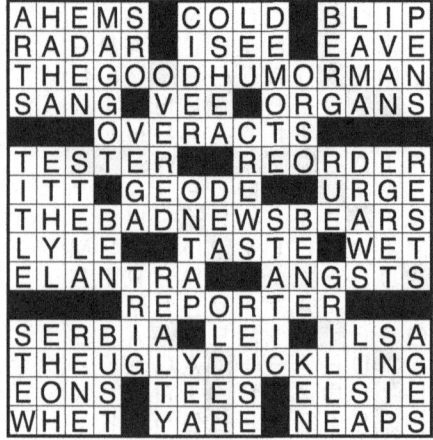

```
BLIND IRKS GABS
RADIO NOAH ABET
AMONG TATI LORE
GALEGORDON LURE
    IDO BRUTAL
STAGED DROOP
TOGAS GRANDPAPA
ABEL EMOTE OTIS
BEDLINENS FLECK
  IRENE SALSAS
WEAVER NET
ALDA GALAAFFAIR
LION ICON ARISE
DART ELSA RENEE
ONES SUES METED
```

Lepidoptera

```
ASLEEP DEPOSITS
SCAMPI OSOLEMIO
SOCIALBUTTERFLY
APER LUG SOB
YES JAY AHS ACT
  BAG GPO OWER
MADAMEBUTTERFLY
ACINI OIL MAULS
BUTTERFLYBALLOT
ETTU OFT LIB
LEO ABO CUL GAP
  AGE ERE DUDE
BUTTERFLYSHRIMP
ORIENTAL KOALAS
TINSTONE YEMENI
```

Spaghetti Feast

```
AHEMS COLD BLIP
RADAR ISEE EAVE
THEGOODHUMORMAN
SANG VEE ORGANS
  OVERACTS
TESTER REORDER
ITT GEODE URGE
THEBADNEWSBEARS
LYLE TASTE WET
ELANTRA ANGSTS
  REPORTER
SERBIA LEI ILSA
THEUGLYDUCKLING
EONS TEES ELSIE
WHET YARE NEAPS
```

3 on a Match

```
SETH BULB AVAST
LURE ASIA MELEE
ARES DELI BLOWN
BOXINGRINGEVENT
  TOES ARE
IMPAIR RPM TRAP
NOUNS UHAUL ALE
CONTESTINTENNIS
ARK SPANS GECKO
NESS OHO RASHES
  OPT TACT
SUCCESSFORYENTA
APRIL ELKE GOAT
ATEAT NOEL GALA
BOWLS DENY SHED
```

11. Think Big

Old Ads

```
OMAHA   FELLA   KPS
LAVAS TOROID   OHO
AXONS ICICLE   SON
FINGERLICKINGOOD
    NED         OVER
ALITTLEDABLLDOYA
HERESY ESSAYS
OVAL   SPADE   TUB
YIN HEREI   SASE
  LABORS   EYELET
SAYITWITHFLOWERS
AFAR       EMU
BECAUSEIMWORTHIT
AAH CONNIE EIEIO
DRT LADDER ONAIR
ODS ARSON   NADIA
```

Time for a Change

```
ORAL CERF   EDSEL
KOLA AXEL   GRAVE
ADAR MUSE   GALES
PINCHEDPENNIES
INSHORE   IONS
    PASSING SHE
PILAU   APO ALEX
STOPPINGONADIME
ACNE MBA   TOPPS
THE PEASANT
  LIRA   BEASTIE
LIVINGQUARTERS
EIEIO OUST ONES
TASER RIEL MONA
ARTSY EDDY PREY
```

Kid Rides

```
PAM PLANA   ANTON
ABA RIMED   RABBI
BACTERIAL AVAIL
SCOOTERLIBBY
TINGE   BRIBER
  ANGST OCELOT
TIL SANEST ALAR
SKATESONTHINICE
ANNA TOOLED SHY
ROCKER FOLIO
  WEEVIL   OLDIE
  BICYCLECARDS
LILAC REUNIFIES
ERECT ERNIE BAA
DESKS SEEDS SLY
```

Coincidence? I Think Not!

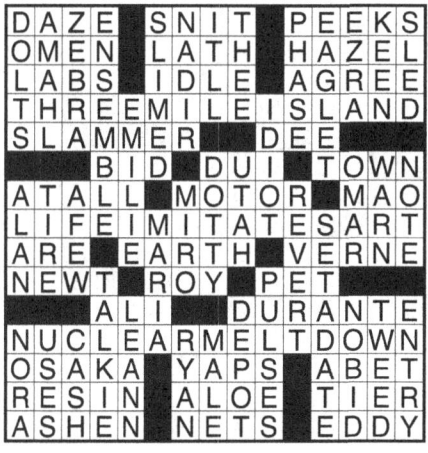

```
DAZE SNIT   PEEKS
OMEN LATH   HAZEL
LABS IDLE   AGREE
THREEMILEISLAND
SLAMMER   DEE
  BID DUI TOWN
ATALL MOTOR MAO
LIFEIMITATESART
ARE EARTH VERNE
NEWT ROY PET
  ALI   DURANTE
NUCLEARMELTDOWN
OSAKA YAPS ABET
RESIN ALOE TIER
ASHEN NETS EDDY
```

Um?

```
ODDS IPASS   AKIN
POOH DEICE   NICE
TWEEDLEDUM GNAT
  KIEV DESIGNS
APPENDED SPED
MALLS ETTU ODD
BRAS BOTHER MAE
LOY RELEARN CIT
ELI ELECTS LOSE
DEN PLOT GAMES
  GORY SPARSEST
OLDGOAT ARIA
SAUL CHEWINGGUM
LIME HORNS NOSE
ORBS ERASE ABEL
```

Drip, Drip, Drip

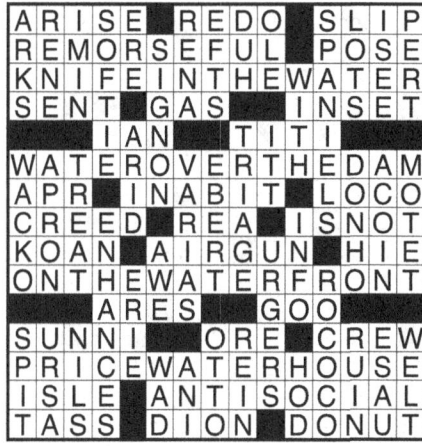

```
ARISE REDO   SLIP
REMORSEFUL POSE
KNIFEINTHEWATER
SENT GAS   INSET
  IAN TITI
WATEROVERTHEDAM
APR INABIT LOCO
CREED REA ISNOT
KOAN AIRGUN HIE
ONTHEWATERFRONT
  ARES   GOO
SUNNI ORE CREW
PRICEWATERHOUSE
ISLE ANTISOCIAL
TASS DION DONUT
```

11. Think Big continued

... Your Boat?

```
ROMP  EPSOM  SNAP
ALOU  MITRE  MALI
PINTHEPARTHENON
TOTTERER   ORATE
    ORIS  EMUS
ISABEL  CRASHPAD
SINE  LORRE   RNA
HEEDTHECOXSWAIN
ANA  HONOR  ONME
MARIETTA  PARKAS
    MISO  MIND
RASPS   FANTASIA
UNNAMEDLITIGANT
STIR  PIANO  ELSE
KEPT  AGNES  SETS
```

Double Double Time

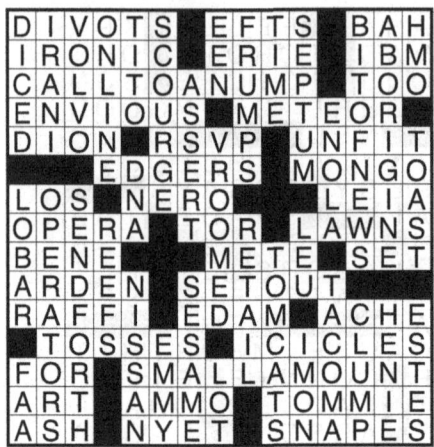

```
DIVOTS  EFTS  BAH
IRONIC  ERIE  IBM
CALLTOANUMP  TOO
ENVIOUS  METEOR
DION  RSVP  UNFIT
    EDGERS  MONGO
LOS  NERO   LEIA
OPERA  TOR  LAWNS
BENE   METE   SET
ARDEN  SETOUT
RAFFI  EDAM  ACHE
 TOSSES  ICICLES
FOR  SMALLAMOUNT
ART  AMMO  TOMMIE
ASH  NYET  SNAPES
```

Of 13

```
WASP  FIBS  VOCAL
AWOL  ISAW  OPERA
TABU  ELLE  LADEN
CREMEDEMENTHE
HERBAL    PEA
    REBA  VIRTUE
 ESPRITDECORPS
TITO  ETO   TEST
ARCDETRIOMPHE
MAHALO  CREE
    IRK  ATONED
 OSCARDELAHOYA
PESCI  AUDI  AMID
UNHAT  ACNE  RAND
TSARS  LEAR  EDGY
```

Playtime

```
CLARA  PLAN  TIPS
AIDER  AONE  ARLO
STAGEPRODUCTION
SEMINARS  TRUSTY
    MAYO  PRAM
SAGE  STALIN  HAS
AGENT   BONIFACE
BUTTONONYOURVCR
REASSURE   MOORE
EST  SCARAB  SCAR
    BELL  DRAT
ATTIRE  EMACIATE
WORKSANTITHESIS
EDIE  THAT  ESTES
DOOR  ELLS  STORE
```

Repeat, No Repeats

```
DELL  GRACE  POOL
RATE  RUNON  LUBE
JUDGMENTOFPARIS
    SENSE  IAN
APR  EAT  SER  CAL
BREAKDOWNLIGHTS
SOIREE  OUD  RUED
   SIR  LOB  EER
POSE  EEE  EGGCUP
BOULEVARDNIGHTS
SHE  LED  ADS  YEA
    TAR  CRIED
TUMBLEDOWNSHACK
APES  SELIG  OBIE
MSRP  TEENS  WEAN
```

Test Your Metal

```
APRIL  SPAR  ISBN
PENNA  TIRE  MILE
BRASSTACKS  PLUS
    PARIS  PROVES
TOTALED  MOORE
ARIDLY  MINSTREL
RENEE  MINDS  BAA
TIPS  EASES  JETS
ADA  ANTED  PULSE
RANAFTER  COLLAR
  ARRAY  THEISTS
SALMON  GEESE
ARLO  GOLDFINGER
PEER  LEAD  ENOLA
SAYS  EDDY  SETIN
```

12. Hitting It Big

Swifties of 11

```
PROEM SLUMP CRT
TABLA TORAH AAA
SHIFTLESSLY UFO
     AORTA LASTS
ADJUDGE   ALIT
CRUSOE RIGIDITY
RIDER TALES CEO
OVID BOILS DALY
SEC SORTS HELLO
SLIPKNOT HARLEM
  OHIO PALMYRA
SQUID VAULT
ITS POINTLESSLY
NIL ANENT ROUTE
SPY DOSES SLEDS
```

Back to the Beach

```
MAHALO ADAM AMI
ELUDED NAVE SUN
SANDYDUNCAN HES
ANT   CIT ORSO
  SHELLEYDUVALL
ARMENIA LARAMIE
COARSE LIRA
TENON MAC NITRO
   AVIS FISHER
ASPIRIN ROULADE
SHELLEYBERMAN
TEAK AIL KEA
RAH SANDYKOUFAX
AVE EDIE INFUSE
YEN TOMS POOLED
```

Intelligence

```
DRAT ULNA ADDLE
DANA RIEL SURER
SMARTBOMB SMEAR
   PIANOS ABASE
BAYONNE KIDDED
IVAN ELGALLO
OAR  IDA RUMS
MING APRON APOP
ELSE RAT FOE
  TEETHES FORE
CESSNA STEERED
SLIMS OCTANE
PILAU PLAYSDUMB
ADORE TOTO EROS
NESTS STEN RITA
```

Strange Fruit

```
TUDOR TROD TAME
UTILE AHSO ALAS
BANANAREPUBLICS
SHOFAR ARBUCKLE
   MIA ELO EEN
APPLEOFMYEYE
IIII SEA STRIP
DELL OWNER HIDE
AREAS ONE ISLE
  CHERRYPICKER
REO RAE ALT
ALFRESCO ASSUME
DATEWITHANANGEL
ATES NONU GALAS
RENT GROG OPINE
```

Tom, Dick, and Harry

```
INCA SCRUB RAFT
NELL HOOHA AFRO
FROMTOPTOBOTTOM
ODDSON   HYGIENE
   NESS LORDS
DOSES EMOTES
ADLAI NANA MAO
FEARLESSFOSDICK
TSP NEHI CACTI
  LADDER OBESE
BACON DEBT
ELASTIC ICEAGE
GIVEEMHELLHARRY
EVER PAPAL SEAR
TESS STABS TAME
```

Let It Ride

```
TODOS HAS LOANS
EMILE YIN ABBOT
NIVEN DOA MESSY
SCOOTERLIBBY
ERRS MOILED NIP
DOC POX GALOOT
 NEPOTIST INNS
 MOPEDAROUND
AXEL ELEVATED
TENANT MAW SEL
EST ALLOUT NCAA
 BICYCLECARDS
UVULA CEO HOIST
HIRED EAU IMPEL
FINDS ENS MITTY
```

12. Hitting It Big continued

Peter, Paul, and Mary

N	O	M	S	G		P	A	W	S		A	L	G	A
O	P	I	N	E		T	S	A	R		T	E	R	N
D	I	M	I	N	I	S	H	W	I	T	H	O	U	T
S	E	E	P	E	D			A	L	I	E	N	E	E
			P	A	R	T		A	N	N	A	L	S	
N	I	T	R	O		O	R	A	N	G	S			
A	C	H	O	O		M	A	R	K		O	W	N	
B	E	A	T	L	E	M	C	C	A	R	T	N	E	Y
S	D	I		F	E	T	A		I	A	M	B	S	
		T	E	F	L	O	N		G	R	E	B	E	
S	A	L	U	T	E		R	E	B	A				
A	V	A	T	A	R	S		I	T	S	E	L	F	
L	I	T	T	L	E	L	A	M	B	O	W	N	E	R
S	A	I	L		N	O	V	A		N	A	I	V	E
A	N	N	E		T	E	E	N		I	N	D	I	E

O Gee, Ogee!

S	A	L	A	D		S	C	R	E	W		Q	E	D
A	R	O	M	A		O	H	A	R	A		U	P	I
S	T	O	P	B	A	N	A	N	A	S		I	O	N
H	E	P			L	I	L			T	I	L	D	E
		S	M	O	C	K	T	U	R	T	L	E	S	
C	A	M	E	A	T		E	V	E	S				
I	L	I	A	D		T	I	M	E	L	A	P	S	E
N	E	M	O		T	A	M	P	A		L	E	A	D
E	X	I	T	R	A	M	P	S		B	I	L	G	E
			T	E	R	I			H	A	V	E	O	N
S	P	I	E	S	A	L	A	M	O	D	E			
C	A	P	R	I		G	O	O			A	C	T	
R	D	A		S	Q	U	I	D	P	R	O	Q	U	O
U	R	N		T	U	L	L	E		E	R	U	P	T
B	E	A		S	A	T	E	S		P	E	A	S	E

The Four Seasons

B	O	U	N	C	E		A	R	E	S		R	A	T
E	N	R	O	L	L		D	E	M	I		I	T	O
D	O	N	N	A	S	U	M	M	E	R		S	A	P
			R	A	P	I	E	R		E	E	R	O	
P	A	S	H	A		S	N	A	I	L	M	A	I	L
A	L	P	O			S	L	O	A	N				
C	U	R	L	S		I	C	U		E	N	D	E	D
E	L	I	O	T		M	A	R		S	A	F	E	R
R	A	N	G	E		L	Y	E		S	T	A	R	E
		G	R	E	C	O			E	L	I	A		
A	F	F	I	D	A	V	I	T		U	S	L	E	D
M	A	I	D		V	I	S	I	O	N				
I	R	E		W	I	N	T	E	R	G	R	E	E	N
G	E	L		B	A	I	L		S	E	E	S	T	O
A	D	D		A	R	T	E		O	R	A	T	O	R

Those Were the Days

A	L	D	O		H	U	S	H	E	D		R	D	A
M	A	I	M		O	L	E	A	R	Y		O	R	B
S	T	V	A	L	E	N	T	I	N	E	S	D	A	Y
O	H	A	R	E		A	I	R	S		A	I	M	S
			O	W	E	N	S		M	Y	N	A	S	
M	A	N	A	G	E			T	H	I	S			
A	G	O	G	O		P	A	Y	I	N		E	G	G
S	U	P	E	R	B	O	W	L	S	U	N	D	A	Y
S	E	E		C	A	R	L	E		T	O	N	U	P
			B	E	A	R		M	E	T	A	L	S	
A	T	B	A	Y		I	S	L	A	M				
F	A	R	R		I	D	L	E		A	U	G	H	T
T	H	A	N	K	S	G	I	V	I	N	G	D	A	Y
E	O	N		I	T	E	M	E	D		H	A	W	K
R	E	D		P	O	S	E	R	S		S	Y	N	E

13. Extreme Theming

4-Letter Words

4-Letter Words 2

4-Letter Words 3

A Lot 1

A Lot 2

A Lot 3

I Spy 1

```
IMAY  SNEER  SSE
RATE  TORRE  EAT
ESTA  ROARS  ALC
STARMAN  EARTH
   NIP  TOWS
BLAST  RAP  ESTE
EEL  ELECT  AHOY
NEAR  ALIST  ORE
DRNO  SAT  OATER
   ACHY  TLC
DERMA  PALATES
OLA  RACES  RARE
PAT  PLANT  IPSE
ENS  SENSE  DEEP
```

I Spy 2

```
ORE  RARE  ESE
EDEN  OVENS  LEAP
SOLE  TENSE  FEST
TRI  OAST  RAISES
ASCENT  STERN
LEER  ANI  GAG
ABEL  SENSES  OIL
SAYSO  JUT  ELUDE
ERE  GREBES  IPSE
ASS  LOC  SATE
BESTS  DISMAL
EFFORT  MADE  ALA
ROAR  ERODE  TOES
LODE  RATON  ARRS
LES  MESS  NIT
```

OOOOO! 1

```
IMA  UHOH  ACE
SLED  NASAL  NATO
WEDS  ARISE  DROP
ATA  NIDE  ASSENT
BALLAD  RODEO
OBEY  NEE  SAM
TEEN  DESERT  ONA
AGNES  AID  ORSON
LAD  TARTAR  AONE
LDS  OWN  YELP
AVAST  TOSSED
GETTER  ASAN  CAR
ERAS  DETER  DATE
LAME  SNEAD  APED
TEA  ERRS  MAN
```

OOOOO! 2

```
TRIMS  LID  AMT
SIREE  TATER  DEN
PORTE  EDEMA  IDO
DIP  MEN  EAT
OPS  CSI  NODULE
AHA  AID  ATNO
ROBUST  PRO  LEO
STONE  DAM  DOLLS
OTC  OUR  DERIDE
LAND  PAT  TIE
ADHERE  ORO  EEK
TEA  ONA  KEN
SIN  MELEE  ALONE
EGG  ASSES  TOPER
ANS  SON  ENTER
```

8 Sounds Good to Me

```
FRO  ARAB  MARE
OIL  TARA  OPEN
USE  AMIR  NEED
LEARN  BAT
AYE  GHOST
STAY  AMIE  CPA
TON  SAT  HAM
ONO  REDO  POSE
PINTA  NUT
ENS  PAUSE
PEER  IDES  TAG
EVEN  RILE  ALA
DALE  EMIT  HEN
```

Food, Wonderful Food 1

```
TOFU  TSP  MOP
OXEN  AHI  AIR
TONIC  FAT  TREE
ACID  SOY
PLA  KEEP
FEU  FOAM
RAKI  BEURRENOIR
OLIN  ADE  ANNA
BURNTSUGAR  PONY
SIDE  AMA
RAPE  MRE
POI  TIES
GHEE  DAL  HAZEL
SOP  OCA  LIME
ATE  CON  SNUG
```

Food, Wonderful Food 2

```
A G E _ _ _ T A B _ _ M A M
D O S _ _ _ A L L _ _ A L A
E A S T _ M I S E _ H E T
_ _ O R E O _ A S T I
P U P P I E S _ C E E
O V A B L T C H E N
T A P A S A M A D U B
_ S E C R U M _ T I P
_ R O B D I P N A T U R
_ R O S A A T E O N O
_ D O C G E H A K T E
_ T A K O N A I L
P R E T O P E U G L I
T U N C I A S O P
S E T H E N A W A
```

Food, Wonderful Food 3

```
P O T _ _ A W A _ _ E P A
O N O _ _ L E G _ _ B A M
G E L _ _ A D E _ P I N A
_ L U N N G R A P E
_ D A U B E R O E
_ O P O R A L L
F D A _ C I B O U L E T T E
L O T T E N A N O R E O S
O C E A N P E R C H A N T
_ M O O O E U F
_ A K U B R A K E
_ L I T E R D U N K
P A C E D U B A H I
A L U A L E R I P
T S P M E L O C A
```

Go Hawaiian 1

```
P A L M A H E M I L E A L
O L E O L E N O P A L M A
P L O W U L A N A P I A N
P E N N A M E O W N A H A
A N A W I N P E E
_ O O N A O E M M A P
I M P A L A A L K A L I N E
L E A H O W E U L N A
I L L U M I N E A P N E A L
A L E A N E A L A E
_ N E O L I L N A M
L A W H E N L E O N I N E
A L A M O O P E N A K I N
M O L A L N I L E P O O L
P E K O E E P E E A N N O
```

Go Hawaiian 2

```
A H E M L O P E H E L L
M A L I I P A N A E L I A
E L A N N I N O N W H E N
N O M I N E E L E O N I N E
_ M O A M A M A
K I P P L E A O K A P I
I L E N E I N O N L A M P
L I N O A N I L E A L P O
L U N E P E K E M I M E O
M E L E E I O W A A L P
_ K L A N A N N
A N A H E I M K N E E P A N
L E N O K O P E K P I L E
M I N K E L O P E A P I A
A L A E E M I L L E A P
```

Go Hawaiian 3

```
P A I L M H O L O N I
A L O U P A U L A A L E E
W A W A A L L E N N I L E
L E A N N E L O O P H O L E
_ N I L P E A
K O P E L L M A I L M A N
H A L L A M I N A L P A P
A K A I A N P O E
N U N P A L O O K A A M A
M A N I L O W A N I L I N
_ O O P H O N
A P E N N I N E U N H E L M
P A L M N I N O N A L I A
I L I A E N O L A L O O K
A L A N E W E E I N E
```

14. Head Games

Head Games 1

```
CRIMP   RAP   ICER
AIRIER  ABU   LOPE
RATTLE  MATTERED
   ELF  STE  NEE
  HER  EITHER
TONS  ROW  RIFLE
AKA    TILE  RUST
RIBS  LATER  OTTO
EELS  ASTA    EAR
 RETES  ENE  RATE
   THIRST  ULE
ERN  NIN  HAM
VOIDANCE  EDMOND
ETTA  GAR  LIENEE
REAM  SSE   TREWS
```

Head Games 2

```
DROIT   HULA   ALL
ENURE   MUSED  RIA
EATEN   EMEND  BEY
   SCARPED   ONE
OAR  HUG   ISSUED
ACE  ENE  ENSURE
THEIST  ANGER
HELM  TAT   ETTA
 PRIER  PURRED
 BREAST  IRT  ORE
READER   NOT  PIN
ATT  ALIGNED
STE  HEAVE  REPAY
EER  OLDER  ELUDE
DDS  PIES  REDOS
```

Head Games 3

```
MAR  THAN   OWLET
EGO  AERIE  GHAST
LAN  RIFTS  LIMEY
TRAITS  ETHER
  SST  RAE  LOW
 MIL  TAR  CAR
RECEPT  RETE  UKE
ANI  ROUNDED  LEE
IDE  ANNA  RELAND
DES  TIC   ERS
 RTE  ETA  ALA
  SPRIT  IONISE
TEASE  OMERS  RCA
OLDEN  NAVES  MAS
EMEND  NARY  ART
```

Head Games 4

```
FLAME   TERI   RAE
RAYON   CARED  ERA
OYERS   ALINE  SIS
  TUMBLED  HIST
ALL  RIB  IRADES
MOO  ELY  UNTIES
IGNORE  URGER
EYER  ALB   ELIA
 ALATE  HIDING
 RECEDE  ROT  ETA
ROLLED  UKE  NOS
AUDE  LANDERS
STE  LINED  ALTER
EER  ENTRY  TEASE
DDS  AGED  EDGED
```

Head Games 5

```
CRAPE   OSO   ALL
ATMAN   REAVE  SEE
DEALS   URGED  TAN
  USE  ERG  OSS
 LAIRS   LIENEE
ROCKETS  OYER
ETHER  CAR  RAPT
ETE   ARA   RAE
 ODOR  PIT  HAIRS
  WIPE  EVOKERS
HERETO   ALARY
ODO  TOP  ANI
RUB  ELAND  SHORE
ACE  RETES  MITER
LED  DEE  STOPS
```

Head Games 6

```
FAR  WAG   AMIAS
ELI  PACER  WOOSH
VON  ANTRA  LOUSY
ENDING   STE
REST  LAVERS  ACE
 ELENA  OSTLER
 TERI  SLED  RING
TOWABLE  RESENTS
ANET  ORAN  ESES
PARERS  LITES
ELS  EERIER  ERIE
  FRO  AIDERS
AMPLE  EATIT  WAS
RATER  SLANT  ETE
ARSES  ERS  DEN
```

Head Games 7

Head Games 8

Printed in the United States
by Baker & Taylor Publisher Services